Planning Sustainability

This book explores the relationship between one of the most important innovations in recent political discourse – environmental sustainability – and an idea which has slipped from public attention recently – planning. The authors, who are all leading scholars in the field of environmental politics, explore the different implications of sustainability for public planning in the industrialised world.

Sustainable development has become one of the most salient issues on the policy agenda of nation-states. However, this book argues that 'planning' is often wrongly ignored by advocates of environmental politics. Three major questions are addressed in this volume:

- what are the consequences of environmental sustainability for current patterns of social steering by the state and socio-economic planning?
- what lessons do earlier experiences of social and economic planning in Western democracies have for future 'sustainability' planners?
- what challenges are generated for conventional socio-economic management by specifically environmental planning?

These topical issues are explored by contributors from different intellectual traditions.

The contributors: Wouter Achterberg, Michael Jacobs, Martin Jänicke, Helge Jörgens, Tim Lang, Charles E. Lindblom, James Meadowcroft, Michael Redclift, William Rees and Paul Selman.

The editors: Michael Kenny and **James Meadowcroft** both lecture in the Department of Politics at Sheffield University.

Environmental politics
Edited by Michael Waller, University of Keele, and
Stephen Young, University of Manchester

The fate of the planet is an issue of major concern to governments throughout
the world and is likely to retain its hold on the agenda of national administrations
due to international pressures. As an object of academic study, environmental
politics is developing an increasingly high profile: there is a great need for definition of the field and for a more comprehensive coverage of its concerns. This new
series will provide this definition and coverage, presenting books in the following
broad categories:

- new social movements and green parties;
- the making and implementations of environmental policy;
- green ideas.

Already available in the series:

Global Warming and Global Politics
Matthew Patterson

Planning Sustainability
Edited by Michael Kenny and James Meadowcroft

Forthcoming in the series:

Ecological Modernisation
Edited by Stephen Young and Jan van der Straaten

Ecology and International Relations
Edited by Eric Laferrière and Peter Stoett

Community, Nature and Politics
Edited by John O'Neill and Michael Jacobs

Planning Sustainability

**Edited by Michael Kenny and
James Meadowcroft**

London and New York

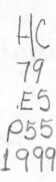

First published 1999
by Routledge
11 New Fetter Lane, London EC4P 4EE

Simultaneously published in the USA and Canada
by Routledge
29 West 35th Street, New York, NY 10001

Routledge is an imprint of the Taylor & Francis Group

Typeset in Baskerville by RefineCatch Limited, Bungay, Suffolk
Printed and bound in Great Britain by
Clays Ltd, St Ives plc

British Library Cataloguing in Publication Data
A catalogue record for this book is available from the British Library

Library of Congress Cataloging in Publication Data
Planning sustainability / edited by Michael Kenny and James
   Meadowcroft.
      p.   cm. – (Environmental politics)
   Papers presented at a conference held in 1995 at Sheffield
University.
   Includes bibliographical references and index.
   ISBN 0–415–16476–1 (hc : alk. paper). – ISBN 0–415–16477–X (pbk. :
   alk. paper)
   1. Sustainable development – Planning – Congresses. I. Kenny,
Michael. II. Meadowcroft, James. III. Series.
HC79.E5P55 1999
338.9 – dc21   98–33290
             CIP

ISBN 0–415–16476–1 (hbk)
ISBN 0–415–16477–X (pbk)

Contents

List of figures and tables

Figures

Tables

List of contributors

Wouter Achterberg is Senior Lecturer in Philosophy at the University of Amsterdam and holds the Socrates Chair of Humanist Philosophy at the University of Wageningen. His recent writings on environmental themes include: *Samenleving, Natuur environment Duurzaamheid* (Assen: Van Gorcum, 1994); 'Sustainability, community and democracy', in B. Doherty and M. de Geus (eds), *Democracy and Green Political Thought* (London: Routledge, 1996); and 'Sustainability and associative democracy', in W. Lafferty and J. Meadowcroft (eds) (Cheltenham: Edward Elgar, 1996).

Michael Jacobs is General Secretary of the Fabian Society and an Associate Research Fellow in the Department of Geography and Environment at the London School of Economics. His publications include *The Green Economy* (London: Pluto Press, 1991) and *Greening the Millennium? The New Politics of the Environment* (edited, Oxford: Blackwell, 1997).

Martin Jänicke is Professor of Comparative Policy and Director of the Environmental Policy Research Unit of the Free University of Berlin. His publications include: 'Conditions for environmental policy success: an international comparison', *The Environmentalist* 12 (1992): 47–58; *Successful Environmental Policy: A Critical Evaluation of 24 Cases* (edited with H. Weidner; Berlin: Edition Sigma, 1995); and *National Environmental Policies – A Comparative Study of Capacity-Building* (edited with H. Weidner and in collaboration with H. Jörgens; Berlin: Springer-Verlag, 1997).

Helge Jörgens is a Research Fellow at the Environmental Policy Research Unit at the University of Berlin. His publications include 'Die Institutionalisierung von Umweltpolitik im internationalen Vergleich', in M. Jänicke (ed.), *Umweltpolitik der Industrieländer. Entwicklung – Bilanz – Erfolgsbedingungen* (Berlin: Edition Sigma, 1996); and (with M. Jänicke and A. Carius), *Nationale Umweltpläne in ausgewählten Industrieländern* (Berlin: Springer, 1997).

Michael Kenny is a lecturer in the Department of Politics at the University of Sheffield. Recent publications include *The First New Left* (London: Lawrence & Wishart, 1995); *Western Political Thought: A Bibliographical Guide to Post-War Writing in English* (with R. Eccleshall; Manchester: Manchester University Press, 1995);

and 'Paradoxes of community', in B. Doherty and M. de Geus (eds), *Democracy and Green Political Thought* (London: Routledge, 1996).

Tim Lang is Professor of Food Studies at the School of Health and Sciences at Thames Valley University. His numerous publications on food-related issues include *The New Protectionism* (with C. Hines; London: Earthscan, 1993); and 'Towards food democracy', in S. Griffiths and J. Wallace (eds), *Consuming Passions: Food in an Age of Anxiety* (Manchester: Manchester University Press, 1998).

Charles E. Lindblom is Emeritus Professor in the Departments of Political Science and Economics at Yale University. His wide ranging contributions include: *The Intelligence of Democracy* (New York: Free Press, 1965); *Politics and Markets* (New York: Basic Books, 1977); and *Inquiry and Change* (New Haven, Conn.: Yale University Press, 1991).

James Meadowcroft is Senior Lecturer in the Department of Politics at University of Sheffield. His recent work on environmental themes includes *Democracy and the Environment* (edited with W. Lafferty; Cheltenham: Edward Elgar, 1996); 'Planning, democracy and the challenge of sustainable development', *International Political Science Review* 18: 167–90; and 'Co-operative management regimes: a way forward?', in Pieter Glasbergen (ed.), *Co-operative Environmental Governance* (Dordrecht: Kluwer, 1998).

Michael Redclift is Professor in the School of Environmental Sciences at the University of Keele. He has written widely on environment-related themes, including *Sustainable Development: Exploring the Contradictions* (London: Methuen, 1987); *Wasted: Counting the Costs of Global Consumption* (London: Earthscan, 1996); and 'Values, needs, rights: reassessing sustainable development', *Environmental Values* 2 (1993): 3–20.

William Rees is Professor and Director of the School of Community and Regional Planning at the University of British Columbia. His recent work includes 'Achieving sustainability: reform or transformation?', *Journal of Planning Literature* 9 (1995): 343–61; 'Revisiting carrying capacity: area based indicators of sustainability', *Population and Environment* 17 (1996): 195–215; and (with M. Wackernagel) *Our Ecological Footprint: Reducing Human Impact on the Earth* (Gabriola Island, BC and New Haven, CT: New Society Publishers, 1996).

Paul Selman is Professor in the Countryside and Community Research Unit at Cheltenham and Gloucester College. His work on planning and the environment includes: *Environmental Planning* (London: Paul Chapman, 1992; second edition 1999); *Local Sustainability: Managing and Planning Ecologically Sound Places* (London: Paul Chapman, 1996); and 'The contribution of landscape ecology' in F. Aalen (ed.), *Landscape Study and Management* (Dublin: Boole Press, 1996).

Acknowledgements

This collection began life as a two-day conference held at Sheffield University, under the auspices of the Political Economy Research Centre. We would like to express our gratitude to: David Marquand (then Director of PERC); Gareth Roberts, the Vice-Chancellor of Sheffield University (for financial assistance); Yorkshire Water (for their sponsorship of the conference); and all the participants at this event. We are especially indebted to Sylvia McColm for all the hard work she put into this conference and her support, commitment and patience throughout.

In bringing this text together we would also like to thank Christine Whittaker, Andrew Gamble, Stephen Young, Claire Annesley and Patrick Proctor.

Introduction

Michael Kenny and James Meadowcroft

This book explores the relationship between one of the most important innovations in recent political discourse – environmental sustainability, and an idea that
has slipped from public attention in recent years – planning. The principal aim
underlying *Planning Sustainability* is to encourage advocates of environmental
politics to consider whether their arguments may gain in analytical precision
and normative power if 'planning' – in all its different senses – were more central
to their thinking. At present one can discern a reluctance not just to utilise the
conceptual vocabulary of planning, but more generally to consider the state as a
conceptual and normative terrain of particular significance in the analysis of
environmental politics.

A RETURN TO PLANNING?

In part this is due to the generally sceptical climate of ideas which now prevails
about planning specifically and state intervention generally within socio-economic
life. Debates about planning in Western democracies have revolved around
issues such as the conditions for successful economic advance, the importance
of redistributive mechanisms and a state-organised welfare net, and the diverse
and potentially contradictory claims of liberty and democracy (Hayward and
Watson 1975; Friedmann 1987). Over time commentators have become
increasingly pessimistic about the chances of achieving desired social objectives
(Rittel and Weber 1973). The history of planning is littered with unintended
consequences and undesired outcomes. Given the imprecision of social science
forecasting too (Ascher 1978), we are entitled to feel doubtful about the prospects for planning in relation to environmental issues, which arguably constitute some of the most complex problems yet faced by modern societies. This
sceptical mood has been reinforced in a number of liberal democratic states by
the de-legitimation of planning which has accompanied the ascendancy of
political perspectives which have poured scorn on the capacities of public
agencies to intervene wisely and effectively (Rydin 1993). This has been
most obviously true following the rise of the New Right in Britain and
the USA (Green 1987; King 1987), but more generally in the wake of the

'marketisation' of political life evident throughout the developed world since the 1980s.

This scepticism, which constitutes one of the most powerful legacies of the past decade, is echoed widely in academic discussions of planning practice and theory. 'Planning', it seems, has fallen from usage because of its association with the more directive, social democratic and occasionally explicitly coercive orientation of socio-economic policy in the 1960s and 1970s. Indeed public administration scholars now proclaim the normative inadequacy as well as the practical limitations of the planning models associated with this earlier era to deal with the uncertainties and risks characteristic of problems in 'complex' contemporary societies (Kooiman 1993).

These doubts find echoes in the academic literature on environmental questions. A great deal of attention has been given to the non-state or even anti-state dimensions of environmental mobilisations, and to the exclusion of 'radical' (often assumed to be authentic) green politics and thinking by the political mainstream (Martell 1994; Dobson 1995). Equally, attempts to define or codify green political thought or ideology have often been fixated by the appearance of anti-state and anti-institutional motifs in the writings of many environmental philosophers. But this is surely a poor reflection of the 'consciousness' of environmentalist-minded citizens in contemporary liberal democracies, and probably tells us more about the analytical preferences of these academics than anything fundamental about green politics.

Equally, approaches to sustainable development favoured in the scholarly and the politically active environmentalist communities have resulted in a rather one-dimensional account of the state, which most frequently depicts it as the servant of entrenched economic elites. Quite commonly sustainable development is defined around the 'core' value of opposition to economic growth which has been deemed to be a product of a drive rooted deeply within the psyche of the modern state. It seems implausible for some, therefore, that the state could ever be more than an agency for the brutalisation of non-human nature. Yet such a conclusion is rather short-sighted politically, and suspect intellectually. The state is surely better regarded as constituting a multi-level terrain over which different social groups and philosophies contend. Certainly it constitutes a series of 'sites' where power is wielded, but authority is rarely exercised in a uniform or coherent way, and underlying the various struggles over the state are the questions of agency and legitimacy. The state offers a vital source of social agency and regulation, as well as of social control (Held 1989). Its different, often contradictory, dimensions need greater consideration by environmentalists.

Definitions of 'sustainability' that hinge upon the reversal of the priority of economic growth might actually lead commentators to acknowledge the significance of public authorities because the latter (at least in theory) possess the resources, legitimacy and powers of co-ordination that such a reversal of socio-economic priorities would entail. Certainly it would be a caricature to suggest that hostility to the state is shared by all analysts of environmental politics. This is clearly not so, but perhaps one legacy of this anti-statist impulse is the lack of systematic attention to the problem of the state within the green literature. Most commonly, it is side-stepped as an analytical and normative problem.

A further impulse within contemporary intellectual debate may also be deemed responsible for the inattention to the issues raised here. This concerns debates pertaining to the globalisation of economic life within the contemporary period (Hirst and Thompson 1996). It has become something of a commonplace for analysts of environmental politics to stress the congruence between (economic) globalisation and the transnational character of many environmental issues. There is much sense in conceiving environmental problems as operative at different spatial scales, though the congruence with transnational economic forces and trends is more dubious. A rather ritualised denunciation of transnational corporations and the environmental 'bads' they generate often substitutes for a hard-headed analysis of these complex processes. More generally, this kind of argument has in some respects been pushed too far, in ways that render the analysis of environmental politics and policy unfeasible and weaken normative arguments for a greener future. It is simply not the case that nationally constituted authorities cannot meaningfully address many environmental problems. On the other hand, few politicians, bureaucrats or policy-minded academics now argue that the nation-state *alone* can deal with the most difficult and dangerous ecological issues. Public authorities at different levels of governance are increasingly required to act in concert with each other, and with other agencies – be they non-governmental organisations (NGOs), companies, or citizen action groups (Glasbergen 1998). Yet within the parameters of the new governance relationships that can be seen to be developing in a number of different policy domains, the nation-state and its attendant institutions remain of great significance. A parallel set of arguments has now grown up around globalisation more generally, with numerous critics questioning the adequacy of 'strong' and even some kinds of 'weak' globalisation theory (Perraton *et al.* 1997). Certainly such a radical argument about the impotence or irrelevance of the 'late' modern state, which does appear to underlie some writing on the international dimensions of environmental politics, requires much greater substantiation.

These suggestions go some way towards explaining the inattention to the state in general and the issues arising from planning in particular. This said, it is not entirely the case that the issues we stress here have been wholly ignored in academic scholarship. Most importantly, the academic study of the histories and problems attendant upon town and country planning deserve a wider audience (Hudson 1979; Sager 1992; Rydin 1993). Within the discipline of geography, other specialised literatures exist on land use planning (Owens 1994) and water resources, for example. These are vital areas of study and are touched on, though not treated extensively, in this collection. Despite these important literatures, planning in terms of the normative, analytical and practical issues at stake when it is considered in the context of environmental sustainability have not been adequately addressed. And though it might be thought that with the arrival of new conceptual categories like 'ecological modernisation' or 'societal steering' the notion of planning had become somewhat 'passé', our suggestion is that there remain untapped and important resources and insights in debates about planning strategies and goals.

PLANNING AND SUSTAINABILITY: BLISSFUL UNION OR GROUNDS FOR DIVORCE?

Sustainability, and the related term sustainable development, should be regarded as 'essentially contested' in definitional terms. The many different understandings and characterisations of sustainability that have emerged from the academic world alone are a testament to this (Mitlin 1992; Dobson 1996). But nearly all definitions concede that it involves the re-orientation of the 'meta objectives' of a given society – by raising questions about different possible social trajectories through which the society may move, and then by promoting some of these as more 'sustainable' than others. It is worth emphasising that the notion of sustainability does *not* in any way imply only one kind of social future as the embodiment of 'the' sustainable society. Environmental sustainability also functions as an 'idealistic benchmark' against which current practices can be critically assessed. Both of these facets lead to the suggestion that only certain conscious human strategies and designs can effect the achievement of a more socially and environmentally responsible range of futures. Thus the discourse of planning remains pertinent for describing the processes of co-ordinating different conceptions of various social futures. It also offers a way of embedding the future orientation of sustainability talk in a highly institutionalised and normatively rich set of intellectual contexts.

In considering agencies which are available to oversee and co-ordinate such a social re-orientation, public authorities, and their attendant capacities, legitimacy and collective experience, have to be regarded as central. After all, the creation of different institutions and agencies within the modern nation-state is a central part of the story of how patterns of socio-economic activity have already been re-orientated in modern history. One of the principal implications of 'planning' in liberal democratic contexts concerns the setting of 'meta-social objectives' by the state, or the 'steering' of economic life to meet pre-determined social goals. The state thus looks like one of the most likely candidates for an agency which may oversee the shift to a (more) sustainable society. In this sense the objective of environmental sustainability, contestable and changing as this is, may well logically entail 'planning' in this meta-level sense.

This theoretical connection is shadowed, in policy terms, by the likelihood that public authorities are uniquely placed to deal with certain kinds of environmental problems, even if they do not always do so effectively or judiciously. As environmentalists have repeatedly reminded us, many of the most pressing and damaging issues facing planetary ecology require co-ordinated responses by an agency acting for the common good. Environmental problems are always of a social character, cutting across the geographical and legal demarcations which frame the social and economic relationships between individuals, organisations and states. Problems and crises of an ecological nature simply do not respect these boundaries, posing 'collective action problems' of urgent and unique kinds (Dryzek 1987). And whilst many greens are perhaps rightly sceptical about any single government's capacity to solve pressing environmental problems, elected governments within sovereign states are integral to the formation of novel patterns and norms governing international collective action. In the responses of public authorities to environmental issues – ranging from air quality in cities and the diminution of fishing stocks, to ozone depletion – the idea of setting goals and targets, and re-orientating existing social and economic patterns of behaviour are ever present. Planning thus may be a practical, as well as a logical, requirement of environmental sustainability.

Arguments for a more sustainable future may in fact be crucial in reviving planning's respectability as a social practice and goal. The urgency of environmentally-related problems and the difficulties which market-based economies experience in generating flexible and long-term solutions, may actually rekindle interest in some older ideas about the ethical and practical merits of state and sub-state planning. Already many commentators have detected a shift in mood in many countries after the 1980s towards a recognition amongst publics at large of the negative consequences of a blind faith in markets, and a recognition of the need for states to co-ordinate a whole range of social activities – from the mundane to the highly complex – for markets to operate at all. The environment may well be a central domain in the next half century in helping re-articulate the relationship between state and economy in liberal democracies.

The problems associated with the environment pose a massive challenge for public authorities. Again a historical perspective on this theme may well be instructive. Earlier developments in the institutional architectures and capacities of liberal democratic states were in part responses to challenges that were perceived at the time as fundamental and, according to some, just as apparently insoluble as ecological threats are today. Thus in the face of the challenges of warfare and welfare, fundamental changes within state apparatuses took place (Offe 1984; Skocpol, Evans and Rueschemeyer 1985; Hall and Ikenberry 1989). But will existing institutional structures and sources of knowledge prove adequate in dealing with the complex and particular character of issues such as pollution, threats to species diversity and the erosion of our non-renewable resource base? Thinking about sustainability and planning in this way should alert us to the dangers of assuming that existing bodies and organisations, which were designed to respond to very different issues, can necessarily be relied upon to deliver environmental sustainability. We need to know much more about the historical processes through which planning agencies have developed and which kinds of social objectives different kinds of planning bodies have succeeded or failed in realising.

Also important here, and central to the evaluation of planning's history that we propose, is the question of democracy and participation within planning processes; and specifically in relation to the goals of ecological sustainability. In some eyes, planning has become irredeemably associated with the denial of democracy and of local and small-scale initiatives and citizen involvement. This can stem from a theoretical rejection of much modern planning discourse as founded upon the provision by experts – looking down on society from 'above' and using rationalistic principles – of solutions to social problems. Planning, when it follows this model, all too often perceives the people as the object of intervention, rather than empowered subjects shaping the planning process. Arguably, when public agencies have intervened in such a way in the urban environment, for instance, disaster has ensued. Having noted these criticisms, it is important to recognise that there is no necessary correlation between planning and anti-democratic practice. In fact, the reverse has often been the case for, without planning, it is hard to imagine a functioning democracy today. Indeed there is a rich and variegated tradition of arguments about how to design democratic or associative planning models that require the consent and participation of key stakeholders. Planning – both as an actuality and ideal – constitutes a terrain which is in many ways as contested as environmental sustainability. As several of the chapters in this book make clear, long established disputes about planning take on a new edge in the context of campaigns and arguments for more environmentally sustainable social economies.

A number of commentators have speculated about the connections between democracy and environmental sustainability in both theoretical and empirical terms (Doherty and de Geus 1996; Lafferty and Meadowcroft 1996). Planning provides a rather different route into these debates, raising as it does questions about social agency, about the responsibility and accountability of state actors, and about who should influence the selection of social objectives. The theoretical and empirical literatures on planning offer many insights from which environmentalists might learn. Here it is vital for academic specialists on environmental matters to recognise that if sustainability does in certain senses entail planning, we have much to learn from the historical failures of particular planning enterprises, as well as more positive lessons to be gleaned from some extraordinary feats of social co-ordination and design undertaken by public authorities in liberal democratic states. A particularly important and burgeoning literature is worth singling out here: the study of social learning in planning processes (Bennett and Howlett 1992). This strand of scholarship explores planning as a recursive and potentially reflexive series of activities and processes in which cognitive and social adaptation are as key to the success of planning practices as traditionally emphasised practices such as goal design and evaluation. This field of study has been fruitfully linked to environmental planning by a number of commentators (Lee 1993; Glasbergen 1996; Grin and van de Graff 1996).

There is a final sense in which we should connect planning with environmental sustainability in our thinking. It is perhaps the most immediately significant of all of the 'bridges' between these two sets of ideas and practices. It involves the recent experiences of actual planning for sustainability which exist at the level of both the nation-state and sub-governmental authority in a number of countries. An important trigger for these developments was the Rio Earth Summit, and the much heralded Agenda 21 initiative. At Rio world leaders formally pledged to make development 'sustainable', and Agenda 21 explicitly called upon states to elaborate 'national strategies, plans, policies and processes' to achieve this (United

Nations Conference on Environment and Development 1992). This call has been answered in the form of a plethora of such plans drawn up by local, national and even transnational bodies, in the case of the EU, and indeed in the adoption of new legislative commitments by many states (Carew-Reid *et al.* 1994; Dalal-Clayton 1996). There is much debate about the nature of the agreements reached at Rio, and the politics that underpinned this and other such events (Kenny *et al.* 1996). Significantly these plans differ enormously in their character and ambition. Disappointingly little attention has so far been paid to these experiences by academic analysts, though in Chapter 8 Jänicke and Jörgens go some way to remedying this in their comparative survey of sustainability planning in different states. Some key questions arise in relation to these experiences. What do they tell us about the viability of different modes of planning in the face of environmental problems? Have states found that existing institutions and agencies are capable of taking on the objectives of sustainability? Have planners in this area learned lessons from earlier experiences of co-ordination and provision in other policy domains?

These different arguments about possible and necessary connections between planning and environmental sustainability provide the backdrop to the contributions collected here, which explore these themes in greater depth. We refer readers to the rich and diverse normative inheritance bound up in debates about 'planning', both in a meta-level sense, and as a set of historically bounded institutions and practices. When considered against the 'problematic' of sustainable development, the idea of planning opens up a field of study and debate bounded by three particular concerns: (a) the challenge of forging associative and effective policy regimes in the wake of environmental problems; (b) the task of devising and legitimating new socio-economic trajectories for liberal democratic states; and (c) arguments about the ethical principles which should underwrite the allocation of resources and responsibilities involved in planning for sustainability. It is within this triangular set of concerns that the debates contained within this text move. If any conclusion emerges from these different ideas it is that planning for sustainable development is a challenge which liberal democratic states are morally obliged to address. Members of the diverse academic communities to which this text is addressed can play a role in exploring and shaping the leading ideas about how this might be undertaken.

In the opening chapter James Meadowcroft considers sustainable development as a particular kind of planning objective. We can learn much, he suggests, from some long-established critiques of planning theories and practices, specifically the ideas of Wildavsky, Lindblom and Hayek. Meadowcroft points to a number of planning 'modalities' – incremental planning, oblique planning and defensive planning – which survive such critical accounts and may well be pertinent for the kind of planning for progress that environmental sustainability involves.

This chapter is followed by an in-depth survey of planning models which have prevailed during the twentieth century by Charles Lindblom, one of the theorists that Meadowcroft considers. Lindblom probes the strengths and weaknesses of these experiences, and points to anomalies underpinning different planning experiments: for instance, the absence of any serious attempt by a democratic state to construct a non-market planning regime. He also reaffirms the importance of the planning modality with which his own work is most closely associated: the process of 'mutual adjustment', as opposed to planning interpreted as the directive intelligence of the bureaucratic state.

While Meadowcroft and Lindblom focus upon planning as a set of historical experiences and associated theories which are of significance for environmental sustainability, the next four chapters focus upon goals and values associated with sustainability, and consider how the state can and should play a role in relation to these. Michael Redclift evaluates sustainability in relation to its wide-ranging implications for our familiar political and intellectual systems. He looks particularly at different ways in which a concern for sustainability might be introduced into current policy choices in developed, industrialised economies, showing that each has important implications for the processes of planning by posing major challenges to prevailing patterns of consumption and production. He also introduces some important theoretical paradigms and shows how their insights may help us to understand the 'problematic' of sustainability in relation to planning in complex and 'risk' societies.

Michael Jacobs focuses too on sustainability, but from a different vantage point. He offers a strong critique of mainstream economic thinking in relation to these questions, suggesting that in key respects (for instance, the 'collective good' character of environmental problems, as well as the scales at which they occur) the neo-classical economic paradigm and related market dominated models offer an inappropriate framework for the comprehension and resolution of environmental dilemmas. The state, Jacobs asserts, needs to be returned to the agenda of environmental economists wrestling with the implications of sustainability.

The question of scale, to which Jacobs alludes, remains one of the most complex and important themes arising from ecological problems, both in terms of the different scales at which these emerge and the difficulties authorities and social actors face in co-ordinating their responses. In his chapter, William Rees explores these issues and focuses on the limitations of quasi-independent sovereign states, with their different levels of spatial jurisdictions and conflicting mandates. He shows how the context for environmental decision-making is changing significantly, and points to the strengths and limitations of some recent multi-scale initiatives in planning for sustainability. He criticises the analytical paradigms located in both classical economics and mainstream science for their failure to comprehend contemporary environmental problems, counterposing the notion of a 'human ecological crisis'. In delineating the latter, he draws upon new scientific paradigms, especially theories associated with 'complexity', 'dynamic systems' and 'chaos', all of which perceive relationships in a non-linear fashion. Yet such ideas contrast dramatically with the monological simplicity of the hegemonic economic philosophy of the era of globalisation.

Wouter Achterberg then explores one possible policy implication of environmental sustainability: the idea of a guaranteed basic income. This policy may represent a way of reconciling the different ethical and practical requirements of both sustainability and commonly understood notions of social justice, at a time when the welfare state is experiencing acute crisis. Achterberg's argument points to the neglect in the environmental politics literature of consideration of tensions between different ethical goals and values – not least social justice – in the wake of the weaknesses of welfare regimes, on the one hand, and the requirements of sustainability, on the other.

Following these discussions of the nature and implications of sustainability for our political and ethical systems, the last three chapters of the collection consider the potential for sustainability planning. Paul Selman reviews the different kinds of environmental planning that have characterised the last three decades, and offers an audit of what we have learned from these in both positive and negative terms. He focuses on two different kinds of planning practice: as a formal process of land management, guiding and controlling built development; and as a generic activity, involving provision for the future and the strategic and tactical allocation of human and physical resources. He notes particularly the different kinds of agencies and resources that have been deployed in these activities, and offers telling observations about the specificities of environmental problems.

The particular character of ecological issues is also the starting point of Martin Jänicke's and Helge Jörgens's chapter. They observe the extreme forms of uncertainty that these generate for policy-makers and offer an authoritative and wide-ranging evaluation of how the different national environmental plans, drawn up since the Rio Earth Summit, have sought to deal with this characteristic. They offer unique insight into the very different ways in which industrialised states have tackled the task of planning for sustainability. Of particular significance is the variation in terms of institutional reform, departmental responsibility and monitoring efforts that they note in the different states under consideration.

Finally, Tim Lang offers a case-study of a particular domain in which sustainability planning seems all too necessary, yet is particularly fraught: food policy. He shows how many of the themes identified by the various contributors to this collection – the question of scale, the impact of the market, the need for state regulation and oversight, and the ethical imperatives of environmental sustainability – lie at the heart of struggles over the future of food policy in Britain. He points to a significant difference of emphasis dividing advocates of sustainability in this domain between those who look to state intervention, monitoring and action, and others who seek to devise a more complex, multi-level and culturally rooted system of governance in this area. Both of these strategies are underpinned by different conceptions of 'planning' in relation to environmental sustainability. It is our hope that this collection will deepen activists', students' and analysts' understanding of the nature and importance of such arguments.

References

Ascher, W. (1978) *Forecasting: An Appraisal*, Baltimore: Johns Hopkins University Press.
Bennett, C. and Howlett. M. (1992) 'The lessons of learning: reconciling theories of policy learning and policy change', *Policy Sciences* 25: 275–92.

Carew-Reid, J., Prescott-Allen, R., Bass, S. and Dalal-Clayton, B. (1994) *Strategies for National Sustainable Development*, London: Earthscan in association with the International Institute for Environment and Development (IIED) and the International Union for the Conservation of Nature and Natural Resources (IUCN).

Dalal-Clayton, B. (1996) *Getting to Grips with Green Plans: National Experience in Industrial Countries*, London: Earthscan.

Dobson, A. (1995) *Green Political Thought*, London: Routledge, 2nd edn.

Dobson, A. (1996) 'Environmental sustainabilities: an analysis and a typology', *Environmental Politics* 5: 401–28.

Doherty, B. and de Geus, M. (1996) *Democracy and Green Political Thought*, London: Routledge.

Dryzek, J. (1987) *Rational Ecology: Environment and Political Economy*, Oxford: Basil Blackwell.

Friedmann, J. (1987) *Planning in the Public Domain*, Princeton, NJ: Princeton University Press.

Glasbergen, P. (1996) 'Learning to manage the environment', in Lafferty and Meadowcroft (1996).

Glasbergen, P. (ed.) (1998) *Co-operative Environmental Governance*, Dordrecht: Kluwer Academic.

Green, D. (1987) *The New Right*, Brighton: Wheatsheaf.

Grin, J. and van de Graff, H. (1996) 'Technology assessment as learning', *Science, Technology and Human Values* 21: 72–99.

Hall, J. and Ikenberry, J. (1989), *The State*, Milton Keynes: Open University Press.

Hayward , J. and Watson, M. (1975) *Planning, Politics and Public Policy: The British, French and Italian Experience*, Cambridge: Cambridge University Press.

Held, D. (1989) *Political Theory and the Modern State*, Cambridge: Polity Press.

Hirst, P. and Thompson, G. (1996) *Globalisation in Question*, Cambridge: Polity Press.

Hudson, B. (1979) 'Comparison of current planning theories: counterparts and contradictions', *Journal of the American Planning Association*: 45: 387–98.

Jänicke, M. and Weider, H. (eds) (1995) *Successful Environmental Policy*, Berlin: Edition Sigma.

Kenny, M., Patterson, M., Thomas, C., Meadowcroft, J. and Ward, S. (1996) 'Debate: re-evaluating Rio', *New Political Economy* 1: 399–416.

King, D. (1987) *The New Right: Policy, Markets and Citizenship*, London: Macmillan.

Kooiman, J. (ed.) (1993) *Modern Governance*, London: Sage.

Lafferty, W. and Meadowcroft, J. (eds) (1996) *Democracy and the Environment: Problems and Prospects*, Cheltenham: Edward Elgar.

Lee, K. (1993) *Compass and Gyroscope*, Washington, DC: Island Press.

Martell, L. (1994) *Ecology and Society*, Cambridge: Polity Press.

Mitlin, D. (1992) 'Sustainable development: a guide to the literature', *Environment and Urbanisation* 4: 111–24.

Offe, C. (1984) *Contradictions of the Welfare State*, London: Hutchinson.

Owens, S. (1994) 'Land, limits and sustainability: a conceptual framework and some dilemmas for the planning system', *Transactions of the Institute of British Geographers* NS 19: 439–56.

Perraton, J., Goldblatt, D., Held, D. and McGrew, A. (1997) 'The Globalisation of Economic Activity', *New Political Economy* 2, 2: 257–78.

Rittel, H. and Weber, M. (1973) 'Dilemmas in a general theory of planning', *Policy Sciences* 4: 155–69.

Rydin, Y. (1993) *The British Planning System*, London: Macmillan.

Sager, T. (1992) 'Why plan? A multi-rationality foundation for planning', *Scandinavian Housing and Planning Research* 9: 129–47.

Skocpol, T., Evans, P. and Rueschemeyer, D. (1985) *Bringing the State Back In*, Cambridge: Cambridge University Press.

United Nations Conference on Environment and Development (1992) *Agenda 21*, New York: United Nations Organisation.

1 Planning for sustainable development: what can be learned from the critics?

James Meadowcroft[1]

It is an intriguing fact of late twentieth-century life that just at the time when philosophers have proclaimed the death of 'meta-narratives', the collapse of grand modernist dreams for re-moulding man and society and consciously shaping the human future – indeed, even the end of 'history' itself – international political leaders have come to identify themselves with an ambitious new project intended to act as the focus of human endeavour in the twenty-first century. Curiously, at a time when 'planning' – particularly macro-scale social and economic planning – is distinctly unfashionable, there is almost universal acclaim for an undertaking which, at least *prima facie*, appears to imply a vast extension of various kinds of planning practice. This new project is 'sustainable development', and the third paragraph of Agenda 21 – the comprehensive document adopted at the Rio Earth Summit in 1992 which sets out the global vision for the first century of the next millennium – calls on governments to elaborate 'national strategies, plans, policies and processes' to ensure the implementation of sustainable development (United Nations Conference on Environment and Development 1992).

Yet experiences with state planning initiatives in the twentieth century have been deeply ambiguous. On one hand, the complex planning mechanisms through which governments seek to structure and orient patterns of social and economic interaction have been associated with real achievements. On the other hand, planning and planners have been linked to a steady stream of policy fiascos and disasters. It is not just that planning techniques have been pressed into the service of dubious ends, but that laudable ends pursued by well-intentioned bodies have so often resulted in acute disappointment: either because the original objectives were never attained, because these objectives were subsequently revealed as ill-conceived or illusory, or because the harvest of anticipated benefits was vitiated by the unintended consequences of the policies designed to secure them.

When contemplating a bold new focus for the work of planners and regulators it is therefore worth pausing to reflect on criticisms which have been levelled at previous planning efforts and to consider how the pursuit of 'sustainable development' might alter the established planning modalities of contemporary democracies.[2] The argument in this chapter is organised in three parts. After a preliminary examination of the character of sustainable development as a policy goal, the discussion moves on to consider the perspectives of three prominent planning critics. Objections to planning practice and potentialities found in the work of Hayek, Wildavsky and Lindblom serve to illuminate difficulties, but also the possibilities, that may be associated with 'planning for sustainable development'.[3] The final section offers some tentative conclusions.

SUSTAINABLE DEVELOPMENT AS A PLANNING OBJECTIVE

Since it was catapaulted to international prominence by the report of the World Commission on Environment and Development in 1987, 'sustainable development' has emerged as the master concept of international discourses of environment and development. The most widely quoted definition of sustainable development – one which underpinned the United Nations Conference on Environment and Development (UNCED) process leading to Rio, and which continues to provide a key reference point for the ongoing United Nations Commission on Sustainable Development (UNCSD) and for Agenda 21 implementation activities – was provided by the Brundtland Commission. According to *Our Common Future*, 'sustainable development' is:

> development that meets the needs of the present without compromising the ability of future generations to meet their own needs. It contains within it two key concepts: the concept of 'needs', in particular the essential needs of the world's poor, to which priority should be given; and the idea of limitations imposed by the state of technology and social organisation in the environment's ability to meet present and future needs.
>
> (World Commission on Environment and Development 1987: 43)

There is no dearth of alternative ways to specify the meaning of sustainable development (Mitlin 1992; Pezzy 1992; Redclift 1992). Furthermore, 'sustainable' and the related term 'sustainability' can be combined with a vast array of terms other than 'development': thus we have 'sustainable growth', 'sustainable biosphere', 'sustainable living', 'sustainable resource management', 'sustainable cities', the 'sustainability of ecosystems', 'cultural sustainability', and so on. This proliferation illustrates the fluidity of conceptual categories and boundaries in the relatively open-textured context of political and social debate. And it reflects the complexity of the themes invoked when development and environment are juxtaposed.

An exhaustive discussion of the idiom of sustainability goes beyond the scope of this chapter, but some broader issues can be clarified by briefly considering usage of four key expressions: 'sustainable yield', 'environmental sustainability', 'sustainable society', and 'sustainable development' itself.

In an environmental context the most straightforward usage is *sustainable yield* from a specific (self-renewing) natural resource: say, the harvest of timber from a forest, or fish from a lake. A sustainable yield is one which can in principle be maintained indefinitely, because it can be accommodated by the regenerative capacities of the underlying natural system. The 'maximum sustainable yield' is the highest yield which can persist over the long run without compromising future harvests. In conceptual terms this is reasonably clear, because the focus is upon a regular (and quantifiable) flow of a single resource which is predicated upon maintenance of an underlying stock. There is a direct parallel with the yield of an interest-bearing security, and the need to maintain the integrity of the investment capital if future income flows are to be secure. Of course, in practice there may be great difficulty in determining the appropriate level of resource extraction. As one moves from considering extraction of a single resource with exclusive reliance upon natural regeneration towards multiple-resource systems and those involving more elaborate human intervention the concept becomes more problematic. Nevertheless, many uses of 'sustainable' implicitly trade upon an analogy with the single self-renewing natural resource harvest model.

Environmental sustainability is a more ambiguous expression. Generally speaking, usage gravitates between two poles. On the one hand, 'environmental sustainability' is taken to suggest the sustainability of the natural environment; on the other, it is associated with the environmental dimension of the sustainability of social institutions and practices. In the first sense the expression relates to the preservation of natural environmental systems and processes. What is to be sustained is 'the environment' itself: either in general, or in particular instances – such as maintenance of specific ecosystems like tropical forests, or of environmental features like 'biodiversity' or the stratospheric ozone layer. The constraint or stress with respect to which such environmental sustainability is assessed is human activity: this is what is taken to threaten the maintenance of natural environmental processes and integrity. In the second case, the expression relates to the necessity of addressing environmental issues if social institutions and processes are to be maintained. What is to be sustained are social practices, and the constraints which threaten sustainability are environmental. The two senses can be related because at least certain natural systems and environments must be 'sustained' if any social practices are to be sustainable. But there are also potential contradictions, because the continuation of many social activities would prove incompatible with the preservation of many natural systems and environments. The two perspectives therefore approach the problem in quite different ways, with the first resonating more strongly with attempts to preserve natural habitats and processes from human despoliation and with the valuation of nature for its own sake; while the second has a particular affinity for human ends, and the management of environmental assets to serve those ends. In both cases human behaviour must be modified to secure sustainability, but the standpoints from which this will be assessed are different. In practice, of course, both conceptualisations of 'environmental sustainability' may be present in any given discussion.

The expression *sustainable society* is usually taken to mean a society that has learned to live within the boundaries established by ecological limits. Society as a collective and ongoing entity can be sustained, because social practices which imposed excessive burdens upon the environment have been reformed or abolished. Such a sustainable society would therefore have achieved 'environmental sustainability' in the second of the two senses described above: its integrity can be maintained because it has adjusted to environmental constraints. It might also be understood as a society which promoted 'environmental sustainability' in the first sense – that is to say a society that sustained the natural environments which it valued for both instrumental and non-instrumental reasons.

Underlying much of the discussion about the nature of a 'sustainable society' is a tension between (a) attainment of a comprehensive social/environmental equilibrium (involving exclusive reliance on renewable resources, stable levels of population and material throughput, and a life in balance with natural processes and systems), and (b) achievement of partial and motile equilibria (perhaps involving continued dependence upon a shifting portfolio of non-renewable resources, and even expanding population levels or throughput volumes, provided provision was made for developing resource substitutes, and key life support systems were not breached). In the first case, a sustainable society is basically in static equilibrium with its surroundings, and in environmental terms its industrial and agricultural practices could be continued indefinitely (or at least until seriously affected by non-anthropogenic environmental change). Yet this would not be a society without movement or the opportunity for bettering the human condition, although change would have to take place within the context of a fixed total environmental loading (Daly 1977). In the second case, the stability is essentially dynamic, and though individual activities will be unsustainable and unsustained, they will form links in an endless chain in which new forms of activity emerge to assure social reproduction.

Nowadays it is increasingly common to link the idea of a sustainable society to sustainable development: thus a sustainable society is understood as a society engaged in sustainable development, or (less commonly) as a social state that will be attained at some future point after sustainable development has effected a significant transformation of existing socio-economic practices. Since sustainable development is usually taken to be more than simply an 'environmental' concept, and also to imply a particular vision of what constitutes genuine 'development', a 'sustainable society' may be understood as one which displays such substantive attributes.

Sustainable development is politically the most significant of these terms today. Crucial to its bearing is the notion of 'development' – for what is to be sustained here is not some particular social form or pre-determined environmental feature, but rather a process called development. In one sense any change might be considered 'development', but as used here it implies improvement or advance, an increase of human welfare, the betterment of material, cultural and moral circumstance; in a word, 'progress'. Sustainable development implies a positive process of social change that proceeds in such a fashion that it avoids generating internal contradictions which would undermine the possibility for future advance.

Sustainable development therefore explicitly engages with the substantial and ongoing debate about the nature of social progress which has concerned political decision-makers, and the social sciences, throughout the twentieth century. The expression has roots in the discourses on development which have grown up since the 1950s around the efforts of the less industrialised states to improve their circumstances. But it has implied a broadening application of the term 'development' to include also the continuing evolution of social, economic and political conditions in the industrialised regions of the globe (World Commission on Environment and Development 1987: 40). Sustainable development raises questions about the character of developmental activities and processes in both North and South, and particularly about the extent to which these can be extended into the future.

As sustainable development has passed into the idiom of international political interchange it has come to be associated with a set of normative principles including a concern to meet human needs, especially the urgent developmental needs of the poor; the protection of environmental resources and global life-support systems; the integration of economic and environmental considerations in decision-making; encouragement of popular participation in environment- and development-related processes; and a recognition of the common but differentiated needs and responsibilities of the countries of the North and South (Lafferty 1996).

Consideration of whether a particular project or set of activities is compatible with 'sustainable development' involves juxtaposition of two dimensions. On the one hand, it implies reflection upon whether the observed or proposed patterns of change should actually be held to constitute 'development' at all – or at least the kind of (genuine) development with which 'sustainable development' is associated. On the other hand, it implies consideration of whether the 'development' in question can be part of an ongoing process of improvement that could without self-contradiction be extended into the future. The first sort of judgement requires assessment of the character (and distribution) of costs and benefits associated with the initiative or orientation, while the second requires analysis of the varied constraints that might preclude continued advance. Both sorts of judgement imply a substantial normative component, for assumptions about the nature and relative worth of various individual and collective goods are necessary to assess the (developmental) value of the putative project or activity and also to define the larger progressive movement with which it is to be compatible.

Since sustainable development focuses upon the maintenance of developmental momentum, it does not necessarily entail the preservation either of existing environmental systems or of prevailing social structures and practices. On the contrary, 'development' implies the potential transformation of both. Of course, without the preservation of much (in terms of planetary life support systems and environmental resources, but also in terms of valued social institutions and practices), continued improvement would be unimaginable. But just what should be preserved and what should be altered is open to argument. Moreover, the boundaries of what can or must be preserved/changed will undoubtedly shift over time as the nature of society, configurations of natural systems, and their inter-relation evolve. Thus, returning to an issue raised above in the context of the discussion of 'sustainable society', sustainable development does *not* depend upon the comprehensive adoption of practices which can themselves be sustained indefinitely, although the term is sometimes used as implying movement towards a society of such a type. Practices that are individually unsustainable could be an acceptable (even an essential) part of a process of sustainable development (Meadowcroft 1997). Here, too, there is a tension between an image which emphasises what might be described as the 'renewable ideal', and one which privileges ascent through the timely succession of non-perpetuable activities.

Elsewhere, I have suggested that it may be helpful to think about sustainable development in terms of a 'social trajectory' (Meadowcroft 1997). Over time, a society may be understood to trace a particular 'development path' as its economic, social and cultural circumstances change (World Commission on Environment and Development 1987: xii, 43). At any given moment a vast array of potential future pathways lie before it, with each phase of social evolution opening up new sets of options but foreclosing others. The challenge of sustainable development would then be to ensure that society moved along a line of advance, avoiding *both* those pathways which constituted a direct deterioration of the social state, and those which lead to points from which further progress was impossible.

This metaphor of developmental trajectory brings a number of issues to the fore. It emphasises that variance in societal behaviour on multiple dimensions can give rise to many alternative futures. Furthermore it suggests that there is no reason to conclude that there is only one pathway of sustainable development – there may be many patterns of possible advance which do not preclude future development. Yet the image of a trajectory also implies that some (perhaps abstractly desirable) social states may now be inaccessible, because they lie too far from the route on which society is presently engaged (path dependence). And since a trajectory represents mass in motion, it hints at the resistance that will confront efforts to deflect society from a well established dynamic.

Two other points are of importance. First, the image of a social trajectory which perpetually 'reads positive' to measures of developmental progress suggests that sustainable development is sensitive to shifting judgements about the nature of authentic development. Change the nature or mix of criteria by which developmental advance is assessed, and different families of social trajectory will emerge as representing potentially sustainable (or unsustainable) futures. Second, there is the implication that sustainable development might appear to be predicated on an unrealistically optimistic notion of social change. History suggests human societies seldom experience prolonged, uninterrupted, across-the-board advance (Mannermaa 1995). More typical are situations where different dimensions of social life display a mix of progression and regression, or where phases of general advance are followed by periods of decay, stagnation and crisis, which may (or may not) open the way to further positive development. Does the idea of sustainable development run foul of this observation? Not necessarily. Endorsement of sustainable development as an objective involves no prediction that social life will evolve smoothly. Neither is there an implication that the pace of progress must be constant, or evenly distributed across social domains. And of course there can be no promise that opportunities bequeathed to the future will actually be used by later generations in ways that correspond with our ideas of progress. To talk of sustainable development does not necessarily imply endorsement of a naive belief that things 'are bound to improve', or a denial that crisis and conflict inevitably accompany human enterprise. Rather it can be taken as reflecting an aspiration to improve human well being, without eroding the environmental foundations upon which the lives of future generations depend. It is a normative standard which we can use today, to assess activities we are currently undertaking (or considering): it impels us to enquire whether their pursuit is compatible with long-term development, and whether they could form part of a positive movement that does not undermine its own preconditions.

The image of a social trajectory can also help us reflect on the implications of the challenge of public planning for sustainable development. It suggests that such planning implies some form of conscious effort to orient society away from certain trajectories and towards preferred pathways. It suggests an element of deliberate social choice to privilege certain patterns of development over others. Of course, no one believes that a society can 'choose' a development trajectory with the same ease with which it may decide to alter its national anthem. Development pathways result from the interaction of vast arrays of complex factors, from choices made by individuals and organisations spread across time and space. Still, the notion of public planning for sustainable development seems to imply some form of conscious intervention by public authorities in an attempt to influence the path that will ultimately be realised.

Planning for sustainable development implies a degree of forward-oriented thought and action by government. Yet it does *not* require directing society towards some comprehensively pre-determined social end state. Nor does planning for sustainable development imply an ambitious exercise in pattern matching, attempting to ensure that the detailed character of the development which is actually taking place 'fits' with the profile of some comprehensively pre-designed social trajectory. Rather, planning for sustainable development involves the more modest task of displacing the direction of social movement (to a certain extent, and in certain dimensions) so that current (authentic) developmental priorities are attained, while the preconditions for subsequent social advance are not eroded.

PLANNING CRITICS

Arguments over the appropriate scope and character of governmental planning have been close to the centre of political controversy in the developed industrial states for much of the twentieth century. On the most abstract level there has been a running 'meta-debate' about the potentialities of planning, and the place of rationality and conscious design in perfecting human social institutions. This discussion will be approached here by focusing on the work of three well-known contributors to such debates: Frederick Hayek, Aaron Wildavsky and Charles Lindblom.

The original thrust of Hayek's criticism of planning was directed against the command economy, against a system where private property had been abolished, the competitive price mechanism suppressed, and economic life was directed by the administrative fiat of central planners. Writing during the Second World War, he argued that while in one sense the term 'planning' could suggest merely that we should manage our affairs rationally, and 'in this sense everybody who is not a complete fatalist is a planner' and 'every political act is (or ought to be) an act of planning', in fact the word had been appropriated by those who wished to establish centralised state control over the economy in order to achieve a pre-determined ('just') pattern of distribution. Hayek explained that the rift between liberals and socialist planners was a dispute over whether it was better:

> that the holder of coercive power should confine himself in general to cre-ating the conditions under which the knowledge and initiative of individuals is given the best scope so that *they* can plan most successfully; or whether a rational utilisation of our resources requires *central* direction and organisation of all our activities according to some consciously constructed 'blueprint'.
>
> (Hayek 1944: 26)

By the end of the 1950s Hayek concluded that the original socialist project of abolishing all private enterprise and establishing a command economy had lost support in Western Europe, and thereafter much of his attention was devoted to repudiating features of the emerging welfare state. Crucial to Hayek's case against more attenuated forms of planning were arguments concerning the dispersal of knowledge, the opposition between spontaneously formed and designed orders, progress, the limited role of reason in human affairs, and the 'rule of law'.

According to Hayek, the 'great problem' of social life is how 'we can all profit' from the vast sum of social knowledge which 'exists nowhere as an integrated whole', but which is embedded in inherited social institutions, traditions and practices, and is dispersed in the minds of many men (Hayek 1960: 25). The fundamental value of freedom is that it permits individuals to make use of knowledge they do not consciously possess. The competitive market allows the co-ordination of dispersed agents based upon information of individualised experience which is in principle beyond the reach of any centralised govern-ment organisation.

Hayek contrasted spontaneously formed social orders which evolved over time (such as language, law, morals and the market), with designed orders created by conscious intent. While human beings could deliberately establish particular organisations to further specific ends, more ambitious projects to consciously re-order the elements of social life according to a pre-conceived plan could only be carried through by compromising the liberty on which genuine progress depended, and they were in any case destined to fail because human reason was not capable of consciously apprehending the full complexity of social life or the full range of factors which had led to the evolution of existing social structures and institutions. Hayek rebuked 'constructivist' or 'design' theorists for failing to appreciate the enduring value and subtlety of spontaneously evolved orders, and for assuming that 'rational' must mean consciously laid out. He suggested that the 'idea of intelligent men coming together for deliberation about how to make the world anew is perhaps the most characteristic outcome' of such 'design theories' (Hayek 1960: 57).

With respect to 'progress', he argued that it represented a voyage into the unknown, for the course of future social evolution could not be anticipated in advance. Progress was 'a process of formation and modification of the human intellect, a process of adaptation and learning in which not only the possibilities known to us but also our values and desires continually change' (Hayek 1960: 40). He insisted, 'human reason can neither predict nor deliberately shape its own future. Its advances consist in finding out where it has been wrong' (Hayek 1960: 41). Thus the notion of 'planning for progress' was ridiculous. Favourable advance emerged from the unplanned interaction of countless factors; at best one could maintain conditions favourable to further progress – especially the impulse and opportunity for experimentation and innovation provided by a market economy and a free society.

Hayek believed the most essential function of the state was to uphold 'the rule of law', that is to say to uphold the set of rules of conduct (which had themselves evolved through complex processes over time) which established the parameters within which individual action was permitted. Law (*nomos*) was by its nature general in character, applying not to particulars but to society as a whole, and so framed that it could be administered impartially by the judiciary. Freedom under the law means 'that what we may do is not dependent on the approval of any person or authority and is limited only by the same abstract rules that apply equally to all' (Hayek 1960: 155). Thus the 'task of the lawgiver is not to set up a particular order but merely to create conditions in which an orderly arrangement can establish and ever renew itself' (Hayek 1960: 161).

Hayek recognised that government would assume a variety of tasks beyond its fundamental obligation to maintain a general framework of law (including rules which made functioning markets possible): its coercive power might support regulation designed to secure public ends (sanitary or factory regulations, for example); and government could perform service functions which involved compulsion only to the extent that they relied upon taxation (provision of public roads or libraries, organisation of relief for the poor, and so on). It was essential that all regulations be framed 'in the form of general rules specifying conditions which everybody who engages in a certain activity must satisfy' (Hayek 1960: 224), that taxation should not approach confiscation, and that government should refrain from attempts to secure some pre-conceived pattern of distribution.

The basic thrust of the argument against conventional governmental planning advanced by Wildavsky was that it simply would not work. It could not fulfil the grandiose hopes of its proponents because the complexity of social life precluded comprehensive control over future circumstances. As he put it, planning 'does not work because no large and complex society can figure out what simple and unambiguous things it wants to do, or in what clear order of priority, or how to get them done' (Wildavsky 1973: 148). Its failures 'are not peripheral or accidental, but integral to its very nature' (Wildavsky 1973: 128). Proponents of planning were in the habit of emphasising the 'rational' character of their activity: is it not eminently reasonable to 'attempt to obtain a more desirable future by working toward it in the present'? But Wildavsky challenged this perspective by enquiring whether it can be 'rational to fail'. If planning cannot work, to continue planning cannot be reasonable. Much of his discussion is actually concerned with assessing the various stratagems planning advocates employ to justify their enterprise in the face of the overwhelming evidence of failure. Ultimately he concludes that 'man' cannot abandon the dream of planning because to do so would be to admit that we cannot control 'our own destiny' and to recognise that man remains at the mercy of 'strange and unpredictable forces'. As 'God is dead', man has built a new faith around reason: but 'since he can only create the future he desires on paper, he transfers his loyalties to the plan', and 'since the end is never in sight, he sanctifies the journey'. Planning has become an article of faith. Wildavsky concludes: 'if governments perseverate [*sic*] in national planning, it must be because their will to believe triumphs over their experience. Planning is not so much a subject for the social scientist as for the theologian' (Wildavsky 1973: 153).

Recognising the many different ways in which planning can be defined, Wildavsky privileged an approach which identified planning with 'future control'. It is 'the ability to control the future by current acts', and 'the more consequences we control, the more we have succeeded in planning' (Wildavsky 1973: 128). The problem is that any significant degree of control over future events requires impossibly stringent conditions: in particular, it requires adequate causal theories which link actions and consequences. Such theories are simply not available. The state of our understanding of economic and social processes and of interaction among societal variables is inadequate. But without such causal knowledge, the prediction of consequences is impossible, and so 'planning' can be no more than a dream.

Wildavsky examined various ideas associated with planning. He notes that 'planning assumes power', for without power it is impossible to get people to 'act differently than they otherwise would': that is to say, to oblige them to conform to the plan. He observes that planning is linked with 'rationality', but different forms of rationality may be applied to different spheres of social life, and there can be no single 'rational' way of selecting national goals. Planners are supposed to co-ordinate, but 'co-ordination' can imply 'efficiency' (accomplish most with the least effort) and 'reliability' (allow redundancy to ensure performance), with 'coercion' (to guarantee compliance with the plan) and 'consent' (through bargaining). How are such mutually contradictory orientations to be reconciled? Planners are urged to be consistent, but they must also adapt to changing circumstances: how can they do both? Thus Wildavsky concludes: 'the injunction to plan (!!) is empty. The key terms associated with it are proverbs or platitudes. Pursue goals! Consider alternatives! Obtain knowledge! Exercise power! Obtain consent!

Or be flexible but do not alter your course. Planning stands for unresolved conflicts' (Wildavsky 1973: 146).

In a piece published some years later, Wildavsky took a slightly different approach. Although he continued to refer to planning as 'future control', he also described 'pure planning' as an ideal type of social decision procedure based upon deployment of the intellect (Wildavsky 1979). It was contrasted with 'markets' and 'pure politics' where outputs were determined by interaction among social actors. Wildavsky insisted that 'politics' was about accommodating mutable 'preferences', while 'planning' was about calculating the right course of action. 'Politics' depended on social participation (bargaining among the many), while planning was 'single-minded' and monocentric. Yet society could not rely entirely on interactive decision-making because this did not necessarily produce just or otherwise desirable outcomes. Theory was required to observe and make intelligible the effects of interaction on participants, to discern patterns and formalise 'rules' bounding interaction, and to guide efforts at re-designing interactive processes. Wildavsky confessed that his own preference was for a 'hybrid of social interaction and intellectual cogitation' ('called policy analysis') composed of 'two thirds politics and one third planning' (Wildavsky 1979: 124).

Charles Lindblom has been a consistent critic of 'rational comprehensive' or 'synoptic' approaches to planning and policy analysis. This is the model in which decision-makers are urged to start by prioritising values, then to analyse systematically all possible means of achieving desired ends, and ultimately to settle on the option that maximises outputs at lowest cost. Lindblom argues that effective decision-makers in the real world do not even attempt to approximate this idealised schema. Instead, they invoke stratagems to simplify radically their analytical tasks, opting generally for solutions that lie close to existing policy or experience. Moreover, he claims that better decisions result from such approaches than from the misplaced pursuit of synoptic ambition.

Two concepts figure prominently in Lindblom's argument, 'incrementalism' and 'partisan mutual adjustment'. The first revolves around the idea of small steps: that analysts and policy-makers will normally focus on a limited range of options which represent but modest departures from existing practice. The second emphasises the advantages of a fragmented decision process, in which groups of actors and analysts adjust their conduct to each other's behaviour. Lindblom suggests that the upshot of such processes may be more 'rational' than conscious attempts to co-ordinate all action from a single centre. Both these ideas were present in 'The science of "muddling through"' (Lindblom 1959), but they were subsequently extended and revised. In a later essay Lindblom distinguished various sorts of 'incrementalism' (Lindblom 1979). First, he contrasted 'incremental politics' (the politics of change through small steps) with 'incremental analysis' (policy analysis reliant upon simplifying assumptions). Then, he cited three different meanings of 'incremental analysis': 'simple incrementalism' (analysis that explored policy options which differed only incrementally from existing practice); 'disjointed incrementalism' (a particular decision strategy that invoked a specific set of simplifying assumptions); and 'strategic analysis' (any conscious strategy to simplify radically analysis of policy choices). 'Disjointed incrementalism' was one form of 'strategic analysis', a form which invoked 'simple incrementalism' as a simplifying device. Other elements of the disjointed incrementalist package included:

a) limitation of analysis to a few somewhat familiar policy alternatives; b) an intertwining of analysis of policy goals and other values with the empirical aspects of the problems; c) a greater analytical preoccupation with ills to be remedied than positive goals to be sought; d) a sequence of trials, errors and revised trials; e) analysis that explores only some, not all, of the important possible consequences of a considered alternative; [and] f) fragmentation of analytical work to many (partisan) participants in policy making.

(Lindblom 1979: 517)

'Strategic analysis' rests on the premise that complex social problems can never be analysed completely. Policy-makers should shun the delusory chimera of 'comprehensive' or 'synoptic analysis', for by seeking to approximate an impossible idea they will 'fall into worse patterns of analysis and decision' than those who pursue 'the guiding ideal of strategic analysis' and 'knowingly and openly' muddle 'with some skill' (Lindblom 1979: 518) 'Disjointed incrementalism' had flaws, but this was true of any form of policy analysis practised in the real world. As an approach to reform, 'political incrementalism' recognises that in democratic systems change can normally be realised most effectively through small steps. Political incrementalism does not necessarily imply slow reform, because a rapid succession of small steps can lead quickly to significant innovation. For the most part, grand political objectives that represent a radical departure from existing patterns such as 'a comprehensive energy programme' for the USA, 'one big implemented solution to environmental decay', or 'an actually operative development plan for developing country' are simply not possible (Lindblom 1979: 521).

Although present in all political systems, 'partisan mutual adjustment' is typical of decision processes in contemporary pluralist democracies. Here a wide range of participants and interests contribute to outcomes, and policies are often 'better described as happening' rather than as having been 'decided upon'. Since participants 'act for diverse reasons', the 'connection between a policy' and the 'good reasons' for it may be 'obscure'. Furthermore, interaction among participants will 'to some degree co-ordinate them as policy makers' even in the absence of central direction. Lindblom emphasises that 'partisan mutual adjustment' represents a partial 'substitution of politics for analysis'. Co-ordination is achieved on the ground, through conflict and accommodation, rather than through the synthetic intervention of a guiding agency. Yet partisan mutual adjustment also involves characteristic analytical elements, because participants are 'constantly engaged in analysis designed to find grounds on which their political adversaries or indifferent participants might be converted to allies or acquiescents'. Lindblom admits that in such pluralist processes interests are not represented equally, but he rejects the assumption that centralisation and conscious integration will provide better or more equitable policy outcomes. Above all, he emphasises that 'fragmentation of policy making and consequent political interaction among many participants' is not just a mechanism for 'curbing power' (as understood by Montesquieu and the American founding fathers), but also 'of raising the level of information and rationality brought to bear on decisions' (Lindblom 1979: 524).

Many common themes are apparent in this brief discussion of these theorists' writings. Each thinker displays profound scepticism about the ability of government to plan and direct large-scale social projects. They share a concern with the informational deficit which plagues public decision-makers, and with the complexity of the analytical challenge confronting comprehensive planning exercises. There is a common pre-occupation with the role of value-judgements in political decision processes, and emphasis on the social significance of integration through interactions among self-directed agents, rather than via central analysis and intervention. Yet substantial contrasts are evident. Most importantly, Hayek betrays a deep scepticism of politics and democracy, emphasising reconciliation through market and 'private' action, while Wildavsky and Lindblom see politics, too, as a medium though which (spontaneous) social co-ordination can be achieved. Though Hayek is opposed in principle to redistributive intervention, fearing it will erode individual freedom and market-based incentive structures, and lead to an extension of coercive interventions throughout the economy, Wildavsky and Lindblom have no such fundamental reservations.

Hayek would have been least sympathetic to the deliberate pursuit of 'sustainable development'. Certainly he would have dismissed it as a permanent and overriding object of government. Only in time of war, or some other *temporary* disaster, was government justified in orienting its activity towards a single substantive purpose. But Hayek would have balked also at making sustainable development a less transcendent (but still fundamental and ongoing) focus of government action. He was deeply sceptical of state intervention to protect 'the needs of future generations', believing this could best be secured by passing on to the future a free economy and a free society that would allow the next generation to satisfy its own desires. Certainly the state could have no privileged access to knowledge about the sorts of action that might benefit futurity. Put simply, Hayek believed: 'let people alone', and by and large 'development' would run into productive channels. Above all, the (re-)distributional implications of sustainable development (both within and between nations), which have formed such an essential dimension of the concept as endorsed by international gatherings such as UNCED, would have been anathema.

One could imagine a sort of neo-Hayekian accommodation with the idiom of 'sustainable development' if the term was shorn of all redistributive connotations, and understood as an automatic by-product of a 'liberal order' which protected certain essential environmental amenities. Here, the state would maintain a framework of universal rules within which individuals and groups could pursue their projects, but these rules would include regulations to prevent environmental damage that reduced collective welfare or threatened global life-support systems. Leverage could be gained from Hayek's observations about 'neighbourhood effects' (referred to today as 'externalities'), for it could be argued that such effects are more comprehensive and complex than was appreciated by Hayek's generation. Indeed, the increase in human numbers, and changing scale and character of our technology, suggest that in certain respects a whole region, indeed the entire planet, may resemble Hayek's 'city life', where costs and benefits of economic activities spill over on to other parties. In such a 'full-world' economy, regulation is required to handle such (environmentally deleterious) effects. On this reading, for example, greenhouse gas emission could be characterised as a 'neighbourhood effect' (externality), and hence a suitable candidate for regulatory control, provided there was scientific evidence that global warming was potentially serious, and that regulation took a form that did not threaten competition and the price system. Neither would a Hayekian environmental policy be entirely without instruments to manage natural resource issues. Hayek recognised the problem of so-called 'fugitive resources' (game, fish, water, oil, and so on) where no individual operator in a particular area had an interest in conservation, because whatever he left could be harvested by a competitor. Hayek argued that here the solution must lie either with conferring property rights in the resource, or with 'alternative forms of regulation'. Needless to say he was more disposed to the 'property rights' solution. Referring to rapid clearing of forest cover in the USA, he noted that most of the destruction was because forests 'did not become private property, but were retained as public land and given over to private exploitation on terms which gave the exploiters no incentive for conservation' (Hayek 1960: 368). In any case, on any neo-Hayekian reading (a non-redistributive) 'sustainable development' could not form the direct object of government policy; rather it would emerge as an indirect (spontaneous) result of policies designed to secure optimum conditions for individuals and groups to pursue their own ends.

Even if one rejects the desirability or plausibility of such a Hayekian model, this perspective contains many insights. Consider Hayek's argument that we cannot plan for progress because it is impossible to discern in advance in what progress will consist. In his view, society is being shaped by evolutionary forces whose complexity renders them opaque to rational analysis. We cannot know in which directions social innovation or scientific and technical discovery will take us. The movement of a whole civilisation (in contrast to the 'progress' of an individual or organisation which involves advance towards a known goal) can only fully be understood retrospectively. Thus for Hayek the appreciation of progress is much like Hegel's 'philosophy': 'the owl of Minerva spreads its wings only with the falling of the dusk' (Hegel 1952: 13). Yet even as Hayek insists that our civilisation depends on continued advance – in material living conditions and in scientific and technical mastery over nature – he also recognised what one might describe as the 'pathos of progress'. He observed that progress constantly erodes much of what people hold dear; patterns of living valued not only by those who experience them, but also by others in society (such as the life of the peasant farmer or rural craftsman) are marginalised and eradicated. Hayek even goes so far as to suggest that we cannot determine whether progress has on the whole actually improved the life of moderns as compared with people who lived several thousand years ago. Still, Hayek remains firmly committed to progress, spurning John Stuart Mill's 'stationary state', and urging us to reconcile ourselves to the fact that we cannot pick and choose which dimensions of the onward movement to accept. Progress is like an elemental force sweeping us along; its dynamism and rapidity a product of the free society, with competition and opportunity to experiment driving forward change. We are reminded here of Marx's (1961) description of capitalism as continuously revolutionising production and social life, or of Schumpeter's (1943) 'gales of creative destruction'.

The value of Hayek's remarks is that they remind us of the essential unpredictability of social change: scientific and technological discoveries, shifting patterns of cultural and economic interaction, can open up (but also foreclose) social possibilities which can never comprehensively be imagined in advance. Hayek is right that we cannot anticipate which inventions will open up new vistas for human development and which will prove to be blind alleys. Unexpected consequences of one change may spread like ripples through a pond, disturbing established patterns of social interaction and dissolving much that many have valued. But Hayek goes much further, for in his perspective not only can progress not be planned, but the '*not-planning*' is *the best guarantee* that progress will in fact be achieved. One may draw out from this the notion that 'oversteering' may be counter-productive: that in attempting too rigidly to constrain social development along a pre-programmed trajectory, government may preclude other (potentially more favourable) lines of societal advance. Indeed, Hayek boldly stated that 'there can be no doubt that man owes some of his greatest successes in the past to the fact that he has *not* been able to control social life' (Hayek 1960: 38). And yet surely this statement demands a counterpoint: the balancing affirmation that humans also owe some of their greatest successes to the fact that at certain times and to a certain extent they *have* been able to devise mechanisms to 'control' specific dimensions of social life. And here is the problem: Hayek greatly overstates his case. For if in the grandest sense we cannot know where future social development will lead, that does not mean that there are not many and varied (though perhaps sometimes mundane) domains in which we know very well what will constitute improvement. It is true that we cannot possibly know all future repercussions of acting to realise a particular advance; but since we also cannot know all the repercussions of not acting to secure it, we may well conclude that public action to secure a known good, or right a known wrong, is preferable to inaction. Of course there are innumerable problems which might command the attention of government; moreover often we do not know how to tackle a problem, or perhaps we think we do, only to find out to our sorrow that we did not. Yet from this it only follows that priorities must be established and lessons learned.

This suggests (*pace* Hayek) that 'planning for progress' – and thus also planning for sustainable development – is possible in several senses. First, it is possible to identify specific priorities and objectives, based on current knowledge of what constitutes social improvement: attempting to secure known 'goods' and avoid known bads. Goals can vary across the range of social conditions, extending from a public health campaign to eradicate a contagious disease to the prohibition of indentured servitude. Such advances clearly represent 'progress' in terms of being improvements to our social state as we understand it; and they are advances that can be 'planned for' – that is to say they can be effected by conscious intervention decided upon through political processes. Of course, this does not remove the possibility that a government may try to realise misplaced objectives, that unforeseen consequences may have grave repercussions, or that the results of current planning efforts may ultimately be repudiated as 'regressive' by future generations. But these dangers do not change the fact that governments can (and certainly will) 'plan for progress' in this sense – an exercise which we might describe as *bounded* or *incremental* 'planning for progress'.

Second, it is also possible for governments to attempt to establish conditions which facilitate 'progress', by structuring social interactions so that groups and individuals are placed within a context which encourages innovation, and which facilitates replication of positive advances which do emerge. This might be called *oblique* planning: it involves government acting to secure circumstances that will maximise the possibilities for progressive social movement, even though at present it is impossible to specify very precisely the nature of the social objectives that will be realised. Such an approach derives inspiration from Hayek's 'liberal regime', except in this context its orientation would be innovation favourable to sustainable development. Now, while Hayek himself constantly emphasises individual freedom as the precondition of this spontaneously oriented and orienting movement of progress, this is a freedom predicated upon law: for only a system of general rules can establish individual liberty. Once this is recognised, it becomes possible to consider which kinds of rules (and which kinds of liberties) are likely to facilitate general social movement towards innovations compatible with sustainable development.

One might tease out a further dimension of 'planning for progress': that is, planning to address negative consequences that arise from broadly positive processes of social change. Change, even change which on the whole marks an improvement, seldom occurs without dislocation. Although overall gains may outweigh losses, particular individuals, groups and communities may suffer from the fallout of even the most 'progressive' innovation. The attempt to anticipate and mitigate such effects might be considered *'defensive'* planning for progress: planning to alleviate the burdens 'progress' imposes on specific individuals and communities.

Another strand of Hayek's argument is also of potential relevance to the project of planning for sustainable development. This is its deep scepticism concerning the possibility of rationally re-making the social order, and his insistence upon the value of social practices and institutions which have emerged spontaneously. Following a long line of social thinkers (including Smith, Hume and Spencer), Hayek emphasises the importance of spontaneous orders for commodious human social life. Patterned interactions, such as morality, language and the market, appear to have grown up without conscious, authoritative intervention; rather, they are outcomes of protracted evolutionary processes involving the self-oriented actions of numerous independent agents. In contrast, consciously designed orders played a subordinate role in social life, successfully addressing more bounded phenomena.

The value of Hayek's perspective is that it draws attention to the complex, iterative and selective mechanisms that shape social process and structures. Yet, like his other dichotomies, this one is overdrawn. For 'designed' and 'spontaneously generated' orders are so intertwined in social life that every practice involves both sorts of 'order', and in most cases it is impossible to distinguish with certainty their respective contributions to the resultant pattern. 'Designed' orders begin to change as soon as they are founded; while 'spontaneous' orders are shaped, codified and re-designed by conscious intervention. Nevertheless, Hayek's perspective suggests at least two things. First, it implies that ambitious efforts at comprehensive social re-design are highly problematic: social complexity and unintended consequences make the likelihood of 'success' minimal. This is a counsel to prudence and a rejection of the hyper-rationalist dream of remaking the world at one go – of utterly transforming human nature and the content of social relations. It suggests reform efforts should be focused on clearly identified and circumscribed problem areas. Once elements of some specific practice or institution have been 'redesigned', attention can shift to other provinces of social life. Thus, one can draw inspiration from Hayek's observation (following Popper) that:

> what can be done to improve it [society] must be done by working with these forces rather than against them. In all our endeavours at improvement we must always work inside this given whole, aim at piecemeal, rather than total, construction, and use at each stage, the historical material at hand and improve details step by step, rather than attempt to redesign the whole.
>
> (Hayek 1960: 70)

Of course, this perspective probably exaggerates the extent to which society can be considered a single 'whole', and the degree to which its dimensions and patterns are systematically integrated. In at least some senses there are multiple social 'wholes', depending on the angle from which collective life is approached. Precisely because there are various 'wholes', many kinds of leverage can be gained to transform particular modes of social interaction. And with time, localised efforts at redesign can substantially alter the configuration of 'wholes'.

Second, Hayek's discussion points to the possibility that spontaneous forces may be harnessed to achieve 'designed' ends, that *deliberate* institutional reforms may alter the outputs of spontaneous interaction. This is not an issue Hayek wants us to take up, although his own rationalistic programme of constitutional reform (which would have confined the state within its province and guaranteed the free rein of liberty) was implicitly such an exercise, as is governmental intervention to rectify (spontaneously occurring) market-failure. But it is one that comes to the fore as soon as the exaggerated separation between rational design and spontaneous growth is overcome.

Wildavsky's colourful critique of planning also raises interesting points, although his discussion is not without confusion and inconsistency. Consider his definition of planning as 'future control'. Wildavsky argues that planning must be considered in this way – as the successful determination of future outcomes – because when planning is separated from the achievement of pre-determined ends it becomes impossible to appraise its causal impact, and 'planning' can be confused with any intentional behaviour. He explains, 'attempts to plan are no more planning than the desire to be wise may be called wisdom or the wish to be rich entitles a man to be called wealthy' (Wildavsky 1973: 129). And the 'determination of whether planning has taken place must rest on an assessment of whether and to what degree future control has been achieved'. Furthermore, 'separating goals from achievements, as most definitions do by emphasising intention over accomplishment, blurs the distinction between planning and other purposeful behaviour' (Wildavsky 1973: 130–1).

The problem here is that Wildavsky's enthusiasm to evaluate planning by its results (what has actually been changed, and has the future successfully been controlled?) has spilled over into his understanding of what constitutes planning itself. Wildavsky's analogies are misplaced: 'planning' should not be equated with an end state (such as 'wisdom' or 'wealth') which can then be contrasted with the 'desire' or 'wish' to achieve the given condition. Instead, planning is a practice or activity, and more appropriate parallels might be 'the quest for' wisdom, or 'the pursuit of' wealth: enterprises which may be motivated by a desire or wish, and which are directed towards a specific goal, but which may be said to have been undertaken whether or nor wisdom or wealth are ultimately attained. Consider an alternative analogy: plotting by a group of conspirators. It is perfectly intelligible to conclude that plotting took place, even though the plot failed. To maintain that plotting only occurs if conspirators' objectives are realised is to write a curious form of history. Indeed, it only serves to obscure the search for causal understandings of various sorts of consequences of the plotters' actions. Furthermore, it is only by recognising that an activity occurred (despite the fact that intended objectives were not achieved), that it becomes intelligible to assess it as having 'failed'. Thus Wildavsky cannot apply his own 'definition' of planning consistently, for to do so would imply not that 'planning always fails' (as he continually repeats), but rather that planning has never existed (because only successful future control would be 'planning'). Moreover, this 'success' criterion cannot usefully distinguish 'planning' from 'other purposeful behaviour' because such behaviour may also fail to achieve intended goals. To the extent that planning (of the type with which we are concerned here) is to be distinguished from other intentional action, it must be on the basis of issues such as the formality of the decision process, the time frame and character of the issues involved, and the nature of the agents or agencies concerned.

Another feature of Wildavsky's discussion is that he shifts back and forth between an understanding of 'planning' that locates it as a comprehensive social phenomenon and one that identifies it as the specific province of dedicated planning agencies and commissions. His definition of planning as 'future control' implies a broad approach, in which planning can be associated with many spheres of governmental endeavour, and even with domains outside the formal political structure. On this reading, 'planners are presidents, ministers, bureaucrats, party leaders, scientists, entrepreneurs – anybody whose acts have large future consequences' (Wildavsky 1973: 133). This is the 'planning is everything' to which the title of the article refers. And yet, Wildavsky explains, 'the act of governing need not necessarily involve planning: intentions in actions may be unrealised'. Thus while all may aspire to plan, none may succeed. And this is the 'maybe it's nothing' included in the title of his essay. On the other hand, much of Wildavsky's commentary is actually concerned with the specific failures of professional planners and dedicated planning agencies – what he sometimes describes as 'formal planning'. The problem is that he slips back and forth between these two modes of analysis, using the critique of the failures of dedicated planning bodies (particularly the national agencies responsible for socio-economic planning in the USSR, France, Japan and the developing world) to draw much more sweeping conclusions about the impossibilities of planning in general. Furthermore, he often invokes a distinction between planning and 'normal' government decision-making. Indeed, he suggests that the incoherence of the notion of 'adaptive' planning (planning that recasts its goals in light of ongoing experience) is that it effaces this contrast between planning and ordinary decision-making: 'by making planning reasonable, it becomes inseparable from the processes of decision it was designed to supplant' (Wildavsky 1973: 135). Such a distinction between 'planning' and 'normal' decision-making is partially intelligible if by 'normal' decisions are meant simply those not taken by 'formal planning' institutions. But it is misleading to the extent that 'normal' government decisions involve planning – in the sense of attempts to control future outcomes – just as much as do decisions taken within dedicated planning bodies. What may differ, of course, is the type of processes that are to be controlled, the range of outcomes and streering strategies to be considered, the time frames of analysis, the kinds of decision techniques employed, and so on. Nevertheless, in some sense there is no escape from planning – and thus all Wildavsky's bluster is for nothing. Attempts to control future circumstances lie at the heart of modern governmental activity, and the real issues are to what ends and how such attempts should be organised; in this, 'formal planning' processes as well as less structured government decision-making must equally be assessed.

Despite such incoherences, Wildavsky's critique can direct us towards issues pertinent to planning for sustainable development. His scathing attack on justifications for planning exercises, and his catalogue of the costs they may impose, provide a fertile basis for reflection. Wildavsky argues that regular failure drives advocates of the formal planning process to seek reasons other than successful goal attainment to justify their projects. This he represents as a shift in the terms of 'discussion from goals to process' (Wildavsky 1973: 139). According to Wildavsky, desirable 'process' outcomes cited by planners include: inculcating 'habits of mind that lead to more rational choice', familiarising officials with the idea of opportunity costs, introducing individuals with economic skills into government, collecting useful data, and expanding the 'time-horizons' of decision-makers by making the future 'part of present decisions'. Unsurprisingly, Wildavsky is sceptical of all such effects, summing up the essence of this defence of planning as: 'Planning is good, therefore, not so much for what it does but for how it goes about not doing it.'

Among the specific costs he believes 'formal planning' imposes upon society are that it may constitute a substitute for action, absorb scarce human resources, encourage over-investment (planners are spenders) and oversized projects (larger units make for administrative simplicity), and encourage exaggerated expectations among the populace. Of course 'formal planning' may bring advantages unrelated to its official (unrealisable) purposes: it may serve the professional interests of planners or politicians, or help a country meet externally imposed conditions for the receipt of foreign aid. Wildavsky also wryly proposed one way in which formal planning could make an unambiguously positive contribution to national economic development through 'buying off the apostles of rationality by involving them in tasks that take them away from real decisions' (Wildavsky 1973: 150).

Such costs and dangers must be considered; but they should be balanced against potential gains which particular planning exercises may secure. Wildavsky's polemic against planning works because gains are reduced to zero since planning ends can never be achieved, and 'process' values are ruled irrelevant. But ends appear never to be achieved only because they are cast in the open-ended form of 'future control'. Of course the future can never be controlled comprehensively; but specific happenings can be impelled to occur, and specific eventualities may be avoided, through behaviour founded in foresight. In other words, elements of the future (in specific places, over specific time frames) may be determined through courses of action adopted in the present. There can be no guarantee that planned outcomes will be achieved, or that initial objectives may not subsequently be revised. Yet this does not mean that planned objectives cannot be realised, whether in their original or in adapted form. The real questions are therefore: what kinds of future circumstance are amenable to which forms of conscious control? Is control of some social dimensions excluded by efforts to determine the disposition of others? And within what sorts of parameters can future elements be constrained at what cost? With respect to planning for sustainable development these questions focus attention on just what must be secured over time if sustainable development is to be judged to have been realised: what future dimensions must be controlled, through which means, and within which parameters?

So-called 'process' gains cannot be dismissed as readily as Wildavsky thinks, for planning processes are not just techniques for securing pre-determined ends; they may also be methods of selecting both ends and means, and of legitimating their adoption. More particularly, planning processes can form part of the way in which interactions among actors are structured within a democratic polity. Thus, when Wildavsky insists that 'planning is not a solution to any problem, it is just a way of restating in other language the problems we do not know how to solve' (Wildavsky 1973, p. 149), he misses the point. In politics restating or redefining a problem may be a necessary precondition to elaborating solutions; and in a democracy participatory planning processes can contribute towards such purposes.

Wildavsky's 'policy analysis' is at least an attempt to reconcile intellectual foresight and practical interaction as modes of social problem-solving. His recognition of the need to purposefully re-design conditions framing spontaneous interactions is both an advance on Hayek and fertile with possibilities for sustainable development planning. Wildavsky explained: 'Analysis supplements social interaction by using the theoretical mode to formulate and test hypotheses that can help bring precision to the judgement of decision-makers. Analysis uses social interaction both to understand what is happening and to suggest how it might be altered' (Wildavsky 1979: 126).

It is also true that his insistence upon the importance of causal theories for planning efforts, and on their relative scarcity in the social domain, provides a valuable reminder of the difficulties of realising large-scale planned outcomes. This suggests that sustainable development planning may do well to focus upon specific domains of social or economic life in which causal theories are already more adequate, or may more easily be formulated and tested, because of the (relative) insulation of these sub-systems from broader social process. By fixing objectives and designing and implementing policy in clearly defined contexts and/or pre-existing policy areas, possibilities for grasping the mutual influences of salient variables (and hence for effective control) can be enhanced.

What of Lindblom's concepts of 'incrementalism' and 'partisan mutual adjustment'? To begin with, it is worth noting that both ideas owe a significant debt to economic modes of analysis. Like Hayek, Lindblom started his career as an economist and, particularly in his early writing, the influence of economic theory is tangible. 'The science of "muddling through"' explicitly discusses 'incrementalism' in terms of policy adjustments 'at the margin', and the parallel with production/consumption decisions is obvious. Moreover, the notion of 'partisan mutual adjustment' echoes market-mediated adjustment among economic producers, with the policy 'co-ordination' understood to result from partisan interaction corresponding to the socially beneficially economic integration generated as independent economic agents pursue self-interested ends. Indeed, the ideas of spontaneous order and paradoxical collective gain which result from the behaviour of self-orienting agents, that have formed a staple of two-and-a-half centuries of economic theorising, are central to Lindblom's argument. As Lindblom and Hirschman commented in an early collaborative essay, this perspective 'insist[s] on the rationality and usefulness of certain processes and modes of behaviour which are ordinarily considered to be irrational, wasteful and generally abominable' (Hirschman and Lindblom 1962: 218).

Consideration of Lindblom's 'incrementalism' has been complicated by confusions over whether it is an analytic or a political strategy, a realist description or a procedural ideal. There is also the difficulty of distinguishing 'small' from 'large' steps. Yet there is wide acceptance that the model captures something of the spirit of decision-making in bureaucratic contexts. Typically, public officials cannot attempt comprehensive analysis or clean-slate solutions; they muddle through, adapting existing policies, borrowing ideas from related domains, tinkering and improvising. But few theorists are as sanguine as Lindblom about accepting 'incrementalism' as the cornerstone of a reform strategy or an ideal analytic mode. One recent review identified four fundamental criticisms of incrementalism commonly found in the policy literature: that it is '1) insufficiently proactive, goal oriented and ambitious; 2) excessively conservative, because increments are small and bargaining favours organised elites; 3) useful in too limited a range of decision contexts; and 4) too hostile to analysis' (Weiss and Woodhouse 1992: 258).

In some ways these are precisely the kinds of criticisms which environmentalists have typically made of existing policy processes: administrators are prepared to contemplate only minor deviations from existing practices, they are too closely tied to established economic interests, they are incapable of taking dramatic action in crises, and their partial analyses overlook long-term consequences or links among disparate spheres of social activity. Indeed, thorough-going integration of policy-making across environmental media, and between economic and environmental domains, has been a core concern of those working for environmental causes for many years. Does this therefore imply that incrementalist modes of politics and analysis should have little relevance for 'planning for sustainable development'?

With respect to political strategy 'incrementalism' might simply be interpreted as a restatement of the obvious fact that radical change is the exception, not the rule. But it can also be taken to raise intriguing questions about the range of factors that influence the pace and scope of policy reform. For example, what sort of incremental change can serve to open the way for further reform, rather than constituting an additional obstacle to such reform? How can one identify 'turn-key' reforms, incremental changes which serve to shift patterns of institutional behaviour in ways that generate increased pressure for additional change? Can incremental changes be structured to avoid generating 'countervailing forces' that will become active to block further reform? These are precisely the sorts of issues which those interested in improving environmental performance must address.

With respect to analysis Lindblom's argument focuses on the fact that it is *impossible* for policy-makers to consider all alternatives and consequences. Thus they do better to acknowledge this frankly, to set aside synoptic ambitions, and to devise workable strategies to adapt policy in the face of pervasive uncertainty. And this challenge appears central to public planning efforts in relation to a complex domain such as sustainable development. Whether Lindblom's 'disjointed incrementalism' is the best analytical strategy, however, remains an open question. But it could be argued that its careful application might raise the analytical sophistication of sustainable development-related decisions currently being taken. Certainly elements four (trial and error) and six (fragmentation of analytical work among diverse agencies) of the model would find a place in most techniques for sustainable development-related decision-making.

In any case, Lindblom was well aware that disjointed incrementalism had serious shortcomings. In particular, he recognised that it might do no better than find 'a "local" optimum', neglecting a vastly superior but more innovative policy option. Others have noted the strategy's vulnerability to 'threshold' and 'sleeper' effects, which are especially important in the environmental context (Weiss and Woodhouse 1992: 265). Still, no analytical strategy could guarantee to pick these up. Lindblom himself has suggested techniques to complement disjointed incrementalism. One is to supplement incremental analysis with other modes of policy-relevant analysis, such as (a) 'speculative and sometimes utopian thinking', as well as (b) detailed examinations of 'one or a few pivotal issues or variables critical to policy choice' (Lindblom 1979: 522). Other decision theorists have suggested similar strategies that combine detailed search of a relatively familiar domain with a wide-ranging survey for outlying solutions and unexpected effects (consider, for example, Etzioni's (1967) 'mixed scanning'). Of course, for Lindblom a major corrective to analytical failures is 'partisan mutual adjustment': practical interaction among competing analysts, but more fundamentally among partisan groups and currents.

If one source of the idea of partisan mutual adjustment is to be found in economic theory, the other lies with political pluralism. So it is not surprising that criticism of the perspective has echoed traditional reservations about pluralist democracy: that it mistakenly assumes all interests will receive appropriate representation, neglecting structural conditions which prevent certain perspectives from being adequately articulated, which accord some groups policy vetoes, and which exclude some matters from the political arena altogether. Yet Lindblom freely acknowledges the seriousness of such difficulties, even admitting that 'on grand issues pertaining to the fundamental structure of politico-economic life' (including 'the distribution of income and wealth', 'the distribution of political power' and 'corporate prerogatives'), partisan mutual adjustment 'is weak or absent' (Lindblom 1979: 523). Nevertheless, he remains convinced that the solution lies not in abandoning interactive intelligence in favour of more extensive centralised co-ordination, but rather in seeking to extend the range of issues which can be brought within the sphere of interactive politics, for partisan mutual adjustment can balance and reconcile behaviours beyond the scope or foresight of any single integrative agency. He explained:

> The co-ordination of participants is in some large part left to their political interaction with each other and, in any case, is not centrally directed analysed co-ordination as co-ordination might be in the mind of a sufficiently cerebral co-ordinator. Their patterns of interaction may be designed – that is, various authorities may be required to interact with each other – or the patterns may have taken form without design.
>
> (Lindblom 1979: 524)

True, one might not want to go so far as to accept Lindblom's verdict that 'partisan analysis' (developed by contending groups) is the 'most productive' 'analytical input into politics'. And one might worry that much of this analysis relates to manipulating processes rather than to finding sound arguments to convert disinterested publics. Nevertheless, the adjustive processes to which Lindblom points are potentially of enormous significance to the project of planning for sustainable development. They suggest the possibility of co-ordinating complex changes across a range of social spheres by radically decentralising analytical responsibility and encouraging practical interaction, and the potential of a reform strategy which emphasises institutional design directed to re-configuring spontaneous adjustive mechanisms to favour sustainable development friendly policy outcomes.

A RADICALLY DISJOINTED PLANNING REGIME

Discussion of the perspectives of these three planning critics has cast some light upon the possibilities of planning for sustainable development. The limitation of human abilities to channel social development into programmed pathways was emphasised by all three thinkers. Yet in contrast to Hayek it has been argued here that some sorts of 'planning for progress' are realisable, in particular *incremental planning, oblique planning* and *defensive planning*. The importance of focusing reform efforts in clearly defined areas of social endeavour, and of engaging in experimental modes of policy design can also be distilled from the discussion. The notion of deliberately re-designing social institutions so that 'spontaneous' forces achieve desired outcomes was another critical insight. So, too, was the significance of *ex-post facto* co-ordination through collision and mutual adjustment.

Discourses of environmental sustainability frequently intimate a vision of an ecologically balanced society, with stable institutions designed to assure equilibrium within tolerances the natural environment can support. But the dynamism of social development and the contingencies of social life ensure this image can never entirely be realised. It is simply not possible at any particular point in time to make a single set of strategic choices, or to design once-and-for-all a set of institutions which can be guaranteed to be best suited to secure sustainable development into the far future. Human inventiveness and the rhythm of technological development fostered by existing socio-economic structures ensure that new materials, processes, products and practices will inevitably emerge to dissolve any equilibrium. Novel environmental impacts will be experienced and new patterns of development activity created. Thus discussions of planning processes and outcomes – understood both as exercises in 'strategic choice' and as exercises in 'institutional design' (Meadowcroft 1997) – will need to be ongoing and iterative.

Another staple of much environmentalist literature is the concept of 'holistic' decision-making: that only by taking into account all the different dimensions of a problem – by examining the situation as a totality – can sound environment and development policy be formulated. Certainly it is true that sustainable development implies the integration of at least three different kinds of factors in decision-making processes: (a) *multiple time scales*: the present, and the near and farther futures; (b) *various dimensions of social life*: economy, environment and social equity;

and (c) *diverse social and ecological scales*: globe, nation, region and locality. And yet, as the planning critics canvassed above were at pains to point out, it is a mistake to believe that integration can only, or even most effectively, be achieved by the conscious intervention of a suitably empowered planner. Markets and political processes also achieve social co-ordination; and while the costs of retrospective reconciliation may be high, these must be weighed up against the costs and the limited deliverables associated with central co-ordination. Moreover it is not necessarily true that problems are best approached in an all-round, all-embracing or comprehensive manner. Often the more widely an issue is defined, the more elusive a solution proves to be, as the analytical tasks, as well as the practical challenges of putting together a reform coalition, grow in complexity. While no-one can ignore the counsel to see things 'in the round', the advocacy of 'holistic' decision-making can all too easily open the door to policy paralysis or deadlock. Thus, from the fact that sustainable development is an ambitious meta-objective that may be related to many areas of governmental competence, one should *not* conclude that it can always be promoted most effectively through recourse to comprehensive, synthetic and centrally integrated planning modalities.

A wide variety of planning structures already exist in contemporary developed democracies, including the state budgetary cycle, ministry and agency centred programmes, resource and waste management strategies, land use planning, and regional development programmes. In some ways the most straightforward way to promote sustainable development is to integrate the normative standards with which it is associated into the ongoing activities of such bodies. This can be understood as co-ordination by normative steering: the harmonisation of policy initiatives through the adoption of a common normative frame.

New planning modalities are also coming into being – consider the recent trend towards preparing national environmental policy plans and 'strategies' for sustainable development (Dalal-Clayton 1996; Jänicke and Jörgens 1998; Meadowcroft 1999). Yet the ambitions of the current generation of national 'green' plans should not be exaggerated. They can perform an important role in mapping policy linkages, formulating priorities and making known the orientation of environmental policy to broader publics. But even the most ambitious of these exercises assumes a very limited role in guiding ongoing decision-making, or attempting to harmonise all the policy domains relevant to sustainable development. Indeed, they seem destined to remain only one strand within a radically disjointed array of planning modalities, organised around different loci, involving varied patterns of social actors, employing contrasting management strategies, and predicated on alternative time scales. Such a pluralistic planning regime, where the initiatives of agencies and programmes may overlap and conflict, where there is redundancy, competition, and often areas that for some time 'fall through the gaps', is a long way from the synoptic ideal – but it may be particularly suited to the pursuit of an internally complex goal (such as sustainable development) that is operative in a domain of such radical uncertainty and indeterminacy.

This is not to say that governments will not be called upon to play the key role in orienting social engagement with sustainable development. There is a need for further institutional reform in the domain of central environmental governance, and the deployment of innovative environmental policy instruments (negotiated agreements, environmental taxes and subsidies, and so on) certainly requires governmental initiative and sanction. Moreover healthy doses of good old fashioned regulation and bureaucratic planning will be required to address many environmental issues. But – barring some unforeseen catastrophe – what is most important is the exercise of strategic choice, and the design of institutional reforms that channel 'spontaneous' processes in directions compatible with sustainable development. If there is one lesson of twentieth-century political life it is surely that the juxtaposition of state *versus* market is misplaced; rather the issue is how markets can be structured by governmental activity to secure socially desirable outcomes. In the case of sustainable development, this means designing economic and political reforms which orient the social dynamic in ways conducive to environmentally sustainable development.

Whether or not one is individually enthused by the idiom of sustainable development, it appears clear that the issues with which it engages are not likely to go away. This reflects the increasing human impact on the non-human natural world rooted in the growing power of technology and the rise of human numbers over the course of the twentieth century. There is the urgency of the development imperative facing the less industrialised countries, and the growing interdependence of human economic activities, and of social and political systems. In the short term we are already committed to continued transformation of global environments and the radical simplification of many ecosystems. Experiences with planning over the past century suggest that the future will be both more different and more familiar than we can possibly imagine today.

There is no doubt that sustainable development is a complex and ambitious social objective. Engaging with sustainable development is not about implementing a particular programme, or about achieving some specific policy outcome. Instead, sustainable development is best thought of as both a long-term social 'meta-objective', and as an idealistic benchmark by which to assess current practices. It is both the result that ensues when genuine development stays within the frontiers of environmental prudence, and a demanding normative standard which requires the balancing of environment, economic activity and social equity in current decision-making. Thus sustainable development is 'open ended'. Since it refers to a process and a standard – and not to an end state – each generation must take up the challenge anew, determining in what directions their development objectives lie, what constitutes the boundaries of the environmentally possible and the environmentally desirable, and what is their understanding of the requirements of social justice.

Notes

1 I would like to acknowledge the generous assistance of the Centre for Research and Documentation for a Sustainable Society (ProSus) in Norway for supporting the research on which this chapter is based.

2 The explicit focus of this discussion is the situation of the industrially developed (as opposed to the developing) countries.
3 Throughout this essay I have taken 'planning' in a quite general sense to refer to the structured and forward oriented decision procedures of governmental institutions. The use of planning in such a comprehensive manner is not entirely idiosyncratic: see for example the work of Charles Lindblom.

References

Dalal-Clayton, B. (1996) *Getting to Grips with Green Plans: National Experience in Industrial Countries*, London: Earthscan.

Daly, H. (1977) *Steady-State Economics*, San Francisco: W. H. Freeman.

Etzioni, A. (1967) 'Mixed-scanning: a "third" approach to decision making', *Public Administration Review* 27: 385–92.

Hayek, F. A (1944) *The Road to Serfdom*, London: Routledge & Kegan Paul.

Hayek, F. A. (1960) *The Constitution of Liberty*, London: Routledge & Kegan Paul.

Hegel, G. W. (1952) *The Philosophy of Right*, translated by T. M. Knox, Oxford: Oxford University Press.

Hirschman, A. and Lindblom, C. (1962) 'Economic development, research and development, policy making: some converging views', *Behavioural Science* 7: 211–22.

Jänicke, M. and Jörgens, H. (1998) 'National environmental policy planning in OECD countries: preliminary lessons from cross-national comparisons', *Environmental Politics* 7: 27–54.

Lafferty, W. (1996) 'The politics of sustainable development: global norms for national implementation', *Environmental Politics* 5: 185–208.

Lindblom, C. (1959) 'The science of "muddling through"', *Public Administration Review* 19: 79–88.

Lindblom, C. (1979) 'Still muddling, not yet through', *Public Administration Review* 39: 517–26.

Mannermaa, M. (1995) 'Alternative futures perspectives on sustainability, coherence and chaos', *Journal of Contingencies and Crisis Management* 3: 27–34.

Meadowcroft, J. (1997) 'Planning, democracy and the challenge of sustainable development', *International Political Science Review* 18: 167–90.

Meadowcroft, J. (1999) 'The politics of sustainable development: emergent trends and the challenge for political science', *International Political Science Review* 20: 223–42.

Marx, K. (1961) *Capital*, New York: International Publishers.

Mitlin, D. (1992) 'Sustainable development: a guide to the literature', *Environment and Urbanization* 4: 111–24.

Pezzy, J. (1992) 'Sustainability: an interdisciplinary guide', *Environmental Values* 1: 321–62.

Redclift, M. (1992) 'The meaning of sustainable development', *Geoforum* 23: 395–403.

Schumpeter, J. (1943) *Capitalism, Socialism and Democracy*, London: Allen & Unwin.

United Nations Conference on Environment and Development (1992) *Agenda 21*, New York: United Nations Organisation.

Weiss, A. and Woodhouse, E. (1992) 'Reframing incrementalism: a constructive response to the critics', *Policy Sciences* 25: 255–73.

Wildavsky, A. (1973) 'If planning is everything, maybe it's nothing', *Policy Sciences* 4: 137–53.

Wildavsky, A. (1979) *The Art and Craft of Policy Analysis*, London: Macmillan.

World Commission on Environment and Development (1987) *Our Common Future*, Oxford: Oxford University Press.

2   A century of planning

Charles E. Lindblom[1]

I have been asked for 'a reflective discussion on the history of economic planning in the twentieth century and the lessons to be learned from it'. I respond by selecting and commenting on each of the century's key developments in economic planning, and follow this with an integrating probe.

KEY DEVELOPMENTS IN TWENTIETH-CENTURY PLANNING

The list I am going to produce is not offered as a definitive one – how could there be any such list? It is one person's considered – and fallible – judgement. I begin with some of planning's great failures.

Soviet War Communism

With the catastrophic failure of War Communism, which was a never completed effort to organise an economy without the use of money and prices, there begins, in a near conclusive mammoth lesson, the education of socialist planners in the intricacies of economic planning. (I mean by socialist planners all those except the market planners: hence I include many Fabians, the Webbs, G. D. H. Cole, Bellamy and other utopians, and, of course, Marxists.) It is from War Communism that ambitious planners begin to learn that a national economy is not 'a single office and a single factory', as Lenin thought it was (Tucker 1975: 383). Planning is not simply a large task in administration, an 'in principle' straightforward simple task of formulating directives. Here planners begin to get a glimmer of daunting intellectual problems that they have to solve: above all, of *evaluating* (rather than merely formulating) alternative possibilities, a problem not of weighing a few alternatives but millions of choices among possible products, qualities, and techniques for producing them. Even the slow learners began to catch on that planning economic life requires a detail and intricacy of co-ordination to which they had never faced up before, and that was beyond the competence of War Communism.

They began to learn some further lessons. Prodigious as Marx's analytical accomplishments were in the eyes of communist planners, they began to realise that he had let them down on what to do after the revolution. Indeed some of them appear to have realised that Marx's brevity on how to plan had been at least one source of their mistaken belief that planning is not a difficult and challenging problem.[2]

A lesson of broader value – because not limited to a Marxist audience – was that money and prices were not just or merely attributes of capitalism but socially useful devices for any society, like language, accounting or wireless transmission of messages. Some planners continued to dissent from that finding, and I think it correct to say that even those who accepted it could not yet explain, even to themselves, just why it was true. That is to say, they could not specify the social functions of money and prices; what they observed was that communism could not do without them.

Troubled by an inadequate understanding of money and prices, the Soviets were, I think, nevertheless driven by the failures of War Communism to make money and prices core elements in the planning that was then constructed and maintained until Gorbachev. If the Soviets never learned – not even by 1990 – how to use money and prices effectively to solve their problems in the evaluation of alternatives, from War Communism they learned how to use them for counting, for crude record keeping and to simplify administration. In administration, they also learned that selling products at a price was far simpler than operating a rationing system, and much less irritating to consumers.

Soviet economic planning

The vision and intent

Whatever one may think of the success or failure of Soviet-style economic planning, it is a great historical fact that it provided a design for what we came to call planned economies over the face of much of the globe from Eastern Europe to China. More than that, it was the first great attempt – at least in the eyes of some of its key players – to organise a national society rationally for the benefit of the whole population. It was, in their view, the first great departure from both the rigidities of traditional agriculture and the chaos, as they saw it, of the market. Information, intelligence and reason were to replace, for the first time in history, the blindness of tradition, the irrationalities of the market and the exploitation of masses by elites. It intended and actually set out to achieve a greater social transformation than had ever been imagined outside the fancies of utopian thought. It was a great vision; and for the first time in human history, such a vision was lodged in the minds of men who held the highest positions of power in their societies.

What a vision and intent! It came to be shared – and defended against deprecators – by many millions of people all over the world, including many intellectuals who examined it before becoming advocates. Its appeal to intelligence and morality was often overwhelming. In our day, having seen the failure of the Soviet venture, we perhaps need to remind ourselves that it was an extraordinary vision and effort and that it appealed, or major elements of it appealed, to what we often say is the most moral and most intelligent in human aspiration.

Of course it did not appeal to everyone. Not to most elites, especially propertied elites, who had much to lose in the contemplated new society. Not to millions of indoctrinated and ignorant people who by habit, timidity or coercion never reached a point from which they could contemplate such a vision. And not to millions of people who shrank from it because of its assault on democracy and its murderous suppression of liberty.[3]

One might also wonder: which of these groups effectively prevented an imitation of the Soviet venture in the UK or in the USA? It is not clear that the Western democracies spurned communism to save liberty and democracy; other explanations may be more valid.

Of those people who were concerned with liberty and democracy – who may or may not have been important to limiting the global expansion of communism – there were at least two kinds: those who believed that in the absence of liberty and democracy, rationality would also disappear (Hayek 1944); and those who saw the vision as posing a choice between liberty and democracy, on one hand, and a rational economic order, on the other.[4] The difference between the two continues to pose an issue today for all kinds of planning, socialist or not. If we plan in order to make economic and social organisation more rational, does success require liberty and democracy in the planning process or, on the other hand, do we have to surrender some democracy and liberty to accomplish the rationality we pursue? Or are both propositions true, in that planning may require some attributes of liberty and democracy yet require the suppression of others?

The failure

Whatever the explanation, the Soviet collapse was of monumental importance in the history of economic planning. But what lesson is to be drawn from this? That the great vision was preposterous? The great effort futile? Non-capitalist planning a certain failure? Many commentators have hurried to tell us that we have learned from the collapse that broad and large-scale economic planning is impossible. To that we need reply that we can have learned no more than that the first great attempt together with its imitators has failed. That leaves open the possibility that another attempt drawing on the experience of the failure might succeed, especially one less crippled by doctrinal rigidities than was the Soviet attempt. Clearly the Soviet failure tells us almost nothing about the possible efficacy of broad and large-scale economic planning using the market system. The Soviet experience did not in any consequential way test the potential of democratic non-market planning, about which we all remain in considerable ignorance. Thus at least three possible designs for a planned economy and hybrids of them survive the Soviet collapse. To these three I shall be making reference from time to time.

1   A *democratic* planned, administered, *non-market* economy using money and prices but, like the Soviet model, using administrative fiat rather than the

market for directing production and allocation resources. So far, this is entirely hypothetical; it has never yet been attempted.

2   A democratic *governed market system*, as evident in one of its forms in the USA and Western Europe, where planning is largely secondary to the market. This would be highly selective (as, for example, in altering the directions or magnitude of capital investment) and is largely focused on specific purposes achieved through a variety of governmental 'interventions' such as environmental protection, worker safety, consumer protection, military defence, education, and income redistribution. The private enterprise form of the governed market system is a real-world model that today dominates the planet. At least hypothetically, another form is a socialist variant of a public enterprise market system (Bardhan and Roemer 1993).

3   A *democratically planned market economy practising not consumer but planner sovereignty*. Thus an economy in which democratic collective authority guides output and resource allocation neither by fiat nor by administrative authority, but by buying the products and services it wants the economy to produce. Instead of administrative orders, this authority would utilise purchases. No individual consumers would place any orders or make any purchases from producers. They would, however, buy from the planners the quantities that the planners have with *their* purchases signalled the producers to produce. This model remains largely but not entirely hypothetical, yet not without promise (Lindblom 1977).

This third and unfamiliar model – planner sovereignty – is practised as a peripheral element in all market systems, as, for example, in the form of government subsidies or taxes that raise or lower the market demand for a product to reflect the priorities of government authorities (for example, taxing tobacco because government wants to curb its use). Subsidies and taxes put government in control of amounts to be produced, yet do so without administrative fiat or commands.

The first model, democratic non-market planning, may turn out to be impossible, and the third, planner sovereignty, may be highly improbable; we do not know. My point here is that we have learned little about either of them from the failure of the Soviet venture. We have been attributing to the Soviet failure lessons that in fact it does not teach. That some have claimed to know something important about the feasibility of democratic planning from the failure of a tyranny suggests that they do not think that the difference between democratic politics and authoritarian politics is consequential. Put that starkly, however, most of us would flee from so dubious a claim.

We nevertheless did learn from the Soviet experience – and again from the Chinese one – that not just money and prices but more fully developed market signals, measures of value and incentives are enormously useful mechanisms for social and economic organisation. We all – even the Russian and Chinese planners themselves – have been learning that these mechanisms are workhorses. They do a job of measurement, calculation and evaluation with far more speed, flexibility and precision than any official or work-group can mobilise at a desk or around a conference table. And, because market relations accomplish all this epiphenomenally – that is, as a by-product of buying and selling rather than as a product of deliberated consultation and collective decision-making – they offer to societies that use markets an enormous scope for individual decision-making, the exercise of individual options, and the somewhat autonomous pursuit of opportunities, even if they do not offer all the liberties that classical market advocates claim. It may be that nothing in the world's experience has so greatly illuminated the technical, practical, non-ideological merits of market mechanisms as both the crippling of the Soviet economy because of their absence and the testimony of Soviet planners to that effect.[5]

What does the Soviet failure tell us about the original vision of rational non-exploitative social organisation and about efforts towards it? The failure is being used to discredit such a vision and effort, and clearly the failure tells us that the effort may quickly turn into new forms of irrationality and exploitation. Still, the aspiration towards rationality, enriched in many societies by a parallel aspiration towards liberty and democracy rather than exploitation, seems to characterise much contemporary thinking about planning. It is a great vision, not invalidated by Freud and others who have rubbed our noses in the fact of human irrationality; and it still motivates great efforts, even if they are more cautious, and more sensitive to feedback and correction, than the early efforts of the Bolsheviks.

Governed market systems

The century's greatest success in planning, broadly defined, has been the second model above: government's shaping of the results of the market. Older forms of market system have for the most part been converted into more sophisticated market systems – prodded, steered, shaped and regulated by government. The consequences have been so large and pervasive that we have come to neglect giving them the attention they deserve. These consequences include a drastic reduction in individual insecurity, enlarged investment in human resources, some significant movement away from extremes of inequality in income and wealth, and in recent decades measures for sustaining an earthly environment favourable to human life.

If your idea of a utopia is a Spencerian struggle for survival, a dog fight, you will not applaud the results of democratic planning of this kind. But most of us do loudly applaud it. We do not think older market systems afforded acceptable levels of security against threats to jobs, income and health. Most of us do not hesitate long in agreeing that the great mass of persons in these market systems can and do live more comfortable lives and enjoy a greater variety of rewarding experiences than their grandparents. This is the great accomplishment of market planning, outstripping anything ever approximated by any nation's experience with non-market socialist planning.

You might hesitate to use the term 'planning' to designate the various activities through which governments alter the results of the market system. But they do constitute planning in the sense of the term used by the editors of this volume.

Moreover, they represent the employment of deliberative intelligence to alter the future, which is what many people would mean by planning. Only if 'planning' must always denote highly centralised deployment of intelligence in shaping the future without the help of the market do these activities fall outside the concept of planning. But surely in reflecting on the history and prospects of planning, we do not wish to exclude by definition all but highly centralised efforts.

For this second model, I use the term 'governed market systems' for several reasons that may illuminate the planning elements in them. The more usual term is 'mixed economies' but that term says nothing about what the elements are that are mixed. I want to call attention to the two elements: government and market. Why not simply call them regulated market systems? Because I want to specify the regulator. Even more important, the role of government in these markets is not simply regulation, if you mean by regulation a process of imposing constraints on business enterprises to curb what would otherwise be their excesses.

More than regulation

Just what are the forms of governance of the market system that account for the extraordinary success of these systems in making life more secure and humane? Transfer payments for one. They do not constrain business enterprises, except to tax them; and they are often financed by taxes other than those on enterprises. Another category, far removed from regulation, is encouragement to business through a long list of benefits such as education of the young, maintenance of law and order, enforcement of contracts, protection of property, exploration and development of new markets overseas, miscellaneous infrastructure services such as mapping and weather surveillance, provision of capital infrastructure, loans and loan guarantees, subsidies: a long and ever-changing list as the needs of business change. Regulation is no more than a third category.

I emphasise the non-regulatory activities of government in the market to make clear that government does not operate largely as a no-sayer but instead shapes the results of the market in a great many ways, and is often itself entrepreneurial and innovative rather than constraining. Government in a contemporary market economy is subject to demands and pressures that enforce on it a generalised standing responsibility to maintain the health of the system and enlarge its product. Instead of simply regulating, it therefore constantly reshapes, pushes, stimulates, and helps the economy in various ways.[6]

Some historic events and developments that fall under the heading of governed markets are, I think, worth listing because of their significance for future planning.

(a) *The use of taxation and transfer payments to redistribute income and wealth.* So familiar as to need no comment.

(b) *The management of money and credit and of other variables to dampen fluctuations in production and employment.* So familiar as to need little comment. I call attention, however, to the degree to which economic stabilisation was epiphenomenal. By that I mean that to some degree it was achieved as a by-product of instruments and policies not designed for economic stabilisation; for example, military spending. Economic stabilisation also seems to demonstrate the gap between cognitive capacity and social complexity. The euphoria among economists that led them about 1960 to speak ambitiously about 'fine tuning' the economy did not last long, as structural changes in the economy began to outpace theoretical understandings of it. Despite the embarrassments of attempts at fine tuning, however, stabilisation policies have so successfully dampened down economic fluctuations as to have raised, in the industrialised market societies, almost everyone's aspirations for economic planning. We have learned from its successes that economic planning of appropriate kinds can make a harsh society at least tolerable.

(c) *Planning for economic mobilisation for the Second World War.* Even before the successes of stabilisation policy after the Second World War, American and British success in drawing resources into the war marked a pivotal event in our thinking about planning. We inferred that at least some governments – democratic governments at that – were able to carry out prodigious tasks of organisation and co-ordination. This was a lesson more impressive for Americans than for the British because Americans more than the British had doubted that capacity. In the USA, a common belief is that successes in war mobilisation were important in producing, after the war, demands and legislation for government planning to stabilise the economy. A frequent oblique inference from the success of democratic war mobilisation was that even on grounds of efficiency democracies were better than we had thought and dictatorships worse. The democracies successfully mobilised for sustained war; the Nazis did not. Intending a very short war, they did not think it necessary to mobilise as did the UK and the USA; and perhaps they could have mobilised if they had tried. But then again, that they had made so great a miscalculation itself cast doubt on their efficiency.[7]

(d) *Through continuing international negotiation, the remarkable invention and maintenance of instruments for organising the international monetary system and thus for world economic order.* Bretton Woods, the creation of the International Monetary Fund and the World Bank, the General Agreement on Tariff and Trades (GATT), and subsequent agreements to cope with emerging problems all constitute a conspicuous and major success of economic planning, remarkable both for its stability and adaptiveness, on one hand, and for its having been achieved without a central or co-ordinating authority, on the other. This experience tells us, perhaps more loudly than any other, that planning does not necessarily require a planner or planning authority.

(e) *The identification in recent decades of industrial policy as a focus for planning.* In market systems, government policies inescapably influence industrial development; and frequently, as in Alexander Hamilton's *Report on Manufactures* or in contemporary Third World economic planning, governments explicitly tackle the task of promoting industrial growth. The element new in emphasis is governmental concern with the nation's competitive position and a consequent debate, open in almost any nation you observe, on how far government should go, and with what instruments, in guiding industry into lines of production thought most promising for success in international markets. The advocates of industrial policy of this kind go far in proposing to constrain business decisions within a frame of governmentally planned decisions, thus to strike harder at traditional conventional business pre-rogatives than the earlier blows represented, for example, by anti-monopoly and fair trade regulation, by labour legislation, and by central bank management of money and credit. The industrial policy debate opens up the possibility of a drastic subordination of some market-determined priorities to selected government-determined priorities for capital investment and production.[8]

(f) *Human resource investment.* Even non-democratic governments usually see the need, in order to increase production, for some investment in the health and, if not that, at least the education of the children destined to become its workforce. That minimum interest in human resources has in recent decades ballooned into a concern, urgent in some nations, for greatly expanded human resource develop-ment, as, for example, in enlarging the flow of students through secondary schools, through the universities, and especially through scientific and engineering programmes in the universities. It also often includes programmes of occu-pational re-training needed for persons already in the workforce. These practical efforts have been encouraged by economic research findings which indicate that some shift of investment from physical to human capital would be productive in all nations. The result is that in some circles human resource planning is as sharply focused a policy area as, say, monetary management, city planning or environmental protection. And it is, I think, a policy area without any major failures, perhaps because human resource investment has been so starved.[9]

(g) *Science and technology development; research and development.* For various reasons, weapons development sometimes the most important among them, governments have funded research, technological innovation and applications, as well as sub-sidising them. They have in many other ways indirectly come to their aid, as, for example, through funds for graduate training in the universities. In the USA, government aid to research and development has a long and strong history in the establishment of agricultural universities together with their research arms. I think, however, that what governments did to improve agricultural technology was independent of their programmes, say, for military research and develop-ment. Only in recent decades have governments' varied aids to science, engineer-ing, technology, research and development come to be viewed, though even now only in some circles, as a potentially coherent whole calling for some co-ordinating authority. It is not at all clear, however, that co-ordination authorities for pro-grammes earlier independent of each other will in any way improve these programmes. So far, there is no such lesson to learn.

(h) *City planning?* I mention it to acknowledge it, but I also want to question it. City planning shows a long record of what many critics call failure and of such dubious accomplishments as cause its advocates to display caution in claiming success. Of the various aspects of planning in market systems that we have so far discussed, it has been most conspicuously the arena of professionals called 'plan-ners' and of organisations called 'planning authorities'. In the eyes of its critics, professional city planners, like early communist planners, do not understand the complexities of urban life; hence they deal simplistically with delicate phenomena of human relationships – movement, neighbourhood solidarity, security and adventure among them – just as communist planners made their distinctive mistake by overlooking complex problems in evaluation. An inference to ponder is the possibility that, just as we now often remind ourselves that war is too important to leave to the generals, city planning is too important to leave to the city planners.[10]

(i) *Environmental planning.* Although communist planning represents a frightening failure to sustain desirable environmental qualities, environmental planning in the market democracies has achieved modest successes and is probably gaining in both strength and intelligence. Clearly in recent decades it has become a major focus for government, a focus as ever present in public discourse as venerable problems like inflation and unemployment. But there are others who know more about environmental sustainability than I do. So, having put it on my list of great events and developments in twentieth-century planning, I will stick to my role as a commentator on planning in general.

With respect to all of these specific areas or foci of governed market planning – from (a) to (i) – we can take note of four features.

One is that each illustrates a process, not of setting existing institutions aside and solving the whole problem from scratch (whether it is a problem of stimulating research and development or a problem of protecting the environment), but instead a process of adjusting or tuning a mechanism that carries the main burden of solving the problem. I would like to repeat this using other words, because it is a point, even if obvious, of enormous importance. We count on the market to organise, say, research and development or investment in human resources or an international division of labour. We then move in with what we call planning to amend those aspects of market results that we do not want. Planning of this kind is not a free-standing method of social organisation or social change but a method of refining an existing method (like tuning a piano). Compared to starting from scratch, planning of this kind excuses planners from vast analytical and organisational tasks very probably beyond their competencies. Understanding this teaches a planner a very practical lesson: *one must never ask how to plan in order to organise* x *but how to plan to alter the existing social mechanisms, whether market or not, that govern* x.

The second feature of each of these listed areas of foci of governed market planning is that each tackles no more than a segment of economic life and copes with it with only minimal – sometimes zero – attention to what planners intend to do in each of the other segments. It is focused, specialised and even narrow, rather than vast, synoptic and broad. Professional planners and advocates of formal planning are consequently often discontented; they strain towards the breadth and synopsis denied them. Many of them do not realise that their successes arise out of their specialised focus; it is a focus tolerably consistent with human cognitive capacities while broad synoptic planning is not. A very practical lesson for planners emerges: modesty. Acknowledge that social complexity cannot be wholly grasped by any mind or committee, even if computer-aided. Bite off only what you can chew. And if, because of your limits, your planning does not co-ordinate well with that of planners in other fields, count on that malco-ordination to be defined as a problem for some other persons or authorities, not for you.

The third common failure is that these focused planning efforts only rarely succeed through a big step but instead work, if at all, through an endless succession of short and fairly rapid steps.

The fourth is that there may be – we do not yet know enough – big differences between a succession of short rapid steps that is influenced by a long-term perspective and a succession that is not, the former probably being the more successful form of planning and decision-making.[11]

The Great Depression

All these specific events and successes of governed market planning are noteworthy. But let us not forget the Great Depression of the 1930s as also a monumental event in the history of twentieth-century planning. From it we learned that a market economy under some circumstances can produce a social disaster. 'Disaster' is not too strong a word: the Depression persisted year after year; and for a time one-third of the American workforce was 'evicted' from the market system, a degree of collapse and disorganisation comparable with recent Russian economic experience. Some kinds of, some degrees of, planning are required for a minimum acceptability of a market economy.

It is significant for the prospects of planning that despite a continuing colossal breakdown of the market, not many citizens in the democracies – and not many politicians – opted to disband the market system in favour of some alternative. You may wish to infer that they had the good sense to stay with it. That would not be my inference. Mine is that because they should have at least been debating alternatives but did not, their minds were not very free or inventive. In other words, the passive continuing acceptance of a grossly malfunctioning economic system is evidence of low levels of enquiry, poor judgement and conformist thinking, about which I will say more shortly. I am not suggesting that we should have abandoned the market system, only that widespread debate on whether to do so was called for by market breakdown; and the absence of that debate says that we wear blinkers, are trapped in traditional ways of thinking, and do not have the intellectual capacities to plan as well as otherwise we might.[12]

Note also that, whether because of blinkers or other reasons, we did not have the competence to climb out of the Depression. It was brought to an end only by war expenditures.

Other governed market failures

While I have just been claiming that the long-term result of governed markets has been a smashing success for economic planning so conceived, I do not want to conceal its many historical shortcomings, aside from the Depression. In the USA, for example, among other failures planning still shies away from appropriate action on housing; wastes the potential labour of many of its young people, especially blacks; bungles medical care; cannot maintain safe streets; and leaves citizens deeply discontent with public education. It is also a poor manager of its own finances. What is to be learned from such failures?

One lesson is that the human mind cannot cope well with the complexity of the social world and, consequently, even highly successful planning (in the light of history) is a miserable record of an excess of mistakes. From that lesson we should perhaps learn modesty in planning.

However, another lesson from failure is that planning is not the mobilisation of intelligence for the alteration of a passive social structure but is instead the mobilisation of intelligence to overcome people who are mobilising intelligence to obstruct. It has been difficult to plan to improve low-income housing because many people in the political system plan and fight against it. Old-age pensions were slow to come to the USA because of opposition rather than system inertness. Extended medical care is now blocked by insurance companies who profit from the existing limited medical care system. The potential for the kind of planning that will extend the mass benefits of the last hundred years of market-oriented planning lies less in better design than in more effective development of majorities to overcome the resistance of highly advantaged minorities. It is not the professional planners or policy analysts who need help so much as it is the left-of-centre politicians. (That assumes again that your utopia is not Spencerian.)

The power of elitist and class-based resistances to steering the market away from traditional inequalities, as well as towards more security, tells us two important things about market planning. First, this power of resistance explains why, despite all the historic successes of governed markets, there are still pockets – and very large pockets – of poverty and insecurity, as well as many other inhumane features of market societies, such as marked inequality before the law or, for another example, political inequalities arising out of the influence of money in politics. Second, the history of power – because it is in many societies a history of declining elite power – promises better planning in the future. We are still pushing back the opponents of steering the market in the direction of a wider and more equitable distribution of its continuing benefits and reduction of its harshness. Then too, we have not reached the peak of our technical competence to govern the market; our cognitive capacities are not strained to their limits.

Not very democratic 'democracies'

In the light of the failures of governed markets, I think it appropriate to list at this point, as a fifth major attribute of twentieth-century planning, that it was never or rarely very democratic. Genuinely democratic planning either still lies in our not-so-close future or is impossible. Democratic planning has not been and is not now very democratic for the following reasons.

1 Inequalities in income and wealth drown the formal equality of the vote. Ask a party whether it would not rather have a $1,000 contribution than your vote. That universal suffrage provides an approximation to democratic equality of political influence or power is close to nonsense, and I think it

possible to document that it is a taught myth, long taught and still taught by people fearful of democracy and protective of their own advantages.

2   Easy organisation and financing of political influence by business enterprises and associations gives them grossly disproportionate political power. If you or I want to help fund a political campaign, we must take the money out of our own pockets, but enterprises can charge much of what they put into politics as a business expense rather than as a charge against personal income.

3   Socio-economic stratification, through its effects on education, civic experience, political access and confidence, strengthens the political influence of some segments of the population and saps others.

4   Planning has to make headway against beliefs directly or indirectly hostile to it, beliefs long inculcated in populations by elites intending to curb masses, beliefs such as those that endorse inequality, hierarchy, deference to authority, political docility and so on.

5   Public discourse on political and economic issues is heavily unilateral in the hands of elites rather than multilateral. Through press and broadcasting small numbers can unilaterally profoundly influence large numbers, a situation far removed from an idealised democratic competition of ideas.

Each of you can add to or refine this list of democratic flaws, even if our habit of calling the North American and Western European nations 'democracies' tends to curtail our thinking about whether they are. We need a great and never-ending debate on whether we have pretty much reached the upper limits of feasible democracy, hence feasible democratic planning, or are still only at its early stages.

To anticipate or make a transition to a seventh major development to be listed, I call your attention to the fact that a number of points I have been talking about raise the old question: precisely what is the connection between market and democracy? Conversely, what is the relation between non-market planning and democracy? Many of the mass benefits of markets are available even in the absence of democracy. We trace, for example, significant early steps towards social security in Bismarck's Germany and can trace a continuity, say, to Kuwait and Taiwan. Yet high standards of living have usually risen out of a combination of democracy and markets. Classical liberal thought claims another connection between the two: democracy, it is claimed, is impossible without a market system; hence democratic economic planning is impossible in the absence of market system. Is this true? We do not know. But we do know that so far no democratic nation-state has been established except with a market system. An extraordinary proposition! Lessons to be learned for planning? Not yet clear. But in thinking about the market-planning-democracy connection, one, two or three of the following may be possible.

- If democracy is impossible except in market societies, wide-ranging or pervasive democratic planning other than market planning is ruled out.[13]
- The contrary: although democracy, such as we so far know it, has always

rested on a market economy, the connection may not hold for a more fully democratic future, leaving open, then, the possibility of wide-ranging pervasive democratic non-market planning (model 1 above).[14]

- And, of course, as critics of democratic market planning never tire of repeating, even if initially successful such planning might itself at some point or under some circumstances undermine democracy.[15]
- But more market and non-market planning might both be necessary to cope with severe imperfections in democracy such as those arising from inequalities of income and wealth and consequent political inequality.[16]

For all the successes of democratic governed market planning for a century and a half, these four inferences from it continue to be disputed, and there is little probability of a resolution of the dispute.

No democratic attempt to operate a non-market system

It is in the light of these contested hypotheses about the market-planning-democracy connection that I now want to call attention to a non-event so extraordinary that its absence has to be listed as number 7 in this list of great developments in twentieth-century planning. In the entire twentieth century – for that matter in all history – no democratic state has ever attempted a democratic non-market economy (model 1 above)! I am not saying simply that none ever succeeded; I am saying that none ever made the attempt. None chose to try, none ever even blundered into the attempt. In a wide variety of countries, socialist thought advocated such a venture, made a case for it that was persuasive to many informed and thoughtful people. But that is as far as it ever went; no government ever tried.

How can that be? One might explain it by saying that such a venture would have been a mistake. But we all know that governments often make mistakes, even democratic governments. So even if an attempt at a non-market system would have been a mistake, we would expect that at some point in the century at least one government would have at least for a short time tried. Clearly this reason is invalid. Moreover, while governments may have *believed* a move to a non-market economy would be a mistake, they could not have *known* it to be so. It was never so known, and it is still not known, even if belief runs strong on the point. So we have to ask: why, in the absence of knowledge, would all governments at all times believe that a non-market economy would be a mistake? What accounts for the uniformity of thought on the issue? Why not diversity of opinion instead?

Do you want to interrupt me by claiming that you at least do *know* that a non-market economy would be a mistake? You are perhaps confusing firm belief with knowledge. So long as many highly educated, thoughtful and informed people, professors, engineers and other experts among them, do not believe it would be a mistake, I think you cannot claim that you *know* and they do not. All you can claim is that you believe, just as they believe the contrary. That there are more of you than there are of them does not mean that you *know* and they do not.

This suggests another explanation for the absence of a single venture into a non-market economy: in no system at any time has there been a majority in its favour. But we know that so-called democratic governments often try policies contrary to majority preference. So we have to discard that explanation. In itself it raises a question: is it possible that at no time in any country has a majority for a non-market economy developed? If it has never developed, why not? Why, despite maldistribution of income and wealth and why, given the miseries of the Great Depression, did such a majority not develop in at least one country?

I suggest that to explain the absence of not even one temporary majority for a non-market system in more than a hundred years, we have to conclude that in market societies our minds are systematically shaped, as I have already briefly suggested. Non-market systems are excluded from the thinking of most people and deprecated in the minds of those who do think about them. Such a programme of what might be called 'thought control' is to be expected in any society in which those segments of the population that can speak through the media are the same segments that are advantaged by existing institutions and wish to protect them against criticism. And that is precisely the state of affairs in most societies, market societies among them. A fair or rigorous competition of ideas is nowhere to be found.

At the same time that we are taught the benefits of the market, we are systematically taught the alleged virtues of hierarchy, inequality, deference, respect for authority and so on. A principal quality of these teachings is that they induce a population to follow its elites in a veneration of existing institutions.[17]

Do you want to reject my argument that our minds have been played upon to keep us from thinking certain thoughts? Then your explanation of why no democratic government has ever tried for a non-market economy must be that, despite an occasional majority for a non-market economy, governments have successfully persisted in avoiding such a venture. Either way, the explanation is that ostensibly democratic governments are not very democratic, either because the discussion of issues and alternatives is not in fact very open or because majorities can be thwarted. That, I suggest, is the great significance of the consistent refusal of all ostensibly democratic governments ever to venture into a non-market economy. That is further evidence, about as far as we ever get on big issues in social science, of the generalisation argued above: that the world has not yet advanced very far in democratic control of economic and social change.

The Marshall Plan and foreign aid

Setting aside now these interlocked concerns with planning, market and democracy, I am inclined to list the Marshall Plan and subsequent aid of the industrial nations to Third World development as a great development in the history of economic planning. The USA vastly extended its old horizons in assuming a major responsibility for European post-war reconstruction; and all the industrialised nations took on significant, even if quantitatively small, responsibilities for giving help to the developing world. The ambition and reach of normal peacetime national policy thus underwent a transformation that has turned out to be significant not only for economic development but for the character of policy-making in other areas, environmental sustainability among them. The industrialised nations now constitute a community of nations with communal responsibilities.

Bureaucratisation

The next development on my list – number 9 – is located from a different vantage point. While for at least 150 years many of us have been passionately debating socialism versus capitalism, almost all societies – democracies or not – have been put through a transformation possibly greater than if we had moved from capitalism to socialism. Rarely making a big issue of the change, we have slid into the bureaucratic organisation of many aspects of life. In their frequency of impact on us, the bureaus of government eclipse parliaments and cabinets. In the economy, we are all familiar with the rise of great bureaucratic organisations known as corporations. Education and health care are heavily bureaucratised; and so is leisure in that we are entertained by films bureaucratically created and distributed, and by sporting events that pit one bureaucratically organised team against another.

Are there inferences or lessons we can learn from these developments? One is that we had better keep our eye on the ball. Perhaps the great issues pertinent to social change are not the issues concerning planning that we have long debated. Perhaps, for example, problems, say, of institutional loyalty or programme inflexibility loom larger. Second, as we all know, bureaucratisation has made planning within corporations and other bureaucracies a major rather than a peripheral phenomenon and problem area. Third, since a bureaucracy constitutes an island of hierarchy and command in a market sea, we should take note that bureaucratisation greatly reduces, along some lines, the scope of market organisation and correspondingly enlarges the scope of 'private' non-market planning.

The multinational corporation

In the form of the large multinational corporation, bureaucratisation has vastly increased the scope of corporate planning, specifically of bringing into a single system of management decisions earlier left to the market system. It has also in some ways diminished the powers of nation-states to govern or plan. For small enough nations, the assets and capacity to spend of the corporation are more than a match for the financial resources of the state. For all nations, the multinationals become instruments through which movements of capital can be organised to threaten or penalise governments that pursue, or might pursue, policies opposed by the corporations.

Market socialism in Yugoslavia

When I was a graduate student in economics, Oskar Lange's now classic paper, 'On the Economic Theory of Socialism', was much discussed (Lange and Taylor 1938). In it he laid out a design for market socialism as an alternative to the command socialism of the Soviet Union. Some of our teachers assured us that, interesting as the design was, we could be sure that no real-world approximation to it was possible.

They were mistaken, for the Yugoslav experience brought into the real world this new possibility of economic organisation. Its second significance is that market socialism worked; it was for a time relatively, even conspicuously, successful, in reaching production levels well beyond those of earlier central planning. But, third, its collapse has muddied the waters of discussion on market socialism by encouraging rash, negative conclusions about market socialism.

Yugoslavia was a poor location for an experiment, torn as it was by religious, ethnic linguistic and national divisions, and Yugoslav market socialism never tested the possibilities of *democratic* socialism. Hence while some critics have hurried to dismiss market socialism as demonstrably unacceptable, others have pointed to its accomplishments, the special political reasons for its difficulties, and its democratic potential still untested. The Yugoslav experience has not been well sifted.

Nazism

I am inclined to add to this list of great twentieth-century developments in planning the Nazi German episode. I doubt that there is anything pivotal to learn from the Nazi economic system. But Nazism as a political force taught us that even the most civilised of nations could support a government that pursued unspeakable violations of the practices of what we thought was civilised behaviour. We had reason to find frightening and dismaying both the policies of the government and the passivity of acceptance of them by the population; and those of us outside Germany have had to contemplate troubling questions about our own bystander passivity.

Lessons for planning? That the state – even a more or less democratic state, which is the instrument to which we turn to plan for us – can turn into a monster and that we – both elites and masses – may be unable to curb it and may not even wish to do so. Can you think of any other lesson about planning that is more significant? Should I here mention two voices that helped us learn this lesson: Orwell in his *1984* and Huxley in his *Brave New World*?

Failures of planning in the developing economies

With the development among the industrialised nations after the Second World War of a significant, even if still stingy, commitment to economic growth in the 'Third World', donor and lender organisations such as the World Bank and the US Agency for International Development undertook to require synoptic capital investment planning by those less developed countries that wished to qualify for aid. Considering that most of the lenders and donors ideologically opposed capital planning of the same kind in their own economies, their urging of it on borrowers is noteworthy. Perhaps they found it easy to imagine that investment planning in a small not yet industrialised country – their typical client – posed no great difficulties in planning. Perhaps they brought to their aid programmes a banker mentality: show us your plans if you want the money. Perhaps they were arrogant in imposing on the client nation whatever suited their own convenience, patronising and self-interested as they typically were.

In any case, they soon found reasons to back away from their demands for synoptic planning. In many cases, the client nation had no competence to plan: no planning competence either in the civil service or in any professional stratum that could be tapped. Or the civil service turned out formal plans that, meeting the lender's requirement, represented no significant national political commitment to the plans. Or the client nation contracted with foreign experts like those of the Harvard Development Group to write a plan, in which case the gap between plans on paper and political commitment was widened; at an extreme the plans themselves were not intelligible to the political officials for whom they were ostensibly written. The lessons here are obvious; I need not spell them out. Only less synoptic, less formal, open-ended interventions to steer the market worked well.

The Chinese turn towards the market

If it is still too early to assess the importance of current developments in Chinese planning, one can hardly neglect the consequences of change in so vast a country. China shares, it appears, the Soviet disillusionment with non-market planning; but has set a new course not in extremity, as in the Soviet Union, but in time to avert the disorganisation that now burdens the once Soviet area. Moreover, its success in introducing ever new elements of the market seems to run well beyond the success, if it can be called that, of Russia and Eastern Europe, for its GNP is rising at a remarkable rate during the continuing transition. It would seem that China might be able to teach Eastern Europe how to transform itself and might provide more competent assistance to Eastern Europe than is now being offered by Western economists and business people. China is also a testing ground for the proposition that market has to precede democracy rather than follow it, and some might suggest that it will also test, though inconclusively, the thesis that democracy *must* follow market.[18]

Still no theory of planning

At this late date, we have no general theory, either descriptive or prescriptive, of planning. I do not regret that we lack it; I only note that we lack it. We have both a descriptive and prescriptive theory of the market economy which, even with its significant imperfections, is a powerful intellectual construct. We have a prescriptive theory of market socialism governed by what economists call 'consumer sovereignty'. We also have threads of a prescriptive theory of market socialism coupled with planners' sovereignty. Quite aside from the absence of descriptive theory about the two models of market socialism, we have no general theory about non-market planning or even about governmental policy-making. Many generalisations are offered, often ambitiously labelled as theory even if not always by their authors: Simon's 'satisficing', for example, or my own 'incrementalism'. We also have formal decision theory, and a variety of attempts to systematise our knowledge of public choice. Yet if I am asked by a bright student where she can find an exposition of the governmental process, or of the policy-making or planning process, that approximates as a coherent theoretical construction the theory of the market system, I have to wring my hands in frustration. And I do not expect this frustration would be relieved if I were to live a hundred more years.[19]

Even so, we almost certainly think more systematically about planning problems than we used to. Various formal analytical strategies are of limited help: systems analysis, for example, or cost-benefit analysis. Electronic computation vastly extends our analytic capacities, even if it does not at all tackle the problem of weighing alternatives. Keynesian theory harnessed together with national income accounting transformed the abilities of government to cope with economic instability.

Yet imprecise, question-begging, and obfuscating habits of ideological thinking persist in most quarters. Perhaps I am simply perverse in thinking that ideology's persistence is more significant than departures from it. Perhaps in Europe I would see the decline in ideology more sharply. Perhaps it is in the USA that its persistence is conspicuous. I make here only one point about ideological thought. The case for the market system is closely – extremely closely – tied in most minds to the case both for private property and for today's distribution of it. The case for steering or governing the market is tied to attacks on private property and its present distribution. It is, then, not surprising that ostensible attempts to analyse problems in planning are often only disguises for not very clear-headed defences of, or attacks on, private property and its distribution, as though no other issues could match these in importance. Instead of analysing questions about the design of good institutions, we degenerate into passionate attempts to hang on to or enlarge our property claims.

In the absence of theory, what to do? Perhaps pursue some fundamental understandings of planning, inconclusive as they may be. At this point, I have finished my list of developments in twentieth-century planning and seek that fuller understanding through a theme suggested by the list.

FUNDAMENTAL ALTERNATIVES IN PLANNING

Several themes in fact emerge from the foregoing commentary on planning events of the twentieth century: for example, the daunting cognitive difficulties of planning, and the successes of focused, sometime piecemeal, planning. Rather than probe every theme we can identify, I propose to probe only one integrating theme. In its vast implications, it is critical, fundamental, pivotal to planning of all kinds and everywhere. It illuminates all the other issues.

Put the theme as a distinction: between unilateral planning and mutually adjustive planning: for example, land-use planning in the hands of one powerful agency versus land-use planning that engages the community's political leadership, its business leadership, and other concerned parties. I put it again as a more fundamental distinction: between centrally co-ordinated social organisation, both small and large, and mutually adjusted social organisation: for example, governing rules within a family, set on one hand by a parent or, on the other hand, emerging from family interchanges. I also put it as an explicit issue for choice: for tasks of social organisation, which of the two shall we choose: the centrally placed authority, mind or committee, or mutual adjustment among participants? To take an example from the discouraging history of US federal budgetary reform: shall we increasingly move towards unilateral authority within a budget bureau, or shall we try to improve legislative negotiation? Or I can put it as a thesis: our thinking about social organisation, including political organisation and planning, carries a powerful bias in favour of the authoritative mind. Or, finally, as a prescription: it is high time to expose and get rid of that bias.

Some of you will know that this is a long-standing theme of mine. I am inclined to think that in the social sciences there is no greater theme, at least no more pervasive and significant an error than this bias. I shall hope here to do more than repeat what I have written before (Lindblom 1965).

First, let me say that I am not talking about administrative centralisation versus decentralisation, a common topic in the literatures on administration and planning. Administrative decentralisation refers to a devolution of primary decision responsibilities to lower levels whose decisions are then subsequently centrally co-ordinated. It is therefore simply another form of what I here call centralisation or unilateral decision-making.

What I mean by non-central or unilateral is organisation or co-ordination achieved without a supervising or overarching power, achieved because persons to be co-ordinated take account of, adjust to, and influence each other. They are organised or co-ordinated with each other by their interactions rather than by a supervising authority. They control and are controlled by each other rather than by a supervising control. Call this method of social organisation mutual adjustment, or call it multilateral control instead of unilateral control.

Further examples? The co-ordination on the field of a soccer team; the movement of intersecting pedestrians at a crowded intersection; the emptying and refilling of an auditorium at intermission time.

More significant examples? The creation of a highly co-ordinated set of symbols and sounds that permit millions of people to communicate with each other. Every language is an accomplishment of co-ordination, achieved almost wholly without unilateral supervision. The development of a society's moral code is another mammoth exercise in mutual adjustment.

Although I put the distinction sharply, in actuality the two forms of organisation are always mixed. A soccer team is coached before the game, as well as governed by rules, even if during the game itself it is largely dependent on mutual adjustment. Even language creation is to some small degree centrally guided, as in French governmental attempts to protect the language from American corruptions.

The example of organisation through mutual adjustment rather than unilateral authority that seems most germane to us is, of course, economic organisation through the market system. In the twentieth century we have slowly learned – with a recent acceleration of learning as communist systems collapsed – that the market system is a prodigious organiser and co-ordinator. Like all other human institutions it is full of problems, severely defective when compared with an ideal, yet nevertheless a great organiser: so great that the whole historical anti-market Marxian tradition together with a gigantic and sustained seventy-year effort to get along without the market, ended with a turn to the market in communist systems. Almost everyone now seems to grasp that the market system is not simply an attribute of capitalism but a multi-purpose co-ordinating mechanism that many – perhaps all – kinds of regimes can put to use.

As a form of mutual adjustment, the market system has accomplished the largest and most detailed feat of social organisation in human history. It is a co-ordination embracing most adults the world over, a co-ordination that engages them in co-operating with each other for the achievements of ends each cannot alone achieve. It co-ordinates a far-away coffee grower with those of you who drank a cup of coffee at breakfast this very day – it is not by chance that there was coffee in your cup. To bring the coffee to you, the market co-ordinated coffee bean buyers, shippers, insurers and roasters. But shippers could only play their role because ships had been built, and this in turn depended upon the mining of ore and the smelting of steel. A single cup of coffee for you is a consequence of organised, non-random, systematic patterns of co-ordination embracing many millions of people.

This world-over intricacy of co-ordination represents by far the greatest feat of social organisation or co-ordination in human experience. Nothing comes close to it. No nation-state – not even a giant like China – engages so many people in such detailed co-ordination. No international organisation – no United Nations, no North Atlantic Treaty Organisation – even distantly approximates this feat of co-ordination.

The theme I want to voice is not the usefulness of the market, however. It is the usefulness of mutual adjustment of other kinds – non-market kinds – that are not yet sufficiently either recognised or appreciated – and specifically, mutual adjustment in politics and planning. Despite our new appreciation of market mutual adjustment, we have a great deal yet to learn about mutual adjustment in general and especially in politics.

My examples of mutual adjustment in language construction, the creation of a moral code, and in the market should be sufficient to suggest very strongly that, for organisation, co-ordination and planning, societies across the board in fact depend more heavily on mutual adjustment than on unilateral decision. Although I am willing to go that far, it is not necessary to my current argument.

All I need to claim is that mutual adjustment carries a very large part of the task of social co-ordination, that unilateral co-ordination is not in any *obvious* way more useful, and that long-established habits of thought carry a bias towards the unilateral that ought to be removed so that we can better master the arts of social organisation.

Let us look at that bias. In English, it shows up in terminology. 'To co-ordinate' means both 'to bring into a co-ordinated state' and 'to play a co-ordinating role', as though only through the centrality of the role can the co-ordinated state be achieved. In American politics, it shows up in our habit of appointing a 'czar' to cope with an especially tough task in organisation, as though centrality were the only remedy for malco-ordination. But the bias has a long history in the study of social order.

In the history of thought, the great minds have, with few exceptions, cast the study of social order – how people can live with each other – as a problem of curbing the potential subversion of the mass against the elite. The great philosophers from Plato on, as members of elites or candidates for membership, have been self-serving in assuming that order is possible only with unilateral rather than multilateral controls; and, of course, for much of history military power has joined with religious authority to insist on mass docility as a requisite of social order. Among very few others, Montesquieu toyed with the possibility of order through mutual adjustment, as did Mandeville and Adam Ferguson. Not until Adam Smith, however, does anyone achieve a comprehensive and explicit statement of the possibilities of order through mutual adjustment. Even so, Smith did not generalise from the market system to other arenas of social organisation, with the result that even today those possibilities are slighted. No, not only slighted: also feared. Even in our day, elites of power and intellect still fear masses as sources of disorder and are consequently still disposed to prescribe unilateral rather than multilateral controls.

Another source of bias arises in our very concept of rationality. A rational solution to a problem of organisation – or any other problem – is, we say, an informed and thought-out solution: not a solution reached by a contest of power but one reached by the mind. This, we think, is precisely what unilateral authority offers, a possibility that an overviewing mind or team can find a rational solution or plan. Thus our bias also tells us that a mutually adjusted solution – a negotiation, contest of power, or exercise in reciprocal threats or other manoeuvres – will give us an unreasoned outcome, not a rational solution.

The argument is a mistake. It wrongly assumes that a mind or team can in fact reach a solution that is in some sense correct. It assumes that the centralist mind or team can accomplish a synoptic overview. For complex real-world problem solving and planning, these are mistaken assumptions. The human mind is of finite capacity and can never wholly completely analyse or master a complex social problem.

At least three difficulties can be identified briefly: (i) *inadequate knowledge:* on this ground alone the unilateral solution cannot be shown to be superior to many others; (ii) *cognitive complexity* of the problem, all analysis being both defective at points and incomplete: again, on this one ground alone, the unilateral solution cannot be shown to be superior; (iii) *evaluation problems*: with the consequence that for inter-personal or inter-group conflicts of interests there is no agreed criteria for an analytical solution. Thus the resolution of inter-personal conflict has to that degree to be arbitrary, not reasoned. Add to these three obstructions the possibility and frequent probability that the supervising mind will be injudicious, whimsical or even malicious.

Given these obstructions to conclusive analysis, there exists no way to show that what purports to be a rational unilateral solution is superior to a mutually adjusted solution. Judiciously observing centrality and mutual adjustment in various situations, you or I will judge mutual adjustment to be superior here, centrality superior there. But no general rule holds. That the unilateral is usually superior is simply a bias.

I can guess that some of you are objecting. Certainly, you will say, *approximating* a centrally synoptic decision is more rational than a negotiation or contest of power. But this is not certain at all! Let us return to market mutual adjustment for an example. The Soviets spent seventy years trying to approximate centralist synoptic decisions on the economy only to decide finally that the negotiations and conflicts of power of the market system would be superior. For complex social problems and planning we can be sure that every ostensibly unilateral decision falls far short of synopsis, is full of error, will need correction, and may be a disaster; hence it may or may not be superior to mutual adjustment problem-solving and planning.

Mutual adjustment in politics and planning

It is in politics and planning especially that we have underplayed the role of non-market mutual adjustment. Of course, we know that, in administering policies once decided on, unilateral authority is often indispensable. It is in choosing or making policy that we neglect the merits of mutual adjustment.

We know that it exists, but that is not the same as appreciating it. We all know, for example, that governmental decision-making is full of wheeling and dealing, negotiation, compromise. We know that a policy is often set not because those active in it jointly reason it through to a conclusion but because a formula is found that meets the diverse needs of each of those participating. We know that, rather than try to plan an integration of half a dozen planning areas, a prime minister or cabinet may plunge ahead with only one, intending that its chronological priority will compel subsequent decisions in the other areas to adapt. We know that the way some members of a government may deal with issues raised by others is to try to drive them out of office rather than reason with them.

We do indeed know all this. But we often adopt the same disdainful attitude towards these forms of political mutual adjustment that communists long took against market mutual adjustment. We regret rather than appreciate, deplore rather than applaud. Politicians themselves remain apologetic. I suggest that political thought at this date has as little explored the usefulness of political mutual adjustment as the communists explored until about 1980 the usefulness of market mutual adjustment.

There has been, of course, a continuing interest in political thought in a separation of powers and in other forms of mutual adjustment as means by which otherwise dangerous concentrations of power can be blocked. But in some circles – for example, in American pluralist thought – it has been assumed that protecting democracy through a separation of powers comes at a price: a reduction in the competence or efficacy of government. That political mutual adjustment through a separation of powers can actually improve the competence or efficacy of government is still a largely unexplored thesis.

Despite what I have just said about the shortcoming of the centralist mind, many of you will argue something like the following: policy-making and planning through a central mind or committee, for all its defects, still makes a place for analysis and reason. In contrast, mutual adjustment is a contestation of influence and power. That being so, centrality makes more sense. I think I can show you that such an argument and contrast is mistaken.

For no complex problem of policy is any society wholly agreed on criteria for choosing a solution. A society may give a great deal of lip service to ideals such as liberty or equality, but it will not agree on just which liberties in what circumstances should be observed or how far which of many possible equalities should be pursued. Even if it agrees on some more concrete objective such as educating the young, it will not agree wholly on the curriculum, or on the budget, tax burden or management of the school system. For at least 2,500 years, philosophers – others too – have sought formulae for deciding such questions, but we are still far short of agreement. Given disagreements, no cognitive or intellectual solution is possible. *By that I mean that no reasoned policy choice satisfies everyone and that, consequently, any policy choice made will have to be somehow imposed over the reasoned objections of advocates of alternative policies.* Every choice requires imposition, power and politics. Reason alone will not do.

How can we and do we proceed, then, to impose?

The mutual adjustment way is to let the advocates of each of the contesting positions use the vote or any other authority we grant them or might choose to grant them in order to bring influence or power to bear on each other so that an outcome ensues. We might, for example, permit or require each of a half-dozen authorities with a stake in education to negotiate with each other. Or we might, as in the USA, assign some taxing authority to municipal authorities, some budgetary authority to a school board, some supervising authority to state governments, and let their interactions, whether negotiated or at a distance and without negotiation, produce an outcome on educational policy. Each of these interacting participants will bring information and analysis to bear in forming its own position and will thereafter bring persuasion as well as harsher forms of influence and power to bear on the other participants. Beyond some point, the solution is a political or power solution. This is the method of mutual adjustment.

The more familiar unilateral way means that instead of assigning or permitting authority to a variety of interested parties, we assign it exclusively to one and only one: to someone called a chairman, prime minister or mayor; or, if the authority is collective, to a body called a cabinet, board, committee or team. Ask such an authority to think its way through to a solution: that is, to use intellect, not imposition or power.

Now stop here to see the difficulties of the centralist or unilateral way. Such a decision-making person or group can do no more than analyse the problem in the same limited way that each of the mutual adjusters can analyse a problem. A grant of unilateral authority is not a grant of brain power not available to others. Hence the authority cannot reconcile the disagreements that have been with us for at least 2,500 years. Nor can it range as widely over relevant analytical issues as can a number of interacting participants in policy-making. All it can do beyond its limited and always inconclusive analysis is use its grant of authority to impose its policy position on all others. To impose, I said. Hence the unilateral solution is, like the mutually adjusted solution, an imposed or political, rather than a cognitive solution.

You may claim that the unilateral authority can think broadly and take everyone's interests into account. Indeed it may – or may not – think broadly; but it cannot take everyone's interests into account in such a way as to satisfy all. In the absence of a reconciling value or formula, such as has evaded us for at least 2,500 years, it will have to impose its chosen policy, no matter how broadly designed, on others who prefer something different (each of whom, incidentally, may have often thought about policy as broadly as has the unilateral authority).

What then is the real difference between unilateral and mutually adjusted policy-making, planning or co-ordination? The unilateral permits one party to impose its position. Mutual adjustment produces policies and plans that take account of many positions – the positions of many groups and persons. On the face of it, that would seem to be a strong a priori case for mutual adjustment rather than unilateral authority.

To make sure the point is clear, let me say it in words that differ only slightly. Unilateral authority does not think or analyse its way to a universally accepted reasoned solution; it only thinks or analyses its way to a position not universally shared in the society. Beyond that point, it achieves a solution only by politically imposing its position on others. In mutual adjustment, both brains and power are similarly employed; and the final solution, like the unilateral solution, is imposed or political, not cognitive. But a larger set of possible positions is taken into account.

Environmental problems are an example of the need for mutual adjustment. In coping with environmental problems, global interdependence now calls for regional or global co-ordination. Action by a single nation is not enough. But there is no world unilateral authority, no world government; and, I might ask, who could trust either the competence or motives of one if it existed? For global environmental policy-making, mutual adjustment among nations, among organisations from different nations, and among people of different nations, is the only big and open route.

Even within any one nation, problems of environmental sustainability call for attention from more varied interests than can be protected by any one unilateral authority. Good environmental policy has to respond to concerns of various authorities: on energy, roads and highways, land use, city planning, air and rail transport, industrial policy, health and education, among others. I cannot imagine a real-world unilateral authority competent to harmonise these conflicting and complementary concerns. But we can observe around us the complex political mutual adjustments that bring them all to bear on policy. They range from inter-departmental or inter-ministerial committees, through negotiation among political leadership, to mutual adjustment at great distances, in which, for example, a health ministry or department debates whether, for the time being, to fight the inadequate anti-pollution policies of an industrial ministry or, alternatively, simply to adapt its own health efforts to the fact of existing pollution.

From this comparison of unilateral authority and mutual adjustment in politics and planning, I think some lessons can be inferred for scholars, planners, policy analysts, and political officials – well, for that matter, for anyone who is interested in public policy.

- As I have said already, we need to move some distance away from deploring the political, in contrast to the cognitive elements in policy-making and planning.
- We need to accept the impossibility of reasoning all the way to solutions, thus leaving generous room for power and arbitrariness.
- Understanding this, we can break ourselves of the frequent habit of simply imputing intelligence to unilateral authority, the actual competence of which must always be questioned.
- We can then also see that big cognitive tasks of central co-ordination run beyond human capacity while smaller cognitive tasks of participating in mutual adjustment often do not.
- Those of us who play professional roles as planners and policy analysts can learn to refuse to claim to know what society should do, proposing instead to offer to our clients and audiences no more than a considered position worth inserting into the political process in competition with the no less well-considered positions of others.
- We cannot even claim to possess the essential facts, for facts are always inconclusive.
- Given the inescapable disagreements that hover over public policy, it is not findings but choices that are finally called for – not discovery of right courses of action but considered commitments to one course rather than others.
- And, of course, it is society through its political machinery that makes the choice or commitment; it is not a task for professionals, though we can be of some help.

In a hundred years of planning, we are still only slowly learning these lessons, all of precise relevance to the pursuit of environmental sustainability.

Notes

1 With thanks for valuable comments to Kate Bauer, Eric Lindblom and James Meadowcroft.
2 Drawing on the intellectual inheritance of classical economics, some voices, not yet extinguished, protested against the new dominant simplifications of the tasks of planning. See Brutzkus (1935).
3 Among countless interpretations of the Soviet experience, one classic stands out in my mind for its vivid characterisation of both vision and disillusion: Edmund Wilson, *To The Finland Station* (1940).
4 Possible conflict and trade-offs between liberty and democracy, on the one hand, and social rationality, on the other, was the theme problem in Karl Mannheim's classic *Man and Society in an Age of Reconstruction* (1940).
5 Soviet economists, engineers and planners testified to the need for market mechanisms decades before Gorbachev, though cautiously and with indirection. See, for an example of earlier appraisals of internal debate in the USSR Goldman (1963).
6 A relatively early attempt to see not simply a picture of government regulation but a wider picture of government promotion of business in Western Europe and the USA was Shonfield (1987: 3–7).
7 On other influences that, like success in wartime mobilisation, raised levels of confidence in planning, see Friedmann (1987).
8 See for example Johnson, Tyson and Zysman (1989). In it and in much of the debate, the Japanese experience with industrial policy provided the focus.
9 Illustrative of this field of planning is Mihaly Simai (1995).
10 A classic attack of three decades ago on city planning was Jane Jacobs (1961).
11 These last few paragraphs draw on my 'The science of "muddling through"' (Lindblom 1959) and 'Still muddling, not yet through' (Lindblom 1979).
12 For an expansion of the argument, see Lindblom (1977: chs 12 and 15).
13 A familiar position derived from nineteenth-century liberalism, as, for example, in Milton Friedman (1962).
14 A position identified with now familiar 'end of socialism' arguments of recent decades. The number of its advocates continues to decline.
15 This argument is another string in Friedman's bow. An analysis far more favourable to a mutually supporting combination of market planning and democracy is Dahl and Lindblom (1953).
16 A position widely argued, identified with twentieth-century rather than nineteenth-century liberalism, and as prominent in political rhetoric in the democracies as in scholarly discourse.
17 These two paragraphs rest on Part II of my *Inquiry and Change* (Lindblom 1991).
18 The Chinese growth record and its implications for these issues are discussed in Overholt (1993).
19 A brave and intelligent attempt to move as far as possible towards planning theory without ascending to obfuscating heights of abstraction – an excellent piece of work – is John Friedmann (1987).

References

Bardhan, P. and Roemer, J. (eds) (1993) *Market Socialism: The Current Debate*, New York: Oxford University Press.
Brutzkus, B. (1935) *Economic Planning in Soviet Russia*, London: Routledge.
Dahl, R. and Lindblom, C. (1953) *Politics, Economics, and Welfare*, New York: Harper.
Friedman, M. (1962) *Capitalism and Freedom*, Chicago, Ill.: University of Chicago Press.
Friedmann, J. (1987) *Planning in the Public Domain*, Princeton, NJ: Princeton University Press.

Goldman, M. (1963) 'Economic Controversy in the Soviet Union', *Foreign Affairs*, 42.

Hayek, F. (1944) *The Road of Serfdom*, Chicago: University of Chicago Press.

Jacobs, J. (1961) *The Death and Life of Great American Cities*, New York: Random House.

Johnson, C., Tyson, L. and Zysman, J. (1989) *Politics and Productivity*, New York: Harper Business.

Lange, O. and Taylor, F. (1938) *On the Economic Theory of Socialism*, Minneapolis, Minn.: University of Minnesota Press.

Lindblom, C. (1959) 'The science of "muddling through"', *Public Administration Review* 19: 79–88.

Lindblom, C. (1965) *The Intelligence of Democracy*, New York: Free Press.

Lindblom, C. (1977) *Politics and Markets*, New York: Basic Books.

Lindblom, C. (1979) 'Still muddling, not yet through', *Public Administration Review* 39: 517–26.

Lindblom, C. (1991) *Inquiry and Change*, New Haven, Conn.: Yale University Press.

Mannheim, K. (1940) *Man and Society in an Age of Reconstruction*, London: Routledge & Kegan Paul.

Overholt, W. (1993) *The Rise of China*, New York: W. W. Norton.

Shonfield, A. (1987) *Modern Capitalism*, Oxford: Oxford University Press.

Simai, M. (ed.) (1995) *Global Employment*, London: Zed Books, vol. 1.

Tucker, R. (ed.) (1975) *The Lenin Anthology*, New York: W. W. Norton.

Wilson, E. (1940) *To The Finland Station*, New York: Doubleday.

3 Pathways to sustainability: issues, policies and theories

Michael Redclift

INTRODUCTION

When the term 'sustainability' is used in relation to human societies it is often taken to imply a paradigm shift, requiring societies to consider everything in relation to nature. This 'transformative' use of sustainability in social and economic terms compares with an emphasis on 'stability', 'balance' and 'conservation' in the natural sciences. The interest in sustainability is beginning to call into question some of the established modes of disciplinary thinking in the social sciences. Concern with the environment, more generally, has highlighted gaps in the existing disciplinary framework of the social sciences. Environmental economics began the assault by rattling the bars of its disciplinary cage, but this exercise is gradually being taken forward in other disciplines.

The need to incorporate a concern with sustainability into real-world decision-making partly accounts for the interest in sustainable development. Stimulated initially by the Brundtland Commission, which reported in 1987, and the Rio Earth Summit five years later, sustainable development began to carry the hopes and aspirations of peoples and governments. It also came to accumulate more conceptual and political baggage than had encumbered 'sustainability'. Political coalitions have grown, in the South as well as the industrialised countries, that cut across class, gender and ethnic differences, to advance the goals of sustainable development. This has become a rallying point for new forms of social and political activity.

LIVING WITHIN ECOLOGICAL LIMITS

One point of departure for considering the relationship between sustainability and planning is the ecological limits within which human societies need to operate. Living within ecological limits means reducing the negative environmental impacts of human activity, and enhancing the resilience of the environment. The key issue is the extent to which the environment can support an increasing through-put of energy and materials. This means establishing thresholds for economic performance (sustainability indicators) and rigorous methods of assessment for land uses, energy and transport, not only locally, but often at several removes, internationally and globally. The key element in this exercise, in conventional economic jargon, is the management of 'externalities'.

SUSTAINABLE INSTITUTIONS AND SOCIAL PRACTICES

Another, quite different, point of departure, which is much closer to planning as conventionally understood, concerns existing social institutions, knowledge and practices. The concept of sustainability can be integrated into existing research and policy agendas. Sustainability planners might look at the effects of seeking to achieve more sustainable economic performance within competitive markets and regulatory frameworks. They might also examine innovation in technology, and its management, from within a sustainability perspective. In the framework of the EU this could mean developing planning interventions which addressed the two principal ways of internalising environmental costs: through technological changes and the management of consumer demand and preferences. On this reading, sustainability planners would also need to examine behavioural aspects of environmental change, and how best to introduce policies which brought short-term benefits, as well as delivering longer-term transformations in society and culture.

Ultimately sustainability planners would need to address the links between the material systems through which goods and services are produced and consumed, and the symbolic systems of representation which underpin these. In practical terms, they also need to specify the political feasibility of environmental goals, within given time frames: in other words, the specific pathways to sustainability. This means charting a different role for the state, which is both the agent to carry out the desired changes and provides the mechanisms through which sustainability planning would be introduced. Since interest in 'sustainability' has grown partly because of the actions of a state committed to economic development, and one often oblivious to environmental objectives, this is unlikely to prove easy. In a world accustomed to regard NGOs as the principal instrument of environmental activity, and in which green NGOs are often pitted against the regulatory science of state institutions, this may prove doubly difficult.

SUSTAINABILITY PLANNING AND POLICY CHOICES

There are three ways of introducing a concern with sustainability into current policy choices in developed, industrialised economies. Each carries different implications for the process of planning, and seeks to change current patterns of production and consumption.

The first strategy is based upon the acceptance of our present 'wants', but seeks to change their delivery. This would mean satisfying current needs with technologies of vastly improved environmental performance (Ekins 1995). The second strategy is to change wants themselves. By altering these it becomes possible to change the overall package of desired goods and services, in ways that are far less environmentally damaging than at present. The third strategy is a conservative variation on the second: to change wants only where environmental damage is conclusive, and where the production and consumption of environmentally damaging goods and services is not readily amenable to environmental improvement.

The first option is reviewed below. It consists of a more or less radical 'technological fix', sometimes expressed in the concept of 'ecological modernisation'. As we shall see later in this chapter, ecological modernisation means that the productive system is transformed, but the human aspirations which drive it are not. Currently there are difficulties in 'internationalising' sustainable technologies, which sometimes represent a barrier to the participation of the poorer countries in world markets and, arguably, a form of protection for the North.

The second strategy – to change wants themselves, and the underlying social commitments (everyday behaviour and practices) which inform them – would require a major shift in lifestyles in areas like the EU. It would require nothing less than a transformation in consumer preferences, a strategy for which there is little demand in the richer countries. To succeed internationally, it would also require a high level of public commitment and international co-operation, combined with a profound commitment to social change. This strategy would also need to maximise very scarce resources such as institutional creativity, as well as political will and stamina. It would probably necessitate not only a better informed civil society, but also a higher calibre of politician to make such a strategy successful!

The third strategy is commonly known as a 'no regrets' option. This implies that governments take action in areas that carry very broad support, and for which there is every likelihood of legislative success. The emphasis would lie in short-term benefits to health and safety, but without the full exercise of the precautionary principle. A government committed to this strategy would not necessarily endorse sustainability as a primary goal, but it would need to examine carefully the links between this policy goal, and others.

Each of these approaches to sustainability planning has strengths and weaknesses, both in what they can deliver and in the priority they attach to sustainability goals. In strictly political terms they can, and arguably should, be combined. In the next section I want to examine three of the issues that lie behind these approaches: levels of consumption and the management of resource systems; environmental valuation; and the role of citizenship in environmental planning. Finally, the chapter explores the different bodies of theory which inform both these issues and the policy choices which stem from them.

ISSUES IN PLANNING FOR SUSTAINABILITY

Levels of consumption and sustainable resource systems

One of the key issues in planning for sustainability is the way that societies match their levels of consumption to resource systems. The connections between consumption and resources, of course, operate on the global, as well as national and local, levels (Redclift 1996). This issue strikes at the balance between the production of goods and services, and the rate at which we consume resources. Is a 'sustainable' resource system compatible with given levels of consumption, and at what level: local, regional, global? The technical discussion involves notions such as critical loads, carrying capacity, ways of assessing biodiversity losses and non-reversible environmental costs. The much less obvious issue, which scarcely plays any part in most of the academic debate, is not about what constitutes 'sustainable levels' but about how they might be achieved. In this area most suggestions point towards global environmental management usually linked to local action ('Agenda 21' arising from the Earth Summit is particularly important here). As we shall see, arriving at 'rational' grounds for environmental action has proved difficult in practice, and involves important policy choices.

Valuing environmental losses and gains

How do societies arrive at ways of valuing environmental losses and gains? Most of the economists who pose this question answer it in a similar way: by establishing how much people would be willing to pay for the environment. The exceptions are interesting because they take issue, to varying degrees, with the assumptions of neo-classical economics (Daly 1977; Ekins 1992; Jacobs 1991; Norgaard 1994). Again, the formal question obscures a much more important primary issue: do valuation criteria reflect real social choices, and according to whose understanding? The ways in which we arrive at environmental valuations can take several forms, including mechanisms to try to achieve social consensus and (more commonly) the conclusions of 'expert' witnesses. It is notable that the green agenda on decision-making has been advanced almost entirely by what Beck calls 'sub-political' groups, outside conventional political parties (Beck 1992). We need to ask how the economic value of resource use/misuse finds *political* expression. This is one important aspect of environmental planning that is increasingly in need of further elaboration.

Citizenship and environmental planning

The third issue that arises from planning for sustainability concerns how societies influence the social and economic behaviour of their citizens towards concern with sustainability. The tendency for questions to be posed in ways which seek to depoliticise the debate are even more evident in this case. Most of societies' institutions, from the most formal (government, law, church) to the least formal (family, work, community) take no conscious account of 'sustainability'. Can we smuggle it into their codes and values, as most commentators hope, or do we have to begin again and re-design these institutions? Do we need to construct a new social and political agenda around sustainability, or can we adapt existing forms of regulation and management?

Clearly we should begin to consider the institutions that we bequeath future generations, as well as the environment we will hand on to them. However, the fact that the question is posed in this way at all, that sustainability is increasingly viewed as an issue alongside governance, is revealing about the shortage of ready-to-wear clothes in the economic policy closet. Unlike the Keynesian 'medicine' of the post-war period, the remedy this time around looks more challenging, and threatens to require some fundamental shifts in 'our lifestyles'. Rather than being asked to spend more, green economics asks us to spend less.

THREE THEORETICAL APPROACHES

Industrial metabolism

Different kinds of theory inform the issues and policy choices discussed above. There is a series of theoretical approaches that might help us to develop new ideas. One of the most important of these concerns the through-put of energy and materials in an economy, and the technological means through which 'external' environmental costs might be internalised in new, cleaner products and services. In most societies there is an ambiguous relationship between the volume of output and the extent of environmental destruction. High output provides resources for environmental protection, but the benefits of conserving resources may be outweighed by the environmental impact of production and consumption. On the other hand, although low output provides fewer resources for environmental protection, it may be grossly inefficient and do little to prevent environmental degradation. In the 1970s the principal fear in environmental policy circles was of the supposed 'limits to growth' (Meadows, Randers and Behvene 1972). In the 1990s 'limits to sink capacities' (or output) poses an equivalent fear, particularly in the context of global problems such as the destruction of the ozone layer and the enhanced greenhouse effect.

The complex interactions between economic activities and the natural environment depend crucially on the way a society organises its relationship to the environment, and the view that different social groups take of this relationship. Many environmental changes are represented as 'demand driven', in the hands of consumers, rather than 'supply driven', in the hands of the formal economic levers dictating production. In fact, it is almost impossible to separate patterns of consumption, and 'lifestyles', from economic instruments and ideologies. Most production in late industrial societies is geared to increasing volumes, rather than the life-cycle effects of goods and services.

Technology and globalisation

The generation of new materials and productive processes has transformed the ways in which environmental costs are transported in space, and frequently in time, usually to poorer developing countries. At the same time, levels of air pollution, for example, in the newly developing countries of East Asia, are rising more rapidly than their increase in GDP. The social processes at work are not simply in the hands of consumers: they are embodied in the global political economy of market capitalism. Some industries in the North, aware of the costs of employing 'dirty' technologies on their doorstep, have sought either to export their pollution and wastes, or to internalise the problems associated with unmanageable levels of waste. They have turned their attention to changing material flows and waste streams as a focus for technological innovation itself.

The concept of eco-efficiency is a response to the crisis of the growing world economy and the pressures this exerts on the global environment (Goodland 1994). Some companies are learning how to maintain or expand output, while at the same time cutting resource-inputs and environmental impacts to a minimum. In a similar fashion, the same principles can be applied to households rather than companies. One might then examine the use that households could make of resources to improve welfare, without increasing aggregate levels of personal consumption to the point at which they are not sustainable. Examples include the diminutions in product size which facilitate reductions in the time taken to transport goods and services, thereby maximising efficiency in the use of space and time. The combination of the quality of output and environmental protection in single low-impact technologies, such as combined heat and power generation for energy utilities, is another example. Similarly, the agriculture and food sectors provide many illustrations of the huge scope for policies which make a realistic assessment of environmental impacts and benefits, replacing the 'value added' which arises from the industrialisation of food (packaging, expensive inputs, and so on) with benefits from local provisioning, reduced packaging and more attention to the nutritional quality of food. Reducing the shelf-life of a food product, and the costs added by advertising and packaging, is unlikely to be possible until these values are affirmed. At the moment the fortunes of the food industry depend upon denying their relevance.

Space/time dimensions

Such changes in the way products and services are valued also generate significant shifts in the use of space and the allocation of time. Planning for such developments requires a radical overhaul not just of consumer attitudes, but, indeed, of the whole infrastructure of modern living. Exploring the dynamics of consumption and production processes takes us well beyond environmental protection. It affords the possibility, in principle, for societies to use the smaller stock of resources available in a more efficient way. At the moment environmental management is principally concerned with modifying existing human behaviour.

Policies are concerned with reducing the full environmental impact of our actions. The underlying behaviour, or social commitments, associated with lifestyles, is currently viewed as non-negotiable.

In a paper written for the World Bank, Robert Goodland has argued that achieving *per capita* income levels in low income countries of $1,500 to $2,000 (rather than OECD's $21,000 average) is quite possible. This would represent a significant advance in welfare for such countries. 'Moreover', he adds, 'that level of income may provide 80 per cent of the basic welfare provided by a $20,000 income, as measured by life expectancy, nutrition, and education' (Goodland 1994). There might also be measurable gains in personal security and reduced social tensions in societies experiencing this type of transition. Goodland then suggests that '[c]olleagues working on Northern overconsumption should address the corollary. Can $21,000 *per capita* countries cut their consumption by a factor of ten and suffer "only" a 20 per cent loss of basic welfare?' (Goodland 1994: 3). His argument illustrates the way in which thinking about sustainability forces us to reconsider the constituents of social welfare and the political conditions under which gains in both sustainability and welfare might be made.

If underlying commitments are non-negotiable, then there is little point in pressing on with this type of analysis. However, the problem of overconsumption might be approached from the other direction. Given that certain resource limits are binding, how can we live within them, producing and consuming goods and services in a way that carries net benefits for society in the future? Arguably, a better understanding of production and consumption flows could help societies make radical choices, at different levels of analysis and different time scales, which transferred welfare benefits between countries, as well as within them, making 'development' a much more reflexive and redistributive process than it is today.

At this stage it is worth pausing to consider some of the difficulties with this argument: first, theories associated with the notion of the industrial metabolism argue that many environmental problems, such as the management of wastes and pollution, arise out of the inherent differences between 'natural' and 'industrial' systems. The laws of thermodynamics have precedence over those of the market. At a philosophical level, this may be true. However, efforts to quantify the life-cycle costs of the production and use of goods and services are difficult to express in alternative economic terms, which returns us to the problem of economic measures of resource use. It is not easy to arrive at the utilisation values which correspond with actual environmental costs and to substitute them for current market values. Without such utilisation values it is impossible to alter the economic behaviour of individuals, still less that of governments.

Second, being able to arrive at sustainable levels of exploitation in environ- mental terms – conserving resources and enhancing sinks – tells us nothing about the social and economic mechanisms that will be required to achieve these objec- tives. Neither does it tell us about the processes through which sustainability assumes legitimacy with the public. These factors – the social mechanisms to achieve greater sustainability, and the legitimacy of sustainability as a social goal – lie outside the provenance of industrial metabolism as understood in the literature. They are linked to wider questions of engagement in the society. As we shall see, we need to turn to other approaches to understand them fully.

Environmental economics and ecological economics

As we have seen, the second issue for sustainable planning – the way that values are attached to the environment – has been considered most by economists. The point of departure for most economists, particularly those who espouse a neo-classical position, is the trade-off between economic growth and environmental protection. Policies to correct environmental problems, it is argued, inevitably carry costs for economic growth, and with it the level of consumption. This concern with the cost of environmental measures serves to disguise the problem that neo-classical economics has in acknowledging that distributional issues – both within and between generations – lie at the heart of valuation. The 'willingness to pay' axiom, with which environmental goods are accorded market values, sets aside the central issues which beset the policy agenda: who should pay, and when?

Two strategies have been proposed. The first, proposed by neo-classical theory, has developed around ways of imputing market values to environmental costs and benefits, through instruments like contingent valuation. The second strategy is to 'internalise' externalities, an approach associated in Germany and the Netherlands with 'ecological modernisation' (Mol 1994). Citing Joseph Huber, one of the principal exponents of ecological modernisation, Mol refers to this process as 'an ecological switch-over of the industrialization process ... all ways *out of* the environmental crisis lead us further *into industrial society*' (Mol 1994: 11).

Both 'solutions' have problems attached to them. The modified neo-classical position, which imputes market values to nature, starts from a number of assumptions which are open to challenge. First, it assumes that individuals act alone to calculate their advantage from making choices under market conditions. The 'individual rational calculator' approach, which lies at the heart of the neo-classical paradigm, results in an approach to decision-making that reduces human agency to price signals. There is no place for society in this view of the economy, as several writers have observed (Jacobs 1991; Benton and Redclift 1994).

Second, this perspective turns on the relationship between prices and values. We are always in danger, as Oscar Wilde put it, of knowing the price of everything and the value of nothing. We know, for example, that the North Sea possesses different value for different groups of people, and for some of these groups it is not adequate to translate these as 'intrinsic values' or 'existence values', for their meaning lies beyond the provenance of the market.

There are similar problems with ecological modernisation. Externalities are not merely environmental costs which can be refashioned into an environment-friendly good or service. They frequently have distributive consequences and causes, which carry political implications for global markets. It is state power, and that of transnational corporations, which frequently lies behind externalities, determining who bears the costs of pollution, toxic wastes or the effects of pesticide use. Indeed, as Murray (1994) has suggested, in a highly original treatise on pesticide use in Latin America, the behaviour of companies which modify agro-chemicals serves to confirm, rather than alter, the essential relationships of power which drive the diffusion of modern, industrialised agribusiness. There are limits in the extent to which 'modernisation' incorporates ecological considerations.

Finally, by way of critique, it can be observed that some goals of neo-liberal economic theory, such as the liberalisation of trade, actually serve to increase externalities. There are basic contradictions between economic growth in the late twentieth century and the protection and conservation of the natural environment. Ecological modernisation does not alter this conflict.

The paradox at the heart of the economic valuation of the environment is that of distribution. The environment can only be properly 'valued' by successive generations of people, for whom any one generation acts as stewards. Inter-generational equity, moreover, assumes more importance as problems assume 'global' importance, and are increasingly governed by uncertainty. Issues like global warming, the destruction of the ozone layer and the loss of biodiversity make little sense within the neo-classical model. Since unborn generations have no 'rights' it is difficult to rely on efficiency in allocating resources between future and present generations.

The problem of inter-generational equity is matched by that of intra-generational equity. Does every member of the human race count equally in their responsibility for carbon emissions? Do emissions of methane from paddy fields or livestock in poor, rural societies count equally with carbon emissions from vehicles being driven between home and shopping mall in California? The most revealing aspects of carbon budgets for nations is that they display such vast inequalities in consumption, and such different trajectories for future development, that only a complete overhaul of the global economic order would enable any meaningful and lasting international agreements to be made. Intra-generational inequities are such that we might as well abandon any pretence that development can be sustainable.

The basic problem with the neo-classical valuation of the environment is that it relies upon questionable assumptions about human behaviour. As a consequence it emphasises 'efficiency gains' for which the confidence limits are low, over vitally important distributional consequences, for which the confidence limits are high. It succeeds in turning the world on its head. Environmental economics, at least in its mainstream neo-classical version, requires that we ignore the institutional context for decision-making, which itself determines whether economic models are used at all.

Social behaviour and sustainability

To meet even modest environmental goals requires significant changes in human behaviour. But how would such changes in behaviour be brought about? If differences in behaviour are based on different perceptions of risk or uncertainty, then it is necessary to begin by explaining the gap between perceptions and behaviour. We all possess enough anecdotal evidence that perceptions influence behaviour in ways that are frequently perverse. The British Meteorological Office has established, for example, that people turn on their central heating in response to cloudy, rather than cold, weather. Can people be relied upon to behave as 'rational' actors, to avert environmental disasters?

This depends on what is meant by 'rational' action, the question at the heart of the debate about so-called risk society and modernity (Beck 1992). According to Beck, late industrial societies have removed technology from the political arena. In the process such societies make it more difficult for individuals to deal with risk in everyday life. In Beck's view social problems tend to be viewed, in late industrial societies, as problems of *individual failure*, rather than social competence. When people challenge their society's competence, in particular that of its 'experts' and political leaders, it becomes a challenge to public science. Human agency becomes embroiled in challenges to the authority of science. The contrast between this approach and mainstream neo-classical economics could not be greater. While economics has been pushing environmental assessment *towards* market-based, individualised models of human behaviour, sociological theory has been emphasising that environmental risks increasingly reflect *socially constructed differences*. Economics has sought to bring the environment into the ambit of human decision-making by allocating environmental values like any other market value. Sociology is arguing that environmental decision-making actually reflects social concerns and commitments, that the environment is nothing more or less than the battleground on which political interests are contested. Social theory is increasingly concerned with the problems that the environment poses for individuals, rather than by them. The differences do not end there. While economists have difficulties, as we have seen, in incorporating distributional issues (time, space and class) into their methodological canon, sociologists experience difficulties in distinguishing between 'what is happening in actually-existing societies' (realist concerns) and the part played by human societies and consciousness in *interpreting* what is happening (constructivism). Some sociological writing gives the impression that ecological issues can be confined to the margins of society, separated from the social institutions of modern life (the family, work, religion and politics). It is as if our 'getting' and 'spending' were somehow divorced from its social consequences. It also evades a central responsibility that might guide our conduct: what are the material consequences of the way in which we socially construct the environment?

The problem with Beck's analysis is that his society of 'incomplete rationality' invokes an active citizenry committed to the goals of liberation from technological tyranny. Do we possess such a citizenry, or are the ecological politics of the risk society still those of a small, self-conscious minority? There is a wider political issue here as well. Ironically, the social commitments that underlie our everyday consumption habits are generally more powerful than the democratic ideals which lead us to question the social authority of science, or the necessity of being yoked to a technological treadmill. Pervasive underlying social commitments, such as our everyday consumption practices, may be the other side of the same coin: facets of the emergence of uncertainty and risk as social phenomena. If they are, then they explain the ambivalence towards late industrial society, rather than wholehearted rejection of it, which characterises the first 'post-modern' generation.

THE PROBLEM OF SUSTAINABILITY AND HUMAN AGENCY

There is an urgent need to incorporate alternative visions of a more sustainable society into practical political discussion and action. Major shifts in the basis of taxation, for example, which would transfer the burden of fiscal responsibility from labour and capital to pollution and waste, are no longer the monopoly of radical green opinion (Weale 1992; von Weizäcker 1994). Environmental standards assume increasing commercial importance, as constraints on 'free trade', under trade relations which, according to the neo-liberal orthodoxy, are meant to be increasingly free and unencumbered. The meeting of the Conference of the Parties to the Framework Climate Convention, held in Berlin early in 1995, revealed once again a major chasm between environmentalists (and many scientists) and governments about the limits within which the world can continue to consume.

Superficially, the different bodies of theory on which I have drawn refer to different social and economic domains: production processes, market values and human agency. A politics of sustainability which reflected all of them would be heterogeneous and incoherent. But these different theoretical approaches share a common problematic: they require the state to act decisively, on behalf of its citizens. They require priorities to be established, including the priority given to sustainability goals, over materials, energy and environmental values. Finally, they require human agency to be integrated into sustainability planning, so that future environments are not guided primarily by the consequences of our preoccupation with consumption. The idea that we might develop an approach to sustainability that transformed both the way we value resources and the processes through which we realise them is not entirely a novel one. It is one of the principles underlying planning that we are able to determine the direction of social advance, and this is a goal not only of those who advocate planning for sustainability, but also of those early followers of Karl Marx, rather more than a century ago.

References

Beck, U. (1992) *Risk Society: Towards a New Modernity*, London: Sage.
Benton, T. and Redclift, M. (1994) *Social Theory and the Global Environment*, London: Routledge.
Daly, H. (1977) *Steady-State Economics: The Economics of Biophysical Equilibrium and Moral Growth*, London: Earthscan.
Ekins, P. (1992) *Wealth beyond Measure: An Atlas of New Economics*, London: Gaia.

Ekins, P. (1995) *Harnessing Trade to Sustainable Development*, Oxford: Green College Centre for Environmental Policy and Understanding.

Goodland, R. (1994) 'Environmental Sustainability', working paper, Washington, DC: World Bank.

Jacobs, M. (1991) *The Green Economy*, London: Pluto.

Meadows, D., Randers, J. and Behvene, W. (1972) *The Limits to Growth*, London: Pan.

Mol, A. (1994) 'Ecological modernisation and institutional reflexivity', paper presented at the International Studies Association Thirteenth Annual Conference, Bielefeld, Germany.

Murray, D. (1994) *Cultivating Crisis: The Human Costs of Pesticide Use in Latin America*, University of Austin, TX: University of Texas.

Norgaard, R. (1994) *Development Betrayed: The End of Progress and a Coevolutionary Envisioning of the Future*, London: Routledge.

Redclift, M. (1996) *Wasted: Counting the Costs of Global Consumption*, London: Earthscan.

Weale, A. (1992) *The New Politics of Pollution*, Manchester: Manchester University Press.

Weizäcker, E. von (1994) *Earth Politics*, London: Zed Press.

4   Sustainability and markets: on the neo-classical model of environmental economics

Michael Jacobs

This chapter will discuss the role of markets in the concept and practical achievement of environmental sustainability. As in other spheres of political and economic life, markets have become a central organising principle of environmental policy, at least in theory and conceptual framework. The vehicle for this has been the development of neo-classical environmental economics, which has gradually assumed a significant influence on the way environmental policy is perceived. Here I shall argue that the prominent role given to the market in environmental-economic policy debates is misplaced. The neglected issue in environmental policy is the nature of the state: how (and how far) states can influence market behaviour towards environmental ends in a global capitalist economy.

The argument falls into two halves. In the first half three crucial features of sustainability as an environmental-economic objective are set out: its biophysical basis, its collective character, and the scale of the socio-economic changes it requires. The approach to environmental policy taken by neo-classical environmental economics is then explained, including the central role given in this to markets. In the second half I attempt to show how these features of the sustainability objective make the neo-classical 'market model' inadequate. The model cannot describe the concept of sustainability; it fails to illuminate its structural character; and its discussion of different policy instruments is too limited. A brief concluding section suggests some key features required by any coherent theory of the 'sustainability state'.

SUSTAINABILITY AS A BIOPHYSICAL LIMIT

For the purposes of this argument I define environmental sustainability as a path of economic and social development whose impacts on the natural environment are constrained within ecological limits. These limits are defined, in general terms, as those which maintain over time the health or integrity of ecosystems and the capacity of the biosphere to provide essential 'environmental services', such as clean air and water, climate regulation, the maintenance of genetic diversity, nutrient recycling and so on.[1]

This concept of sustainability, now widely accepted within the environmental policy and academic communities, is founded on the notion of biophysical limits to economic activity: that is, it starts from the premise that certain conditions of the natural environment which may be caused by human activity would be intolerable, either because they would involve major ecological disruption or degradation or because of their effects on human health and quality of life. The idea of 'intolerability' makes sustainability a fundamentally social notion: human societies must choose what they regard as (in)tolerable. But sustainability is not *simply* social: it does not permit societies to choose just any condition of the environment and describe that as 'sustainable'. For the term to be meaningful, the argument over what is tolerable must be couched in terms of environmental health and integrity and the capacity of the biosphere to maintain the provision of environmental services over time. There will always be room for argument as to what precisely constitutes these concepts; but they cannot simply be ignored if the term 'sustainability' is to be used.

In this sense sustainability is inescapably biophysical in origin. It is the condition of the natural environment, ultimately, which determines whether or not a society can be described as sustainable; and it is to this that the social argument must refer. It is important to note exactly what this biophysical emphasis does and does not imply, since the notion of 'environmental limits' has been the subject of much misunderstanding. It *does* imply that there are limits to particular uses of environmental stocks and flows of material and energy through the economy. But there is almost no-one who disagrees with this, who thinks (for example) that we can go on adding mercury to rivers or lead to air forever, or that we can concrete over the entire world's agricultural land. These flows and stocks, like others, are subject to the limits of tolerability. But this does *not* imply that therefore there are (imminent) limits to *all* material and energy throughputs: one material can substitute for another, and some new materials (and some sources of energy) might become available in such huge supply, with minimal waste disposal effects, that their physical limits were not relevant. These are ultimately empirical-cum-speculative questions (on which there is much dispute).[2] Certainly sustainability as a concept does not imply that *economic growth* must be subject to limits: this depends on whether the efficiency of resource use can be raised sufficiently (and sufficiently cheaply), which is also an empirical question (Ekins and Jacobs 1995).

Only the first limit, to particular material and energy flows and stocks, is definitely implied by the concept of sustainability. But this is enough, for the scientific evidence appears to show that many of these limits are being, or have already been, reached. Of course, this is where the social construction of sustainability becomes crucial, for (as well as scientific uncertainty) there is by no means universal agreement on where many of the most important limits lie. Disputes arise about the possibility of substitutions and efficiency improvements in relation to future scarcities (Beckerman 1994; Daly 1995), about the nature of ecosystem health and human quality of life (Jacobs 1991; Costanza *et al.* 1992), and about the intrinsic value of the natural world (Sagoff 1995). But so long as these arguments are conducted in terms of the health and integrity of ecosystems and the capacity of the biosphere to provide environmental services, they are about sustainability, not a denial of it.

SUSTAINABILITY AND COLLECTIVITY

The second feature of sustainability which bears on the arguments of this chapter is its inescapably collective character. Nearly all environmental goods are public goods. That is, they are in general 'indivisible' between individuals benefiting from them (the air you breathe is the same air I breathe) and it is difficult to restrict access only to people willing to pay. The 'public good' character of most environmental goods means that they must be collectively provided (individual purchase is always liable to free riding), generally by regulation or taxation. In turn this means that decisions about how much of the environment should be protected, or to what level, must be made collectively and politically, by the community or society as a whole; in practice, by the state.[3]

This much is commonplace. But there is a stronger sense in which sustainability is collective in character. Some environmental goods, such as clean air or beautiful landscapes, can plausibly be represented as contributing to individual welfare or well being, and therefore as objects of individual 'consumption'. Although they must generally be collectively provided, their benefits can meaningfully be described as accruing to individuals. But this cannot be said of many of the goods (and bads) with which sustainability is concerned. Some, perhaps, fall in an inter-mediate category of 'social risks'. Toxic waste, for example, is clearly a contributor to individual 'diswelfare' when and if it causes health problems to people living near disposal sites. But it is not clear that it is an individual or private concern for people not living in these areas. Such people do generally have concerns about such waste (as opinion surveys show), but the problem is surely better described as belonging to the society in which individuals live than directly to the individuals themselves. It is at best an indirect risk.

For most of the major issues with which sustainability is concerned, even a limited ascription of private benefit or disadvantage to individuals appears inappropriate. It makes little sense to speak of an individual 'consuming' the control of climate change, the prevention of desertification or the maintenance of species; to see these goods as making an identifiable contribution to *individual* well being. Rather, they seem to provide the essential life-support framework *within which* individuals can achieve well being. It is of course possible to trace the effects of impairment of such 'environmental services' to the lives of individuals, though probably to my descendants rather than to me. But there is something odd about individualising these issues in this way: quintessentially, if climate change or spe-cies loss occurs, it occurs to society as a whole. This is not to downgrade the importance of differential distributions of environmental goods and bads: some groups of people will suffer much worse effects than others. But it is to assert the inescapably *collective* nature of global environmental problems. The language of the popular sustainability discourse gives a clue to this: overwhelmingly couched in terms of the problems faced by 'the world' and 'our children', caused by 'society', it urges actions which 'we' must take in response (Macnaghten *et al.* 1995). Or to put it another way: individuals cannot be 'sustainable'. Sustainability is either something which the whole of a society achieves, or it does not happen at all.

The scale of the sustainability objective

The third important feature of sustainability is the scale of the changes required to achieve it. Acknowledgement of this is often lacking in discussion of environmental policy. This is unsurprising, since (notwithstanding the rhetoric) most current environmental policy is not designed to reduce environmental degradation to levels which could be described as sustainable. Moreover, individual aspects of environmental policy are generally considered (again, despite the rhetoric of 'policy integration') in isolation from one another. Reducing all the different types of environmental impact simultaneously (energy use, different kinds of materials use, different kinds of polluting emissions, solid waste, land use, and so on) involves change on a much larger scale than does a reduction in just one impact on its own.

What scale of reductions in impact is required for sustainability, and in which aspects of the environment? Given the remarks about definition given above, some broad answers can be suggested.

A recent study by the Wuppertal Institute for Friends of the Earth Europe attempts to calculate sustainable rates of European 'environmental consumption' on the basis of the concept of 'environmental space' (Friends of the Earth Europe 1995). Estimates are made, from scientific evidence and judgement, of total global environmental capacities: that is, those levels of air and water quality, land use, materials consumption, energy consumption and so on which can sustain the ecosystem and human health over time. These global totals are then divided by the figure for current global population to produce global per capita 'allowances' on the equality principle. The allowances represent the amount of 'environmental space' to which each human being would be entitled if the space were shared out equally. These allowances are then compared with current per capita rates of European consumption. The difference – the 'sustainability gap' – represents the extent to which current European consumption is unsustainable. On the basis of these figures the study then calculates the reductions in consumption required to achieve the sustainable *per capita* allowances. Given that these reductions cannot be achieved overnight (2050 is the general target date), the study sets intermediate targets for progress towards sustainability by the year 2010.

The main results are given in Table 4.1. They show that sustainability on the equality principle requires reductions in current European carbon dioxide emissions of 77 per cent, which translates into a halving of fossil fuel use. Key raw materials such as cement, pig iron, aluminium, copper and lead, along with nitrogen, phosphorous and potassium fertilisers, need to be reduced by 85–90 per cent, with chlorine use being stopped altogether. To conserve biodiversity the area of protected land needs to be increased more than ten-fold, with arable and pasture lands cut by around half.

Table 4.1 Requirements and targets for a 'sustainable Europe'

Resource	Present use per capita	Environmental space (per capita)	Change needed (%)	Target 2010	Target 2010 (%)
CO_2 emissions	7.3 t/a	1.7t/a	−77	5.4 t/a	−26
Primary energy use	123 GJ/a	60 GJ/a	−50	56.1 GJ/a	−21
Fossil fuels	100 GJ/a	25 GJ/a	−75	45.0 GJ/a	−55
Nuclear	16 GJ/a	0 GJ/a	−100	0 GJ/a	−100
Renewables	7 GJ/a	35 GJ/a	+400	11.5 GJ/a	+74
Non-renewable raw materials					
Cement	536 kg	80 kg	−85	423 kg	−21
Pig iron	273 kg	36 kg	−87	213 kg	−22
Aluminium	12 kg	1.2 kg	−90	9.2 kg	−23
Chlorine	23 kg	0 kg	−100	17.2 kg	−25
Land use	0.726 ha	—	—	0.64 ha/cap.	−12
Built-up area	0.053 ha	0.0513 ha	−3.2	0.0513 ha/cap.	−3.2
Inland waters	0.009 ha	—	—	0.009 ha/cap.	0
Protected areas	0.003 ha	0.061 ha	+1933	0.064 ha/cap.	+2000
Unprotected wooded area	0.164 ha	0.138 ha	−16	0.138 ha/cap.	−16
Arable area	0.237 ha	0.10 ha	−58	0.15 ha/cap.	−37
Pasture land	0.167 ha	0.09 ha	−47	0.113 ha/cap.	−32
Wood	0.66 m^3	0.56 m^3	−15	0.56 m^3	−15

Notes
t/a   = tonnes per annum
G/J   = Gigajoules per annum
ha   = hectares
ha/cap = hectares per capita

Estimates made by the Wupperthal Institute and published in Friends of the Earth Europe, *Towards Sustainable Europe* (1995)

The basis of these calculations – particularly the original estimations of total available capacity – are obviously open to argument, and the final figures should be regarded as illustrative only. But they suggest the sort of scale of the changes in current patterns of environmental consumption required by the sustainability objective. Other studies suggest similar figures. The Dutch National Environmental Policy Plan, for example, calls for 75–90 per cent reductions in discharges of major pollutants (including organic wastes, heavy metals, certain hydrocarbons and some pesticides) and in the volume of solid waste. Although (in common with other EU countries) the Dutch Government has only made an actual commitment to stabilising carbon dioxide emissions at 1990 levels by 2000, it has accepted a long-term sustainability target of reducing emissions by around 90 per cent (Ministry of Housing, Physical Planning and Environment 1988). Estimates given by the Worldwatch Institute for a range of environmental indicators are of the same order of magnitude (Brown, Falvin and Postel 1992).

All these figures are reductions from current rates of resource use and environmental consumption. If no action is taken, economic growth will in nearly all cases increase current consumption. The required reductions will then become larger.

Economic growth has a second important effect. With respect to raw materials and waste discharges, environmental policy is generally able only to address the rate of environmental consumption *per unit of output*: for example, a new technology can be prescribed which cuts polluting emissions from a manufacturing process by half, but the half relates only to emissions from a constant volume of output. If output doubles, the actual (absolute) emissions remain constant. We have so far expressed sustainability targets in absolute terms. But for the purposes of policy it will often be necessary to express them as improvements to the 'environmental efficiency of production': that is, to the rate of resource use and waste production per unit of output. Do emissions from this industrial technology need to be cut by 20 per cent or 50 per cent? How much more fuel-efficient do cars need to be? But if we do this, we must beware the undermining effect of economic growth. So long as there is growth, reductions in absolute environmental consumption can only be achieved if efficiency improvements are continuous and exponential.

To illustrate this, we can use the simple 'sustainability equation' originally suggested by Commoner (1972) and publicised by Ehrlich (1977):

$$I = PCT$$

where I = environmental impact
      P = population
      C = consumption per capita
      T = environmental impact per unit of consumption (= 1/efficiency).

Given a moderate rate of world economic growth of 2–3 per cent, output will quadruple over the next fifty years. Population is expected to double. Let us say, conservatively, that current environmental impacts must be reduced by 50 per cent in that period. Then T in the year 2045 must be one-sixteenth of its current level; or, put another way, the environmental efficiency of production must improve by 91 per cent. And of course, so long as growth continues, it must carry on improving after 2045 too (Ekins and Jacobs 1995).

What would reductions in environmental impact on this scale mean for production and consumption patterns in an industrial country such as Britain? The Worldwatch Institute and the Friends of the Earth Europe reports, along with many other studies, have provided some pointers. To reduce carbon emissions the efficiency of energy generation and use would have to increase dramatically, entailing an expansion of combined heat and power plants, much higher insulation standards and major improvements in the efficiency of lighting, appliances and industrial machinery. Use of fossil fuels for electricity generation would need to be reduced, and renewables substantially increased. Wind power, photovoltaics and biomass are the most likely sources of renewable energy. Cars and buses will almost certainly have to become electric or alcohol/hydrogen driven, with high fuel efficiencies. The majority of regular urban journeys (such as to work) will need to be made by public transport, bicycle or walking, with changed land-use patterns making this possible. Various social innovations may be predicted: neighbourhood car sharing, home deliveries by supermarkets, and so on. Most long-distance journeys will have to be made by train or coach, with freight using rail and water where possible, transferring to motor vehicles for final delivery (Brown *et al.* 1992).

Solid waste will have to be reduced at source, by changes in production methods, an increase in the durability of products and a reduction in disposable packaging. The re-use, and to a lesser extent the recycling, of materials will need to become standard practice. Consumer durables such as cars and washing machines will probably be leased, with manufacturers responsible for disposal and re-use of materials. Industrial processes will need to change radically, with energy- and water-efficient and 'clean' (low and no-pollution) technologies and production systems introduced. Imports of tropical timber and certain other materials from the South would have to be much reduced. In general, the need to reduce global transport is likely to reduce the growth of international trade and increase local sourcing. Agricultural practices will need to become much less chemical-intensive, with organic and near-organic agriculture the norm and a much greater proportion of land managed specifically for biodiversity conservation (Brown *et al.* 1992; Jackson 1993; Pretty 1995).

None of these possible elements of sustainable production and consumption patterns can be projected with certainty. In particular, whether or not sustainability is compatible with continued economic growth, and/or whether overall consumption or 'standard of living' will have to decline in value terms remains open. It will depend partly on the extent of efficiency improvements and material substitutions in the provision of existing goods and services, and partly on the extent to which new, less-material goods and services (such as education and health care) arise in response to higher material prices. I shall discuss this further below.

What can be stated with reasonable certainty, given the scale of the reductions in material throughput required, is that sustainability is a very tough objective for industrial societies to meet. The changes required will be large.

NEO-CLASSICAL ENVIRONMENTAL ECONOMICS

Over the last few years, at the same time as the concept of sustainability has become more prominent in environmental policy debate, the discourse of neo-classical environmental economics has also come to play an increasingly dominant role. Broadly speaking, the neo-classical approach can be characterised as an attempt to render environmental issues amenable to conventional micro-economic analysis, by turning discrete environmental goods (clean air, species preservation, acceptable climate change, and so on) into priced commodities. This takes place through two 'stages' of policy-making.

The first stage specifies the *objective* of policy, answering the question 'How much environment should be protected?' Drawing on its marginalist traditions, the neo-classical answer to this question is that the environment should be protected up to the point at which the costs of protecting it outweigh the benefits from so doing. This involves a cost-benefit calculus, in which the 'benefits of the environment' must be calculated in monetary terms and then compared over time with the monetary costs of protection. The second stage is then concerned with the *instruments* of policy, answering the question 'How can the objectives best be achieved?' The neo-classical answer focuses in general on the criterion of efficiency: the 'best' achievement of the objective is the one which incurs the least total cost to society. Efficiency is secured, it is generally argued, through the use of 'market-based instruments' such as taxes, charges and tradable pollution permits, which give producers and consumers financial incentives to reduce environmentally damaging behaviour.

At the heart of the neo-classical approach is a model of the market. Environmental problems are seen as examples of 'market failure': cases where markets fail to achieve their otherwise socially optimal result. This failure arises because environmental goods are (in general) not priced.[4] This results in 'external' or 'social' costs (environmental damage) being imposed on third parties. The first stage of policy-making seeks to discover the magnitude of these costs. It does this by discovering the 'market value' or 'shadow price' of different kinds of environmental costs and benefits. The market value is defined as consumers' average willingness to pay for benefits or to avoid costs. This can be discovered either by examining market values for goods associated with the environment (such as travel to the countryside, or houses with pleasant views) or by asking the public their willingness to pay directly in 'contingent valuation' surveys. In either case, the value of the environment is given by consumer behaviour in markets rather than being imposed by government bureaucracies.[5]

Once the values of the external costs have been discovered, the aim of the second stage is then to 'internalise' them: that is, to bring them back within the market by raising the prices of damaging activities via taxes, charges, tradable permits, and so on. This forces those responsible for causing the costs to face them directly. Having to pay higher prices or taxes will change their market behaviour: they will reduce the environmental damage they cause. If the costs have been calculated correctly, and the taxes or other market instruments are effective, the total amount of environmental damage will be reduced to just that point at which its marginal costs equal its marginal benefits. Moreover this will have been achieved at the lowest possible cost to society: in contrast to the use of 'non-market', regulatory ('command and control') instruments, whose inflexibility makes for much higher costs. The market failure will have been eliminated: the market will once again generate the socially optimal result (Pearce and Turner 1990).

This 'market model' of environmental damage and policy response has been intellectually very influential. Even though, for a number of reasons, it has proved difficult to implement precisely in practice, the conceptual framework it provides increasingly underpins official environmental policy thinking in the UK, the USA and other industrialised countries. This is quite explicit: for example, in the UK government's 1990 Environment White Paper, *This Common Inheritance*, in subsequent environmental policy documents and in the 1995 Environmental Act, which requires the new Environment Agency explicitly to balance the costs and benefits of environmental policy. The same approach is being used by the Intergovernmental Panel on Climate Change in relation to global warming policy (Bruce, Lee and Haites 1996).

Indeed, it is arguably *because* of this emphasis on the market that the neo-classical discourse has become so dominant. This emphasis appears to make orthodox environmental economics concordant both with mainstream economic rationality and with neo-liberal ideology. It therefore appeals to those with commitments to these two streams of thought. Neo-classical economics appears to offer a 'market-based' alternative to the traditional approach to environmental policy, which is perceived as dealing with environmental problems through government planning and regulation. Indeed, the approach it recommends is often described as enabling policy to 'use market forces' to achieve environmental objectives.

MARKETS AND THE CONCEPT OF SUSTAINABILITY

The neo-classical model is a powerful intellectual tool which has contributed a great deal to the economic analysis of environmental problems. Because it has risen to prominence at the same time as the concept of sustainability it is not unnaturally assumed (and by the advocates of the neo-classical school, commonly asserted) that the two are connected: that neo-classical economics can contribute to the understanding and achievement of sustainability. But it is this claim that I wish to deny. I want to show that the central role given to markets in the neo-classical model is deeply unhelpful in understanding either the concept of sustainability itself or its policy implementation. This unhelpfulness arises from the three characteristics of sustainability we have discussed: its biophysical basis, its collective nature and the scale of the changes it requires.

The biophysical basis of sustainability represents a fundamental difference between it and the market model of environmental economics. The latter is essentially a branch of welfare economics, concerned with maximising well being in society. The innovation it introduces is the inclusion of unpriced environmental benefits within the measurement of well being; but its goal – the socially optimal result of equilibrating markets in which all external costs have been internalised – is explicitly concerned with the satisfaction of human preferences (Pearce 1993). Sustainability, by contrast, is ultimately concerned with the maintenance over time of biophysical stocks and flows and their environmental effects. There is no necessary connection between these and human preferences. Sustainability may or may not maximise the satisfaction of human preferences, now or in the future: this is not how it is defined.

The neo-classical answer, of course, is that even on a biophysical definition sustainability must involve human judgement of 'tolerability', and this is where the market model enters. It is in the hypothetical markets of the first stage of neo-classical policy-making that such judgements are made. In markets for environmental goods people express their views on what is tolerable.

However, this approach cannot bridge the gap. In markets, people do not 'express their views'; they express their private willingness to pay for environmental benefits. There is no *necessary* reason to suppose that the social optimum in environmental markets (where marginal aggregate willingness to pay just equals the marginal cost of environmental protection) will fall within the biophysical limits of ecosystem health and maintenance of environmental capacities. It may do; it may not – particularly where incomes are low and the (opportunity) cost of environmental protection is high. If it does not, the neo-classical model cannot redefine sustainability out of its biophysical basis, saying that whatever the market chooses just *is* 'sustainable'. Of course, it may be argued that if markets generate this result this is the path society should choose: satisfying market preferences is a more important goal than sustainability. This is perfectly coherent. But it does not mean that the concept of sustainability can be defined or understood through the operation of markets. The biophysical basis of sustainability marks its logical separation from the neo-classical model.

In fact this argument can go further. In proposing that markets are an appropriate institution through which society can make judgements about the tolerability of environmental change, the neo-classical school misunderstands the nature of such judgements. Here it is the collective character of sustainability which raises the problem. We saw above that most of the environmental problems with which sustainability is concerned are not experienced individually and do not directly contribute to individual well being. They provide, rather, the general conditions of life-support and social stability within which individual well being is meaningful. But then the use of markets to decide their fate – leaving it to the private willingness to pay of individuals – seems inappropriate. We might (perhaps) expect people to pay individually for clean air or a beautiful landscape, since these goods provide individual benefit. But there is something profoundly odd about the idea of privately 'purchasing' the control of climate change, prevention of desertification or maintenance of species (or even the elimination of toxic waste). These are quintessentially collective decisions, affecting everyone.

This oddness is less an empirical question – though in fact contingent valuation exercises show that people find great difficulty in 'valuing' primary, collective goods in this way, and even object to being asked to do so (Vadnjal and O'Connor 1994; Clark and Burgess 1997) – than a philosophical one. If sustainability is a collective outcome, affecting society as a whole, decisions about it should be made socially or collectively. Markets, including hypothetical markets, are essentially individualistic institutions, in which individuals make private choices in relation to their own self-interest, and these are aggregated to generate a social preference. But social choices, of which sustainability is one, must be public in character, involving debate and argument about the common good of society as a whole rather than simply the good of individuals. They require the deliberative institution of the 'forum' rather than the aggregative institution of the market (Elster 1986; O'Neill 1994; Jacobs 1997).

There is a specific dimension to this which is of particular importance. Sustainability is a distributive aim. The goal of maintaining environmental capacities over time is often represented and justified as a fair distribution of resources between generations. As we have seen, it must also involve some principle of equity between different countries and regions within the present generation. But fair distribution can only be a political choice, not a market one.

In the first place, the market model is concerned with the allocation of resources, not their distribution. As standard welfare economics acknowledges, the socially optimal result (even adjusted for external costs) is efficient; it need not be equitable. The neo-classical school gets round this difficulty by introducing equity into the model as a consumer preference: people normally value their children's well being, and if they are altruistic they may value other people's too (Pearce 1993). But this move simply fails to understand what equity or fairness is. It does not rely on private concern for other people's welfare, let alone willingness to pay for it. It is a moral outcome in its own right: it stands logically separate from any actual procedures generating particular outcomes. As such it must be the subject of moral and political deliberation about social choices; it cannot simply flow from the aggregation of private preferences. In markets, not only is there no such deliberation, but the aggregated preferences are almost guaranteed not to achieve equity, since any individual's concern for the well being of future and distant people will almost certainly be 'discounted' or undervalued in comparison with such people's concern for themselves.

The inability of the market model to articulate the concept of environmental sustainability is in fact revealed in the rather different notion of sustainability which has been developed within the neo-classical tradition. This is what has become known as 'weak' sustainability: it is defined as the maintenance of capital (including both human-made and 'natural' capital) over time (Pearce and Atkinson 1992). But this is not an environmental objective at all: although it acknowledges that natural capital is part of overall capital, it allows for continuing environmental degradation if human-made capital is rising faster. In fact weak sustainability is now frequently defined as the maintenance of *welfare* over time: definitionally, its environmental component has completely disappeared (Pezzy 1992). The gap between this notion of sustainability and the definition used in this chapter (which is the dominant interpretation used in the wider environmental policy community) arose explicitly because neo-classical economics could not make sense of a biophysically constrained and politically chosen (that is, non-market) conception. The latter, defined in terms of the maintenance of physical stocks of natural capital, was originally identified in the neo-classical literature under the label of 'strong sustainability' (Pearce, Markandya and Barbier 1989). But it has now been dropped.

MARKETS AND STRUCTURAL CHANGE

There is a deeper, if more subtle, way in which the market model fails to illuminate the concept of sustainability. The concept of the market equilibrium depends upon the assumption that demands and preferences (tastes) at given prices do not change. This assumption makes it possible to compare two alternative policy options – for example, one with environmental protection measures, one without – and judge which one is preferable. Only if tastes do not change will the idea of something being 'preferable' have the same meaning in both options. This assumption is at work, notably, in cost-benefit analysis, which the neo-classical school uses to evaluate the effects of policy proposals. It enables economists to say, for example, whether society would be better off (or not) if public funds were to be spent on public transport in order to reduce air pollution; or whether global warming is worth it, given the costs of its prevention.

However, this is not as straightforward as it seems at first sight, or as it is taken to be in the neo-classical model, for the assumption of constant preferences only works in relation to small changes in market conditions over relatively short time scales. Small changes are required because such changes can safely be assumed not to alter the prices of other goods and services in society. If other prices do change, then so will demands and preferences, since these are governed not just by the objective character of different products but by their prices *relative* to one another. If many of these prices are altered, because the policy option involves major changes in market conditions, the assumption fails. Whether or not this happens, the assumption becomes increasingly unstable the longer the time scale over which change is measured. It is hardly realistic to expect demands for goods and services to remain constant over a period of, say, thirty years.

The problem here, it should be clear, is the scale of the changes required by sustainability. It will be recalled that, on plausible calculations of environmental effects and economic growth, these changes are likely to be very large. New industrial technologies and processes will have to be developed, new products will need to be introduced, new kinds of infrastructure put in place. Some important aspects of lifestyles, such as transport demands, are almost certainly going to have to change. These shifts will need to be promoted through regulatory, tax and other measures which will affect the prices of goods and services in the market. For example, energy-intensive products will become more expensive, in order to reduce their use and stimulate efficiency in their production; so will transport; labour-intensive products will probably become cheaper.[6] Certain chemical-based and non-reusable products will become more expensive, organic and recyclable ones cheaper (and so on).

Sustainability will therefore involve major adjustments in relative prices. These adjustments will mean that demands and preferences themselves change. But in turn this will mean that the changes cannot simply be judged from the perspective of the present, when current demands and preferences apply. To put it another way: if sustainability is 'achieved' in, say, thirty years, the people living then will not judge their well being in the same way as people do now. The very fact that substantial changes will have occurred will mean they have different tastes.

There are thus two perspectives from which sustainability can be judged. There is the *ex ante* one, in which demands and preferences are assumed unchanged; and there is the *ex post* one, in which demands and preferences have changed, in ways we cannot predict.[7] The market model of cost-benefit analysis in relation to sustainability therefore does not tell the full story.[8] By concentrating exclusively on the *ex ante* analysis, it fails to capture the sense in which the choice of sustainability is a choice to live in a different kind of society, one in which we (or our descendants) will have different kinds of demands and preferences: perhaps in which we will be different kinds of people altogether.

The inadequacy of the market model here runs very deep. Sustainability, it is clear, requires long-term *structural change* in economy and society: changes not just in the demands for a wide variety of goods and services, but in technologies, infrastructures, lifestyles. But it is precisely these kinds of shift on which the model throws almost no light. It is well suited to understanding small, incremental changes in particular markets, where all else can be assumed constant: prices, tastes, and basic technologies. But these conditions are precisely those which do not hold for the kind of shifts required by sustainability. Here we wish to know how to change these things, or what happens when they change. Our analysis must focus on the dynamic process by which one type or structure of market changes into another, not (or only secondarily) on what happens inside a particular market. The crucial missing element in the market model is *time*. The idea of the equilibrating market is essentially static, when what is needed is an understanding of the dynamics of the economy: of its historical, non-reversible adjustment and development.

Understanding sustainability, therefore, almost certainly requires the use of evolutionary and institutional approaches to economics (Rutherford 1994; Hodgson 1993; Dosi *et al.* 1988). These approaches offer at least four important insights unavailable from the neo-classical market model. First, evolutionary theory offers a conceptual framework for understanding how market systems change over time. Though some economists have used an evolutionary approach to explain how imperfect markets generate optimal equilibria ('natural selection' rewards profit-maximising behaviour: Alchian 1950; Vromen 1995), the crucial insight here is the role played by 'adaptive learning' among individual firms as they react to past experience (Nelson and Winter 1982; Vromen 1995). Achieving sustainability is likely to require particular attention paid to the processes of institutional learning, among consumers and public bodies as well as among firms (Milbrath 1989).

This will require, second, an understanding of the conditions under which such adaptation occurs. Here institutional studies of technological innovation have shown the crucial role played by different organisational forms and cultures within firms, and by the financial and public policy environments in which they operate (Kay 1979; Freeman 1982; Loveridge and Pitt 1990; Lundvall 1992). The price mechanism, the key variable in the market model, is shown to be of rather less importance. This finding has major implications for the kinds of policy instrument necessary to achieve sustainability: it suggests that price incentives such as taxes will need to be supplemented by policies aimed at firm culture and the wider political context. The understanding of 'regulatory regimes' provided by French regulation theory – embracing firm organisation, consumption patterns and public policy – may be of particular help here, showing how different features of industrial and social organisation are inter-related (Boyer 1988).

This in turn leads to a third important insight of evolutionary-institutional models. This is the 'embeddedness', or condition of being 'locked-in', of particular products and forms of production in wider technological and institutional infrastructures (Arthur 1988). Present demands for goods and services make sense only in relation to the technologies and institutions within which such goods and services are produced. The demand for cars, for example, is closely tied to the infrastructure of roads and public transport and the patterns of land-use planning which have grown up in the past forty years, which themselves have been influenced by the demand for cars. Demands for foodstuffs and the unusual structure of the food industry (controlled by retailing firms) are explicable only in relation to the particular post-war circumstances under which the industrialisation of agriculture has occurred. These include the historic price of oil, which has allowed the widespread use of agro-chemicals and the huge growth of the international trade in foods, and the European political context which has supported a high level of agricultural subsidy. One of the hardest tasks in achieving sustainability will be to transform deeply embedded or 'locked-in' products and production processes of these kinds: again, there are obvious implications for the choice of appropriate policy instruments. These will have to address the wider institutional and technological contexts as well as the products or processes themselves.

Embeddedness is one result of the boundedness of technical change. The fifth insight offered by evolutionary-institutional economics is that technical change is limited. Outside specific and rare periods when the whole 'techno-economic paradigm' shifts, technical change occurs along 'technological trajectories'. Innovation occurs within existing basic technologies, forms of social organisation and product ranges (Nelson and Winter 1977; Dosi 1982; Perez 1983). Moreover, such change is 'path dependent': choices are constrained by decisions made in the past, and the circumstances that have arisen from them. Recognising these limitations of technical change is a crucial element in understanding sustainability. There are considerable technological opportunities for improving resource efficiency, but these must occur only within existing trajectories, and will be constrained by the patterns of development which the past has bequeathed us (Kemp and Soete 1992). The utopian projections of some environmental advocates often miss this basic point. An evolutionary and institutional approach to economic analysis will not give simple explanations and prescriptions: the complexity of socio-economic conditions and the uncertainty inherent in innovatory change make this impossible. But it will surely prove more useful than the simplicities of the market model.

The concept of 'market failure' exemplifies the inadequacy of the neo-classical approach. The idea that the current state of unsustainability is a 'failure' of the market system suggests that we should have expected it to be sustainable; it has gone wrong somewhere. But this model offers no help in understanding what has actually happened. Unsustainability is not a failure, since the present system of markets was never intended to be sustainable. Its historical trajectory has been given by other goals and interests. If society now wishes to change that trajectory, it should not see this as a process of 'correcting' markets, but as choosing a different future development path. In this sense sustainability can be described as a choice of 'ecological restructuring': of deliberate changes in the structure of economic activity (and therefore of wider social systems) so as to bring environmental impacts within the boundary of ecosystem health and environmental capacity maintenance (Jackson 1993; Ayres and Simonis 1994; Taylor 1995; Ayres and Weaver 1998).

MARKETS AND INSTRUMENTS

If the neo-classical market model throws little light on the objective of sustainability, it is hardly any clearer in relation to the instruments required to achieve the objective. The dominant distinction made in the second stage of neo-classical policy-making is between market-based and regulatory instruments. The former are sometimes presented as a policy mechanism in tune with 'free markets', while the latter – slyly given the pejorative label 'command and control' by neo-classical economists – are draconian and bureaucratic. But of course this is nonsense. Both kinds of instrument are forms of government intervention in markets. Regulations affect market behaviour just as taxes, charges and tradable permits do. Both change the conditions under which market actors operate.

The force of the neo-classical distinction derives from the overriding criterion of efficiency given by the neo-classical definition of optimality. Regulatory mechanisms (technological standards, legal prohibitions, and so on) are said to achieve given objectives at greater total costs than financial incentives such as taxes and charges. But the scale of the changes required by sustainability makes the criterion of efficiency rather less important than that of *effectiveness*: actually achieving the objective in the first place. Again, the neo-classical model assumes that the changes required will be small: when this is the case, the kind of price adjustments which market mechanisms can effect may well be sufficient. But when the changes required are large – and affect the structures of production and consumption, not simply their marginal quantity or technological detail – price adjustments alone may not achieve the objective.

The standard economic reason for this is that many of the key patterns of demand which sustainability requires to be changed are price-inelastic (insensitive to price changes). What is not often asked is why. Price-inelasticity is generally a function of the embeddedness of particular products in wider technologies, infrastructures, lifestyles and social systems. Unless these change, demand for the products cannot alter very much: firms and households are 'locked into' particular patterns of consumption. Examples include car use, energy use in buildings and industrial production, water use, demand for agro-chemicals, demand for oil in industrial production, and for certain other chemicals (such as chlorine). Small changes in the prices of these commodities, of the kind feasible through taxes, charges and other market-based instruments, will simply not have the required environmental effects. Changing the patterns of demand in significant ways will require changes in basic technologies and infrastructures, and these are not primarily responsive to price.

Of course, if prices are raised enough such change may occur. But very large increases in taxation (of 100 per cent or more, which might well be required in these fields) are rarely politically feasible. Securing changes on the scale required for sustainability requires the sources of the inelasticities themselves to be attacked, by changing the basic technologies and infrastructures. This may be done either through direct public provision, such as in public transport, land-use planning and renewable energy sources; or through subsidy and support for private investment, such as energy efficiency technologies in buildings and production, clean technologies, agricultural subsidy schemes, and so on.

The crucial point is that this requires a mix of instruments, not simply tax increases. This is particularly the case where innovation is required: where sustainable methods of production or consumption actually do not exist at present and must be developed. The market model assumes that innovation is a function of price; but all the evidence suggests that 'cultural' and organisational factors within firms and industries are much more significant (Kay 1979). Stimulating innovative cultures and industrial structures is likely to be a far more hands-on process of partnership-building, financial and marketing support – even of regulatory flexibility – than the model of simple price changes through market mechanisms suggests. The relationship between financial institutions and firms appears to be crucial. Empirical studies of successful environmental innovation bear this out (Gouldson and Murphy 1997).

The fact that major price rises in basic commodities such as energy and water can have extremely regressive distributional effects provides another reason why price incentives alone are not sufficient to achieve sustainability. Such effects will have to be mitigated through other kinds of policy, particularly public investment in and subsidy for domestic energy efficiency, but also possibly through the welfare benefit system (Boardman 1991). Where environmental policy stimulates differential regional employment effects, these too will need to be mitigated (Jacobs 1994).

The point of these arguments is not to deny the importance of market-based instruments in policies for sustainability (they will be essential); it is to expose the seriously misleading character of the market model of intervention. The model suggests that there are just two stages of environmental policy-making: setting objectives, and then adjusting prices to achieve these objectives. Policy implementation in this model is seen as an essentially hands-off process: using taxes and charges to change market prices allows firms and households to make their own decisions about how to respond with the maximum amount of flexibility and market liberty. The detailed intervention in specific production and consumption decisions required by regulatory methods (setting product standards, for example) is no longer necessary: government can simply pull the appropriate price strings from afar.

This model of the policy process, however, is a fiction. There are in fact three stages: in between setting objectives and determining instruments there is the choice of 'techniques'; that is, of the technical and social methods by which the objectives will be achieved. For example, urban transport problems can be reduced by developing electric cars, or improving bus services, or investing in light rail, or reducing the availability of car parking, or introducing congestion charges, or encouraging bicycle use, or changing land-use patterns, or any combination of these. Landfill might be reduced by reducing industrial inputs – by which methods? – or by internal re-use of wastes (ditto?), or by recycling or energy from waste schemes, and so on. These different options are the actual methods by which environmental objectives can be achieved; instruments such as charges and regulations are simply the means to bring them into being.

The market model's emphasis on incentive instruments assumes that governments do not have to be interested in techniques: the market can be left to sort these out on its own. But the importance of basic technologies and infrastructures in achieving sustainable reductions in environmental impact means that in many fields governments will have to get involved in choices of techniques. Much of the infrastructure will have to be publicly provided or regulated: transport, land-use planning, energy supply, water supply, telecommunications networks, waste disposal. Research and development in new basic technologies will almost certainly not be forthcoming from private industry alone. If public support is required, detailed involvement in the choice and assessment of technologies is inevitable. Investment in such technologies will also require detailed partnerships with the private sector, who will not be willing to undertake such investment unless they can be certain that it will be supported by appropriate infrastructure, financial and tax conditions (including quite possibly financial support) and regulatory regimes. Where major structural change is involved, governments cannot avoid hands-on involvement in choices over the form it takes.

MARKETS, PLANNING AND THE STATE

Understood as a process of ecological restructuring, therefore, sustainability will require detailed government involvement: in setting environmental-economic objectives, in choosing techniques, and in the use of instruments. This must be described as a form of planning.

However, it is not planning in opposition to markets. Here again traditional dichotomies merely obscure the argument, in two different ways. On the one hand, 'planning for sustainability' will not get rid of markets. What sustainability requires is changes in the conditions in which markets currently operate: the prices given to them by tax regimes (and by the structure of other markets), the infrastructure in which they are embedded, their legal framework, even their social (cultural and moral) context. This is not a question of *adding* such conditions: markets are already bounded and structured in these ways, both by cultural-historical legacies and deliberate policy (Lindblom 1977). In this sense current environmental outcomes are already 'determined', if only by omission. Altering the outcomes by changing these conditions will redefine many markets, reducing the scale of some, enlarging others; new markets will be created. But though the scale of purposeful intervention will be higher than currently, this will still be a market economy.

On the other hand, there should be few illusions about the freedom of competition in many of the markets which sustainability seeks to change. Planning for sustainability will involve negotiation with transnational corporations wielding significant economic power. In many fields, the process may be less one of trying to change a 'market' than simply trying to influence a small number of very large companies.

For this reason, the term 'planning' may not be the most appropriate. The dynamic nature of structural change, the idea of sustainability being a direction rather than a condition, suggests that the process is more one of 'steering'. In the context of globalisation, it is not clear that national or regional-bloc economies can be 'planned'; but they may still be capable of being steered in a general direction by national or supranational states. Sustainability – the large-scale reduction of environmental impact – is the direction proposed here.

This immediately raises the question of the nature of the state which is expected to perform such a steering function, however. What kind of state would it be? After all, there is no more *logical* connection between sustainability and the state – no a priori reason for the state even to pursue the goal – than between sustainability and the market. This is an absolutely central question for sustainability, but the dominance of the neo-classical theory means that it has barely been addressed in the environmental literature. The deficiency of the market model here is one of omission. The flip-side of the emphasis on markets in environmental debate is the lack of consideration given to the state.

In neo-classical theory the state is a cipher: it is assumed simply to adopt in benign and disinterested fashion the socially optimum objective and to adjust taxes and charges until the optimum is achieved. But of course states are not like this: as the Austrian public-choice schools have pointed out, they engender their own bureaucratic self-interest, they are open to regulatory capture, and they are subject to at least as much 'failure' as markets, if not more (Buchanan 1986; Anderson and Leal 1991). But the solution proposed by these schools – minimising the role of the state by creating private property rights and leaving decisions to markets – is of course no solution for sustainability, for reasons we have already given (even leaving aside all other considerations). Markets cannot guarantee, and are in practice almost certainly unable to achieve, major reductions in environmental impact. Since the most important environmental goods are inescapably public and collective in character, only states can regulate their condition: only states have the coercive power which can overcome the free-riding problems of individual choice.

For this reason sustainability needs a rather more substantive theory of the state in its relations with late modern capitalism. Is the process of 'steering ecological restructuring' feasible? Under what conditions might states engage in such a process? A substantive theory of the 'sustainability state' must be the subject of another paper, but some of the questions it would have to answer can be suggested.

First, such a theory would have to explain the relationship between the state and the processes of capital accumulation under the sustainability objective. Is the process of 'steering ecological restructuring' *economically and technologically feasible*? In capitalist societies it is reasonable to assume that even active states can only pursue economic directions which allow capital accumulation to continue: the collapse of accumulation would undermine the state.[9] But this raises a serious issue for environmental sustainability. Sustainability requires economic activity to remain within biophysical limits. Is this compatible with long-run capital accumulation? If it is, evolutionary change led by the state may be theoretically feasible; if not, the role and nature of the state are not clear at all.

Second, a theory of the 'sustainability state' would need to explain the *political conditions* under which a state would wish to engage in the ecological restructuring project. Even if continuing accumulation is possible, its likely slower pace under the sustainability goal and the changed distributions it would enforce between industries and firms are likely to encounter resistance on the part of capital. In these circumstances, what balance of forces on and within the state, from which interests in society, might be strong enough to push it towards adopting the sustainability objective? Could a sustainability state win the *public legitimacy* to engage in the necessary steering activity?

Third, even if sustainability is economically feasible and has sufficient political motivation, do states have the *power* to direct or influence capital sufficiently to enable it to be pursued? This question requires particular consideration to be given both to the *scale* of the state and to its *form*. In a globalised economy, are national states powerful enough, or are supranational states, or state structures, required? We have argued that sustainability requires considerable government intervention. What kind of state apparatus is required to engage in such levels of intervention?

CONCLUSION

As with other areas of politics, environmental policy has in recent years found its place within broader arguments over markets: over their economic efficiency, their ability to harness entrepreneurial dynamism in the pursuit of wealth, their libertarianism, and so on. Whether in the field of economic policy in developing countries, in the provision of health care and local government services, or in the nature of socialism, it is the concept of the market which dominates argument. This is perhaps to be expected in a post-1989 world, but it does not mean that it is helpful.

In particular, the ways in which markets are understood and the emphasis that they are given in dominant debates in environmental policy has been misplaced. This is not to say that markets are unimportant: examined as empirical structures – different in every sector, socially embedded, constrained by external conditions and forces (both deliberately imposed and not) – the study of markets is crucial to sustainability policy. However, as a foundational conceptual construct – from which political objectives can be derived, the process of environmental change understood and the means of policy implementation designed – markets offer very little help. There has been too much implicit 'ideology' underpinning their advocacy.

The nature of the sustainability objective forces us instead to turn our attention to the state. Here the problem has been too little discussion. It is time that this was changed.

Notes

1 This definition obviously raises the question of what precisely constitutes 'ecosystem health' or 'integrity' or 'the capacity of the biosphere to provide essential environmental services'. This question raises philosophical as well as scientific issues, but neither need be discussed here. For the purposes of this chapter it is sufficient to acknowledge that these concepts are ultimately socially constructed, not objectively 'scientific'. Although science may be able to tell us – with varying degrees of confidence – at what level of human impact some aspect of the environment will undergo change, it cannot distinguish precisely between acceptable and unacceptable change. Similarly, sustainability-related ethical principles (such as equity in the distribution of resources between or within generations, or an acknowledgement of the intrinsic value of the natural world) can help us to think about what 'acceptable' means, but such principles always underdetermine policy: they cannot specify precisely which incremental environmental changes do or do not in practice pass the ethical test. For these reasons there are no single states of 'health', 'integrity' or 'capacity maintenance': these are at best ranges of environmental conditions.
2 See, for example, Simon (1981) and Daly (1992).
3 In some cases, the privatisation of environmental goods and individual payment for them is possible. But even if this is regarded as politically acceptable, it is not a policy for sustainability, since there is no guarantee that market bargaining will generate sustainable outcomes. If such outcomes are imposed on the market, as with tradable pollution and resource extraction permits, this is of course a form of collective regulation. In practice the indivisibility of public goods makes privatisation rarely feasible. For a discussion see Anderson and Leal (1991), Eckersley (1993) and Jacobs (1993).
4 An alternative analysis within the same general economic tradition is that market failure occurs because environmental goods are not subject to well-defined property rights; therefore they get overused. This formulation is the basis of the 'public choice' approach to environmental policy, which seeks the privatisation of environmental assets in order to create well-defined property rights and therefore markets (see Anderson and Leal 1991). Though close to it in originating analysis, this approach is *not* that of neo-classical economics, which prefers government intervention through market-based instruments. The public choice approach has received little interest in Europe and has been largely irrelevant in policy debate, largely because of the practical impossibility of privatising most environmental goods.
5 For an exposition see, for example, Pearce (1993).
6 The switch of taxation from labour and other economic 'goods' to energy and other environmental 'bads' is likely to be an explicit part of a sustainability package. This is

known as 'ecological tax reform'. See von Weizäcker and Jesinghaus (1992); Repetto (1993); Commission of the European Communities (1993); O'Riordan (1997); and Tindale and Holtham (1996).

7 It is possible that as they become cheaper people will come to value labour-intensive and recyclable products more than energy-intensive and toxic ones, which will have become more expensive. On the other hand the shortage of the latter may cause genuine feelings of loss. See Jacobs (1991: ch. 19).

8 Witness, for example, the attempts to conduct cost-benefit analyses of global warming abatement, such as Nordhaus (1991) and Cline (1992). The notion that by comparing base case GDP in 2050 with the GDP that would emerge from major environmental policies – even if such long-range projections are in themselves meaningful – we can read off which type of society would be 'better off' in terms of the satisfaction of its preferences is simply absurd.

9 Such an assumption underpins most modern theories of the state, despite otherwise substantive differences. See, for example, Lindblom (1977), Gough (1979), Offe (1984), Castells (1980), and Jessop (1990). I am concerned only with the state in advanced liberal democracies.

References

Alchian, A. (1950) 'Uncertainty, evolution and economic theory', *Journal of Political Economy* 58: 211–21.

Anderson, T. and Leal, R. (1991) *Free Market Environmentalism*, San Francisco, Ca.: Pacific Research Institute for Public Policy.

Arthur, W. (1988) 'Competing technologies: an overview', in Dosi *et al.* (1988).

Ayres, R. and Simonis, U. (eds) (1994) *Industrial Metabolism: Restructuring for Sustainable Development*, United Nations University Press.

Ayres, R. and Weaver, P. M. (eds) (1998) *Eco-Restructuring: Implications for Sustainable Development*, Tokyo, New York: United Nations University Press.

Beckerman, W. (1994) ' "Sustainable Development": Is It a Useful Concept?', *Environmental Values* 3: 191–209.

Boardman, B. (1991) *Fuel Poverty*, London: Belhaven/Wiley.

Boyer, R. (1988) 'Technical Change and the Theory of Regulation', in Dosi *et al.* (1988).

Brown, L., Flavin, C. and Postel, S. (1992) *Saving the Planet: How to Shape an Environmentally Sustainable Global Economy*, London: Earthscan.

Bruce, J., Lee, H. and Haites, E. (eds) (1996) *Climate Change 1995: Economic and Social Dimensions of Climate Change*, Cambridge: Cambridge University Press.

Buchanan, J. (1986) *Liberty, Market and the State: Political Economy in the 1980s*, Wheatsheaf: Brighton.

Castells, M. (1980) *The Economic Crisis and American Society*, Princeton, NJ: Princeton University Press.

Clark, J. and Burgess, J. (1997) 'Asking Questions about Answering Questions: A Case Study of Public Understanding of a Contingent Valuation Survey', in P. Lowe (ed.) *Environmental Valuation and Policy Appraisal*, CAB International.

Cline, C. (1992) *The Economics of Global Warming*, Washington, DC: Institute for International Economics.

Commission of the European Communities (1993) *Competitiveness, Growth, Employment: The Challenges and Way Forward into the 21st Century*, Brussels: CEC.

Commoner, B. (1972) *The Closing Circle: Confronting the Environmental Crisis*, London: Jonathan Cape.

Costanza, R., Norton B. and Haskell, B. (eds) (1992) *Ecosystem Health: New Goals for Environmental Management*, Washington, DC: Island Press.

Daly, H. (1992) *Steady-State Economics*, London: Earthscan.

Daly, H. (1995) 'On Wilfred Beckerman's Critique of Sustainable Development', *Environmental Values* 4: 49–55.

Dosi, G. (1982) 'Technological Paradigms and Technological Trajectories: A Suggested Reinterpretation of the Determinants and Directions of Technological Change', *Research Policy* 11: 147–62.

Dosi, G., Freemann, C., Nelson, R., Silverberg, G. and Solte, L. (eds) (1988) *Technical Change and Economic Theory*, London: Pinter.

Eckersley, R. (1993) 'Free Market Environmentalists: Friend or Foe?', *Environmental Politics* 2: 1–9.

Ehrlich, P. (1977) *Ecoscience: Population, Resources, Environment*, Oxford: W. H. Freeman.

Ekins, P. and Jacobs, M. (1995) 'Environmental Sustainability and the Growth of GDP: Conditions for Compatibility', in V. Bhaskar and A. Glyn (eds), *The North, the South and the Environment*, London: Earthscan.

Elster, J. (1986) 'The Market and the Forum: Three Varieties of Political Theory', in J. Elster and A. Hylland (eds), *Foundations of Social Choice Theory*, Cambridge: Cambridge University Press;

Freeman, C. (1982) *The Economics of Industrial Innovation*, London: Pinter, 2nd edn.

Friends of the Earth Europe (1995) *Towards Sustainable Europe.*

Gough, I. (1979) *The Political Economy of the Welfare State*, London: Macmillan.

Gouldson, A. and Murphy, J. (1997) *Environmental Policy as Practice: The Implementation and Impact of Industrial Environmental Regulation*, London: Earthscan.

Hodgson, G. (1993) *Economics and Evolution*, Cambridge: Polity Press.

Jackson, T. (ed.) (1993) *Clean Production Strategies: Developing Preventive Environmental Management in the Industrial Economy*, Lewis Publishers.

Jacobs, M. (1991) *The Green Economy*, London: Pluto Press.

Jacobs, M. (1993) 'Free Market Environmentalism: A Response to Eckersley', *Environmental Politics* 2: 238–41.

Jacobs, M. (1994) *Green Jobs? The Employment Implications of Environmental Policy*, Godalming: World Wide Fund for Nature (WWF).

Jacobs, M. (1995) 'Sustainable Development, Capital Substitution and Economic Humility: A Response to Beckerman', *Environmental Values* 4: 57–68.

Jacobs, M. (1997) 'Environmental Valuation, Deliberative Democracy and Public Decision Making Institutions', in J. Foster (ed.) *Valuing Nature? Economics, Ethics and Environment*, London: Routledge.

Jessop, B. (1990) *State Theory: Putting the Capitalist State in its Place*, Cambridge: Polity Press.

Kay, N. (1979) *The Innovating Firm*, London: Macmillan.

Kemp, R. and Soete. L. (1992) 'The Greening of Technological Progress: An Evolutionary Perspective', *Futures* 24: 437–57.

Lindblom, C. (1977) *Politics and Markets: The World's Economic Systems*, New York: Basic Books.

Loveridge, R. and Pitt, M. (eds) (1990) *The Strategic Management of Technological Innovation*, John Wiley & Sons.

Lundvall, B. (ed.) (1992) *National Systems of Innovation*, London: Pinter.

Macnaghten, P., Grove-White, R., Jacobs, M. and Wynne, B. (1995) *Public Perceptions and Sustainability in Lancashire*, Preston: Lancashire County Council.

Milbrath, L. (1989) *Envisioning a Sustainable Society: Learning Our Way Out*, New York: State University of New York Press.

Ministry of Housing, Physical Planning and Environment (1988) *To Choose or To Lose: National Environmental Policy Plan*, The Hague: VROM.

Nelson, R. and Winter, S. (1977) 'In Search of a Useful Theory of Innovation', *Research Policy* 6: 36–77.

Nelson, R. and Winter, S. (1982) *An Evolutionary Theory of Economic Change*, Harvard, Mass.: Harvard University Press.

Nordhaus, W. (1991) 'To Slow Or Not to Slow: The Economics of the Greenhouse Effect', *Economic Journal* 101: 920–37.

Offe, C. (1984) *Contradictions of the Welfare State*, London: Hutchinson.

O'Neill, J. (1994) 'Preferences, Virtues and Institutions', *Analyse and Kritik* 16: 202–16.

O'Riordan, T. (1997) *Ecotaxation*, London: Earthscan.

Pearce, D. (1993) *Economic Values and the Natural World*, London: Earthscan.

Pearce, D., Markandya, A. and Barbier, E. (1989) *Blueprint for a Green Economy*, London: Earthscan.

Pearce, D. and Atkinson, G. (1992) *Are National Economies Sustainable? Measuring Sustainable Development*, CSERGE Working Paper GEC 92–11, London: Centre for Socio-Economic Research on the Global Environment, University College London.

Pearce, D. and Turner, K. (1990) *Economics of Natural Resources and the Environment*, London: Harvester Wheatsheaf.

Perez, C. (1983) 'Structural Change and the Assimilation of New Technologies in the Economic and Social System', *Futures* 15: 357–75.

Pezzy, J. (1992) *Sustainable Development Concepts: An Economic Analysis*, World Bank Environment Paper No. 2, Washington, DC: The World Bank.

Pretty, J. (1995) *Regenerating Agriculture: An Alternative Strategy for Growth*, London: Earthscan.

Repetto, R. (1993) *Green Fees*, Washington, DC: World Resources Institute.

Rutherford, M. (1994) *Institutions and Economics: The Old and the New Institutionalism*, Cambridge: Cambridge University Press.

Sagoff, M (1995) 'Carrying Capacity and Ecological Economics', *BioScience* 45: 610–20

Simon, J. (1981) *The Ultimate Resource*, Oxford: Martin Robertson.

Taylor, M. (ed.) (1995) *Environmental Change: Industry, Power and Policy*, Avebury Press.

Tindale, S. and Holtham, G. (1996) *Green Tax Reform*, London: Institute for Public Policy Research.

Vadnjal, D. and O'Connor, M. (1994) 'What is the Value of Rangitoto Island?', *Environmental Values* 3: 369–80.

Vromen, J. (1995) *Economic Evolution*, London: Routledge.

Weizäcker, E. von and Jesinghaus, J. (1992) *Ecological Tax Reform*, London: Zed.

5 Scale, complexity and the conundrum of sustainability

William Rees

DEFINING THE PROBLEM

In recent decades, a set of powerfully interrelated environmental, economic and cultural factors has elevated problems of scale in space and time to a central place in the sustainable development debate. This poses a practical challenge to a world of quasi-independent sovereign states, each characterised by multiple levels of spatial jurisdictions (states or provinces, counties, regions and municipalities) and by overlapping and/or conflicting mandates. The purpose of this chapter is to examine the evolving context for environmental decision-making, including some less familiar dimensions, and to explore its implications for multi-scale initiatives in planning for sustainability.

The scaling-up of ecological stress has been accompanied by a shift in at least some observers' perception of the nature of the problem. The environmental movement first became a political force in the 1960s. At that time, most of the attention was focused on local hotspots (this factory, this pulp mill, or that nuclear plant or tanker spill), understanding of the problem was often superficial (based on aesthetic considerations such as visible smoke, bad smells and sullied beaches), and society generally perceived such issues as amenable to technical 'quick fixes'. Today, the local problems are still with us, but the greatest concern is reserved for global trends (such as atmospheric change and ozone depletion), and many analysts see these as indicative of deep systemic dysfunction. Most importantly, there is increasing suspicion that global change reflects an entire way of life gone awry. Certainly there appear to be no easy technical solutions.

Easy political solutions may be equally problematic. Significant ecological impacts often span several political jurisdictions and may also impair the global commons. Overfishing on the high seas by competing states is a continuing source of international friction; the consumptive destruction of rain forests for timber and to provide land for agriculture accelerates the loss of biodiversity, may alter global heat distribution, and contributes to greenhouse enhancement, all of which ultimately harm people everywhere. Certainly, too, pollution pays no heed to city, provincial or national boundaries. The mobility of many pollutants means that individual political entities often lack both the capacity and the incentive to take corrective action. Indeed, to the extent that countries can benefit – at least in the short term – from their ability to overexploit global sources (such as deep-sea fisheries) and sinks (like the atmosphere), they are positively driven to continue their damaging practices!

Clearly, the increasing scale of human-induced ecological change is in itself sufficient to suggest certain key questions. How can the global community reconcile local, regional/national and international interests as we seek mutually beneficial responses to global environmental change? What kinds of initiative would enable us both to respect the reasonable rights of sovereign states and to provide adequate protection to the global common pool of resources and functions upon which we all depend? Some of the answers to these questions undoubtedly lie in an evaluation of international environmental agreements, various local planning instruments and the hierarchical linkages among them, particularly those that have already been tested in the arena of *realpolitik*. However, as implied at the outset, the scaling up of environmental stress *per se* is only one relevant factor in the equation and *may not even be a critical one*. Conventional efforts to integrate inter-jurisdictional environmental management initiatives are therefore unlikely to be sufficient to the task. Indeed, it is a central premise of this chapter that despite a decade of impassioned debate, industrial society lacks any appreciation of certain critical dimensions of the sustainability dilemma. For example, it is a deep irony of the human-induced 'environmental crisis' that people have a dismally ill-developed understanding of themselves as ecological beings. Similarly, despite their central relevance to framing the issues, some of the major findings of systems science have barely entered the mainstream debate. The problem here is that 'no amount of ethical axiology, or legal, policy, and technological engineering, is going to solve problems that are misunderstood' (Drengson 1989). The following sections are therefore intended to broaden the conceptual scope of contemporary analysis with a view towards increasing understanding. This necessarily takes the debate on to unconventional ground.

(RE)FRAMING THE ANALYSIS

The economy as forcing mechanism

There is a growing consensus that the current global economic development path is itself inherently unsustainable. The human population is nearing six billion and is growing by eighty-five million per year. By the year 2000, it will have almost doubled twice in this century. All these people, rich and poor alike, have rising material expectations sustained by an economic system that assumes the latter are insatiable. Driven by both population growth and rampant consumerism, the world economy has expanded five-fold in half a century. Unfortunately, it is precisely continuous growth in the 'throughput' of energy and material required to feed aggregate human demand that causes the ecological crisis (Goodland 1991). Resource consumption already exceeds the productive capacity of certain critical

biophysical systems on every continent. Waste production breaches the assimilative capacity of some ecosystems on every scale. As these trends continue, they
have the potential to undermine the long-term stability and vital life-support
functions of the ecosphere permanently.

There is no consensus on how to deal with this emerging reality. Many concerned humanists and techno-optimists remain dedicated to growth and global
consumerism. They see freer markets and a new efficiency revolution as the
only politically feasible solution to both global ecological decline and chronic
Third World poverty. This approach would ostensibly decouple the economy from
the environment. Other more ecocentric and community-oriented groups see
growth-bound consumerism itself as the issue. They argue that beyond a certain
point, there is no evident relationship between income and perceived well being.
Further growth may therefore be unnecessary. From this perspective, the solution
lies more in changing consumer values and behaviour, and in developing policies
to ensure more equitable distribution of the world's present economic output.
These actions would size the economy to the environment.

Even within the economic arena, there are numerous complicating factors. As
intimated above, the growing income inequity between rich and poor both within
countries and between North and South may be the most important. The five-fold
increase in global income since the Second World War has been very unevenly
distributed. While 20 per cent of the world's population enjoys an unprecedented
level of material wellbeing, another 20 per cent remains in abject poverty. Worse,
there is no indication this gap will be bridged any time soon. In 1960 the fraction
of global income enjoyed by the richest 20 per cent of people was 'only' thirty
times greater than the share received by the poorest 20 per cent; by 1990 this ratio
had increased to 60:1 (UNDP 1992). In short, the income gap actually doubled
in thirty years of continuous global growth! No other issue holds greater potential for inter-regional and inter-jurisdictional conflict. Rich countries disdain
mechanisms for redistribution. With no other choice, poor states will not tolerate
constraints on growth. The resultant stalemate contributes to the political attrac-
tiveness in both North and South of 'growth through efficiency', or worse, just
plain growth.

Economics as human ecology

It is a tribute to the strength of the Cartesian dualism that characterises Western
scientific culture that we see our present problem as an 'environmental crisis'
rather than as a human ecological crisis (Rees 1990; 1995). The distinction is not a
trivial one. The idea of an 'environmental crisis' literally externalises the problem,
effectively blaming it on defective ecosystems which then need to be fixed or
managed more effectively. This suggests a supply-side corrective approach which
excludes any notion of constraining demand. By contrast, the idea of a human
ecological crisis places blame squarely where it belongs, on people themselves,
and suggests that it is human wants that need to be better controlled. This is a
demand-management approach which concedes that supply may ultimately be

limited. Recognising the problem as a 'human ecological crisis' is a step beyond seeing it as one of excessive economic scale. The two concepts are, however, closely related. The economy is that set of activities and relationships by which humans acquire, process and allocate the material necessities and wants of life. It therefore includes that sub-set of activities by which humankind interacts with the rest of the ecosphere. If we were dealing with any other species, these relationships would indisputably fall within the realm of ecology. In this light, therefore, much of what we term economics should really be seen as a sub-set of human ecology.

However, there is a structural problem which stems from conventional economic thought. Ecologists study non-human species and the ecosystems that sustain them by measuring and analysing the physical flows of energy, material and information essential to the continuous restructuring and self-organisation of those systems. By contrast, most economic analyses are money-based. They ignore both the biophysical basis of the economic process and the behavioural dynamics of the ecosystems within which it takes place. Thus, economics as presently structured is inherently flawed as (human) ecology. To make matters worse, academic ecologists themselves have spent little effort studying humans as ecological entities. With neither discipline properly focused, it is little wonder that we still have such a poor understanding of human ecology in relation to sustainability (Rees 1996, 1998a). I explore this issue further below.

Humans as 'patch disturbers'

The mere existence of humans means that there will be some impact on the ecosystems that sustain them. For example, the recent palaeo-ecological and archaeological literature tells a convincing story of the extinctions of large mammals and birds that accompanied first contact with, and settlement of their habitats by, human beings. The slow spread of humanity across the face of the earth seems invariably to have been accompanied by significant structural changes in local ecology. The impact of humans on local ecosystems has continually escalated with technological change. With the dawn of agriculture, 10,000 years ago, and the vastly larger human populations it could support, people acquired the capacity to alter entire landscapes permanently. Indeed, the evidence is clear that whole civilisations on every continent have collapsed at least partially because of the over-exploitation of ecosystems that had originally enabled them to flower (Ponting 1991; Diamond 1992; Tainter 1988). Historically, at least, it seems that the material reach of humans has tended to exceed their technological grasp. What is not generally understood is that this historical pattern is the inevitable consequence of two simple biological realities: first, human beings are large animals with correspondingly large individual energy and material requirements; and second, humans are social beings who universally live in extended groups. These simple facts of human ecology, together with productivity data for typical ecosystems, would be enough for an alien ecologist to advance the following hypothesis: in most of the potential habitats on Earth, groups of human hunter-gatherers will quickly overwhelm their local ecosystems and be forced to ramble ever farther afield in search of sustenance.

The productivity of most unaltered ecosystems is simply inadequate to support more than a few people for long in the immediate vicinity of a temporary camp. Thus, in pre-agricultural times, when a group of human foragers had hunted out and picked over a given area, they would simply move on, enabling the abandoned site to recover. The increased food production made possible by agriculture in turn enabled larger populations, permanent settlements, the division of labour, and other manifestations of 'civilisation'. However, it often merely prolonged the process of ecological decline and extended its spatial scale. Eventually, as populations grew too large, primitive technologies failed: soils eroded or became saline or waterlogged, for example, and the weakened society collapsed or succumbed to invasion.

All this is to make the point that humans are a 'typical' patch-disturbance species, a distinction we share with other large mammals from beavers to elephants (*BioScience* 1988).[1] 'Large animals, due to their size, longevity, and food and habitat requirements tend to have a substantial impact on ecosystems' (Naiman 1988). Thus, a patch-disturbance species is any organism which, usually by central place foraging, degrades a small 'central place' greatly and disturbs a much larger area away from the central core to a lesser extent (this is an amended definition of that given in Logan 1996). It seems that from the perspective of basic ecology, the makings of the ecological crisis are programmed into the biology of our species. In fact, despite – or because of – the marvels of modern technology, little has changed but the intensity of disturbance and the scale of the 'patches' we disturb. One manifestation of this is that the earth is currently experiencing the greatest extinction episode since the natural catastrophes at the end of the Palaeozoic and Mesozoic eras (Wilson 1988).

'Upping the ante': human ecological footprints

Clearly, any effort to understand global change and create a more sustainable society must reflect human ecological reality. With this in mind, the author and his students have developed a method to estimate the scale and impact of the human ecological niche. Our approach, called 'ecological footprint analysis', starts from the premise that far from being independent of nature, human beings are integral components of the ecosystems that support them (Rees and Wackernagel 1994; Rees 1996; Wackernagel and Rees 1996). This perspective is a central tenet of the emerging discipline of ecological economics. Ecological footprinting explicitly builds on traditional trophic ecology. We begin by constructing what is, in effect, an elaborate food-web connecting any specified human population to the rest of the ecosphere. This 'niche analysis' involves quantifying the material and energy flows required to support that population and identifying significant sources and sinks. As might be expected, the human 'food-web' differs significantly from those of other species. In addition to the material and energy required to satisfy the metabolic requirements of our bodies, the human food-web must also account for our industrial metabolism, the material demands of the economic process.

Ecological footprinting is further based on the fact that many material and energy flows (resource consumption and waste production) can be converted into land- and water-area equivalents. Thus, the ecological footprint of a specified population is the area of land/water required to produce the resources consumed, and to assimilate the wastes generated, by that population on a continuous basis wherever on Earth that land may be located. It therefore includes the area appropriated through commodity trade and the area needed to produce the referent population's share of certain free land- and water-based services of nature (such as the carbon sink function). In other words, ecological footprinting estimates the area of productive ecosystems all over the world whose biophysical output is appropriated for the exclusive use of a defined human population. As such, it is a measure of the extended 'patch' occupied ecologically, if not spatially, by that population.

Eco-footprints of cities

Our published estimates show that the ecological footprints of typical residents of high-income countries, accounting for average food, fibre and fossil energy consumption,[2] ranges as high as five or six hectares *per capita* (Rees and Wackernagel 1996; Wackernagel and Rees 1996). More comprehensive analyses push the estimate to nine hectares *per capita* (Wackernagel *et al.* 1997). By extrapolation, the ecological footprints of high-income cities are typically two to three orders of magnitude larger than geographic areas they occupy physically. For example, the 472,000 residents of my home city of Vancouver generate an average ecological footprint of at least five hectares *per capita* in order to support their consumer lifestyles. This means that the aggregate eco-footprint of the city proper is 2,360,000 ha, more than 200 times its political-geographical area (11,400 ha). Similarly, in a more comprehensive study, Folke *et al.* (1997) estimate that the twenty-nine largest cities of Baltic Europe appropriate for their resource consumption and waste assimilation an area of forest, agricultural, marine, and wetland ecosystems 565–1,130 times larger than the area of the cities themselves.

These data emphasise what should be obvious but is often forgotten in a rapidly urbanising world: that no city as presently defined can be sustainable on its own. In ecological terms, cities and urbanised regions are intensive nodes of consumption sustained almost entirely by biophysical production and processes occurring outside their political and geographic boundaries (Rees 1996; Rees and Wackernagel 1996).[3] In terms of patch disturbance, cities are the modern equivalent of the highly degraded 'central place' of our foraging ancestors, and the rest of our urban ecological footprints represent the less disturbed areas further afield. Today, of course, because of expanding trade, the 'patches' exploited by wealthy city dwellers extend ever further across the planet. The resultant separation of production from consumption is problematic because it renders urbanites blind to the degradation that results from their consumer life-styles and unconscious of their increasing dependence on a deteriorating resource base.

Global overshoot

It is not just cities that 'overshoot' the productive capacity of local ecosystems. Most high-income countries have an ecological footprint several times larger than their national territories. Since their consumption of nature's goods and services far exceeds domestic consumption, we say that such countries are running a massive ecological deficit with the rest of the world (Rees 1996). In effect, as a result of continuous population growth and rising material demand, the entire planet has become the common 'patch' of humankind. And what is the status of the global patch? Ecological footprinting reveals that in some dimensions, con-sumption by the present human population already exceeds the long-term pro-ductivity of the ecosphere. Wackernagel and Rees (1996) and Wackernagel *et al.* (1997) estimate that with prevailing technologies and average consumption levels, the present world population exceeds global carrying capacity by up to one third. Similarly, Folke *et al.* (1997) show that the carbon dioxide emissions of just 1.1 billion people (19 per cent of humanity) living in 744 large cities exceed the entire sink capacity of the world's forests by 10 per cent. In short, the wealthiest one-fifth of the world's population that consumes nearly 80 per cent of global economic output has unwittingly claimed the entire sustainable biophysical output of the ecosphere.[4] Thus, contrary to prevailing international development models, so-called 'First World' material lifestyles cannot be sustainably extended to the world's population. To put it another way, the evidence suggests that the global patch is not large enough to sustain the aggregate demand of even the present human population, assuming prevailing technology. Ozone depletion, fisheries collapsing, burning forests, record flooding, extreme weather events: all these reflect the inexorable acceleration of global patch disturbance. Unfortunately, unlike our ancestors, modern humans can no longer simply move on to greener pastures when our planetary patch wears out.

THE DIALECTIC OF DENIAL

The past few decades have witnessed two perceptual revolutions, a scientific one and a socio-economic one, that provide additional contexts for the sustainability debate. While the shift in thinking has been dramatic within science itself, its major elements remain at best on the margins of our cultural consciousness. By contrast, the socio-economic shift has swept round the world, dominates geo-politics, and affects the lives of almost everyone. The difference in popular and political appreciation of the two 'revolutions' is critical because their implications for sustainability are often diametrically at odds.

The second scientific revolution

The new science reveals a world both more complex and less tractable than the one our scientific-industrial society has traditionally assumed. According to a prevailing myth within our cultural life, nature is knowable and therefore ultimately malleable to human will. From this perspective, the traditional role of science has been to abolish superstition, reduce uncertainty, and to discover the natural laws or rules that govern the behaviour of energy and matter. The grand objective, of course, is to give humans the power to assume control over the material world.

In just the last three or four decades the shift in thinking in the scientific world has been nothing if not revolutionary. The seeds were planted with the development of Einsteinian relativity and quantum mechanics, but have flowered with new mathematical tools and the astonishing number-crunching capacity of modern computers. Our artificial linear-mechanical paradigm has gradually given way to a view of nature that, while still deterministic at the material level, is 'relentlessly non-linear' (Stewart 1989). Notions such as 'complexity theory', 'deterministic chaos', 'non-linear dynamics', 'autopoiesis', and 'Prigoginian self-organisation' capture the flavour of the paradigm shift fairly well.

A world of chaos . . .

An explosion of theoretical and empirical literature reinforces the idea that the interaction of the simple laws of physics and chemistry can produce systems behaviour of extraordinary complexity and richness. Conversely, systems of inordinate complexity are able to generate patterns of beautiful simplicity (Cohen and Stewart 1994). Perhaps most important in the present context is the recognition that the interplay of even strictly deterministic rules can quickly generate patterns of systems behaviour that are inherently unpredictable even if we possess near-perfect knowledge of the initial state of the system. To the extent that such counter-intuitive behaviour is characteristic of real-world ecosystems, economic systems, and social systems, it requires a serious re-evaluation of our dominant economic model and the prevailing approach to international development.

Two classes of phenomenon are particularly relevant to this. The first is the apparent chaos that can emerge from even the simplest dynamic system. Put simply, a dynamic system is one governed by strict rules such that the state of the system at any point in time unambiguously determines the future state of the system. In theory then, if we know how the system is behaving now, we can predict what it will look like at any point in the future. This requires simply performing an iterative sequence of calculations. The outcome of any calculation in the sequence both determines the next state of the system and provides the starting values for the subsequent iteration. This seems the very essence of predictable order, of Newtonian mechanism in fact: determine the rules governing the behaviour of the system, insert the starting values and the future will unfold without any surprises. Apply such a model to some real-world phenomenon, however, and after just a few iterations the state of the model will bear no evident relationship to reality. The problem usually lies in small errors of measurement. The internal dynamics of the model system are such that these errors are folded back and amplified with each iteration. Given sufficient time, *any* inaccuracy will derail the model. Better measurement does not help; at least, not for long. The tiniest, unavoidable measurement error can render even a perfect model useless as a predictive tool.

The general problem is called 'sensitive dependence on initial conditions' and the behaviour it produces in both mathematical models and real systems – even simple ones – is called chaos. Chaotic behaviour has always existed, but generally went unnoticed in our dedication to 'normal' science. If actually encountered, it was ignored because the mathematical calculations were too difficult. Now that computers are up to the task, 'the dreadful truth has become inescapable: Chaos is everywhere. It is just as common as the nice simple behavior so valued by traditional physics' (Cohen and Stewart 1994: 190). Chaos explains why even the best computer models cannot predict the weather next week.

... and even catastrophe

The second phenomenon is the unexpected, dramatic, or even catastrophic change that can occur in previously stable systems under stress. To understand this behaviour we must recognise that key variables of complex systems, such as ecosystems, may range considerably within broad domains of stability. Within these domains, all points tend to converge towards a centre of gravity called an 'attractor'.[5] Traditional predictable dynamic models may be characterised by a single equilibrium (a point attractor) or a repeating cycle of values (a periodic attractor). Chaotic systems, by contrast, trace a complex, often elegant, highly organised pattern of individually unpredictable paths – a 'strange attractor' – within the stable domain as internal feedback continually changes the system's dynamics. In any of these cases, the system will retain its familiar character and behaviour as long as key variables remain under the influence of their customary attractors.

Now, although it may not initially be obvious, dynamic systems may have several attractors separated from each other by a system of unstable 'ridges' or bifurcations (picture a terrain of watersheds, each isolated from the others by irregular hills and ridges). 'Catastrophe' occurs when a key systems variable, perhaps driven by some persistent change in an important control variable, is displaced far from the centre of its familiar attractor. If the variable reaches a bifurcation, it may be captured by an adjacent attractor instead of returning to its accustomed domain. Suddenly, the quality of the system changes dramatically. Indeed, catastrophe is characterised by large discontinuous changes in system characteristics and behaviour resulting from incrementally small changes in key variables. A last, marginal change in water temperature or fishing pressure and the whole system flips into a new stability domain controlled by a different attractor. This is problematic for sustainability planning since there is no guarantee that the system will ever return to its former state. Indeed, Kay (1991: 487) has been 'unable to find a single example of an ecosystem flipping back after undergoing such a dramatic reorganization'.

Various real-world systems as different as commercial fisheries, acidifying lakes, the Gulf Stream, global climate and even civil society seem to be prone to catastrophic behaviour and there is reason to believe that it is a characteristic of most complex dynamic systems. This is particularly worrying because the situation is actually more complicated than described above. First, neither the existence nor the nature of multiple attractor(s), simple or chaotic, is knowable before some critical variable slips from its historic domain into an adjacent attractor. Second, the very act of exploiting or otherwise manipulating the system changes its internal dynamics and shifts the location of both its attractor(s) and the bifurcations between them. Indeed, some existing attractors may disappear and new ones may emerge spontaneously. Third, the customary attractor may shrink even as systems variability (amplitude) increases under stress. This increases the brittleness (reduces the resilience) of the system. All these changes enhance the probability of catastrophic bifurcation.

In short, complexity theory has two key messages for those who would plan for sustainable development: (a) any persistent incremental stress on a dynamic system may increase the probability of dramatic qualitative and quantitative changes in the future state of the system, and (b) both the nature and magnitude of these changes are inherently unpredictable. We ignore these findings at considerable risk to future global society. Humans have become the driving force of global change, the level of stress is steadily increasing, and there is every reason to believe that ours is a world of dynamic systems characterised by multiple strange attractors.

On self-producing systems and . . .

Two additional structural properties of complex systems, particularly those with living components, are relevant to this discussion. The first concerns the capacity of living systems to respond to modest exogenous changes in ways that maintain their structural and functional integrity. This is not mere negative feedback. The central idea here is that the internal organisation of living systems is such that the systems are able to produce themselves continuously. The organisational property that enables this self-production is called 'autopoiesis' and was first elaborated by Humberto Maturana. Maturana's chief insight was that '[l]iving systems . . . [are] organized in a closed causal circular process that allows for evolutionary change in the way the circularity is maintained, but not for the loss of the circularity itself' (Maturana 1980; Maturana and Varela 1980). The organisation of a system is embodied in a set of interdependent relationships among the system's components. These organisational relationships specify the system as a unit and determine the domain of its operations. 'Causal circularity' resides in the fact that the relationships are in turn essential for the continued maintenance and production of participating components. Thus, autopoiesis is the product of a network of production processes in which each component participates in the production of other components of the network through the relationships specifying the system. The network is continuously 'produced by its components and in turn produces those components' (Capra 1996: 98; see also Maturana and Varela 1980; 1987). Autopoiesis is arguably a property of living systems at every level of biological organisation from individual cells to the intact organism. In other words, the human body is an autopoietic system (Rees 1990). Even entire ecosystems are 'in many respects self-generating – [their] productivity and stability determined largely through [their] internal interactions' (Perry *et al.* 1989). As Lynn Margulis, co-author of the Gaia hypothesis, confidently asserts about the ecosphere: 'There is little doubt that the planetary patina – including ourselves – is autopoietic' (Margulis and Sagan 1986).

. . . dissipative structures

Autopoietic systems can function and persist only as long as they have access to a continuous supply of available energy and material. This requirement forces us to consider the second law of thermodynamics, the law of energy (and material) transformation. The second law states that the entropy of any isolated system always increases. That is, available energy spontaneously dissipates, gradients disappear, and the system becomes increasingly unstructured in an inexorable slide towards thermodynamic equilibrium. This is a state in which 'nothing happens or can happen' (Ayres 1994). Historically, the second law referred to isolated systems very near equilibrium. More recent explorations of the second law recognise that all systems, whether isolated or not, are subject to the same forces of entropic decay. In other words, any integrated, differentiated system has a natural tendency to erode, unravel and dissipate. The reason that complex, self-producing systems such as the human body do not simply run down is that they are able to import available energy and material from their host environments which they use to maintain their internal organisation and integrity. Such systems also export the resultant entropy (degraded energy and material waste) back into their hosts. This modern interpretation of the second law therefore suggests that highly-ordered autopoietic systems develop and grow (increase their internal order) at the expense of increasing disorder at higher levels in the hierarchy of the systems (Schneider and Kay 1992; Kay and Schneider 1994). Because such systems continuously degrade and dissipate available energy and matter they are called 'dissipative structures'. I argue below that the operation of the second law in relation to the materially growing economy (one level in a nested hierarchy of self-producing systems on earth) must inevitably lead to the dissipative disorganisation of the ecosphere.

The globalising economy

In the light of the second scientific revolution, the contemporary socio-cultural revolution seems perversely enigmatic. While the new science reveals a world of dynamic complexity and sudden surprise, the material philosophy of our globalising society assumes vapid simplicity and practical certainty. The past twenty years have witnessed the unprecedented homogenisation of the world's economic system. The most visible manifestation is the near-universal collapse of state socialism in all its historic forms and its rapid substitution by market-based economies. However, this shift represents more than the mere 'triumph of capitalism' over alternative approaches to production and consumption. It heralds an era in which simplistic economic considerations have come to override all other objectives in the arenas of public policy and international development: 'The economic ideology, the dominant intellectual framework in the world today, has reduced practically every human value to the categories of economics: production and consumption, basic needs and satisfiers, human rights, scarcity, nature, energy systems, Cartesian time and space, the assumption that all things are measurable and comparable' (Hunt 1989: 3). Virtually all major governments, corporations, and international institutions, particularly the UN, the World Bank and International Monetary Fund, the Organization for Economic Cooperation and Development (OECD), and their offspring such as the World Trade Organization (WTO), have made economic development their central preoccupation following the urging of US President Roosevelt and the experience of the Marshall Plan (Sachs 1990):

> Development – perceived and defined in the Western sense as maximizing or optimizing economic growth, confirming the sanctity of economies, and building up the material resources of society – has been seen as the real key to people's and society's well-being as well as the principal panacea for the world's problems.
>
> (Schafer 1994: 833)

The major effect of this singular preoccupation has been the impoverishment of public debate on even the major economic issues of the day. In the words of American analyst Stephen Viederman, 'we have allowed the language of conventional economics to become the language of politics, a language without a moral sense (because of its origins), and with a limited relevance to real economic circumstances' (Viederman 1994).

Of course, the 'conventional economics' to which Viederman refers is the neoclassical (neo-liberal) variety, a form of economics that was erected on a foundation borrowed from Newtonian analytic mechanics. It is based on the premise that the simple mechanics of supply and demand as mediated by the competitive interplay of producers and consumers in the marketplace is the most efficient generator of material wealth. In a mechanical world where short-term production efficiency was all that mattered and all players possessed perfect knowledge of the system, a purely market-based approach might well provide safe passage for all humanity into the twenty-first century. However, in view of our emerging (complex systems) understanding of how the world actually works, the simplistic assumptions of market economics provide far too frail a vessel in which to float a whole 'new world order'.

THREE DANGEROUS ABSTRACTIONS

> we are turning away from the truth when, in moral science where everything is connected, we endeavour to isolate a principle and to see nothing but that principle.
>
> Sismondi (1991)

Daly and Cobb note that the relative success of economics (among the social sciences) in becoming a deductive science hinges, in part, on a high level of abstraction. Unfortunately, the ethos of the discipline discourages full acknowledgement of the extent of such abstraction so that 'conclusions are drawn about the real world by deduction from abstractions with little awareness of the dangers involved' (1989: 37). This section touches on only three such abstractions of particular relevance to sustainability.

Welfare is not mere production

The first problem is the virtual equation of human welfare with *per capita* income. As noted, this leads at the policy level to a primary focus on increasing economic efficiency with a view towards maximising production growth. What country does not regard *per capita* GDP as its principal, if not exclusive, indicator of national health? Even in relatively wealthy countries where basic material requirements have long been satisfied, virtually all other values – social justice, distributional equity, environmental protection, public safety – are increasingly compromised in order to minimise public expenditures, maintain the economy's competitive edge in the global marketplace, and generally increase economic output and market share. Accordingly, global commerce is increasingly governed by regional alliances and trade treaties aimed at increasing economic output in both rich and poor countries. Such agreements confer greater freedom and power on corporations and on international tribunals while restricting the authority of electorally accountable governments. Meanwhile, participating countries and firms drastically restructure to exploit their competitive advantages in an increasingly global market. The increased economic efficiencies associated with specialisation (reduced marginal costs) and intensified competition can result in both lower prices and higher wages in successful economies. Demand increases, forcing aggregate energy and material throughput ever higher. Driven by positive feedback, the world economy is expected to expand by a factor of five to ten in the next half century (WCED 1987).

It seems that in apparent denial of the obvious, the world has conceived an approach to international development that can only exacerbate the 'environmental crisis' – *existing* levels of production and consumption are the proximate cause of global ecological change. Not only is this fixation on economic growth ecologically deluded, it is also a perversion of economic theory. Economic theory starts from the assumption that people want to maximise their welfare, but welfare comprises more than greater production and rising incomes. If, at the margin, we value safe communities, public health or local ecosystems more than production, and if preserving community and the environment leads to less production, then less production actually improves welfare. In short, to the extent that our global credo of progress is equated with production growth (at least in high-income countries), 'we are up against a deep-rooted, erroneous notion . . . that is threatening our planet' (Heuting 1996).

People do not behave like *homo economicus*

The second conceptual shortcut relevant to this discussion is *homo economicus*, the neo-classical representation of real human beings. This particular abstraction reduces humans to self-interested utility maximisers with fixed preferences and insatiable material wants. This mythical figure acts as an individual automaton, devoid of community and family and unmoved by other people's needs or suffering. Margaret Thatcher was speaking for this figure when she declared: 'There is no such thing as society.' There is no such thing as nature or environment either, since neither has much to trade in the marketplace. The conception of *homo economicus* leads us to define rational behaviour as maximising individual satisfaction exclusively through participation in the market. Moreover, in the absence of any moral or ethical criteria or context by which to judge relative value, all wants and desires are deemed to be equivalent. This reduces the task of the economy 'to [meeting] as many of these desires as possible, whatever they may be' (Daly and Cobb 1989: 92). This, in turn, is part of the conceptual basis for the wasteful consumerism and expectations of interminable material growth prevalent even in high-income countries today.

Land is not ethereal

The concept of land fares even worse than that of people in the neo-classical model. In one sense, ' "land" as used by economists is the inclusive term for the natural environment' (Daly and Cobb 1989: 97). However, early considerations of land by economists was almost exclusively about production in agriculture and subsequent abstraction has further narrowed the frame of reference. Indeed, there has never been serious contemplation of the myriad other essential biophysical functions services associated with terrestrial ecosystems and no consideration at all for the oceans, the hydrological cycle, the climate, and all the other less land-bound dimensions of nature. In effect, neo-classical economics has turned land into an abstract space and a property relation, with no inherent production value. As such it is 'merely one commodity among others. The "forces of nature," and therefore of nature in general, have disappeared from view. Economics as a discipline floats free from the physical world' (Daly and Cobb 1989: 99).

Such gross simplifications certainly contribute to the methodological tractability of economic analyses. However, they also reveal that at its core, the economic paradigm driving the world today is abstracted from community, offers a shrivelled caricature of human beings, and 'lacks any representation of the materials, energy sources, physical structures, and time dependent processes basic to an ecological [complex systems] approach' (Christensen 1991); or, one might add, the sense of reality essential to any contemplation of sustainability.

JUST WHAT ARE 'THE DANGERS INVOLVED'?

> the big problem facing the planet is the possibility that human activity may tip it over the borderline toward a totally new attractor.
>
> Cohen and Stewart (1994)

Does it matter that global society seems to be so disconnected from biophysical realities? We can approach this question by asking how the neo-classical paradigm fares in the light of complexity theory and modern interpretations of thermo-dynamic law. The second law is the starting point for any analysis of energy and material transformation. Since the economic process in the real world is very much about energy and material transformation, the second law is arguably the ultimate regulator of economic activity (Rees 1990). As previously noted, the material economy can be interpreted as human ecology and analysed as such. However, in addition to accounting for our direct biological needs, we also have to account for the material and energy flows associated with building and maintaining our consumer and capital goods, our houses, factories, the service infrastructure; in fact, all the accoutrements of modern life. Indeed, since the beginning of the industrial revolution, this industrial metabolism has grown vastly to exceed humans' own biological demands on the ecosphere.

Now, also like our bodies, the economy is a highly-ordered, dynamic, far-from-equilibrium dissipative structure (Rees 1996; 1998a). At the same time, it is an open, growing, sub-system of the materially closed, non-growing ecosphere (Daly 1992). It follows that the economy can grow and develop (that is, remain in a dynamic non-equilibrium state) only because it continuously extracts the energy and materials it requires from the ecosphere and discharges its wastes back into it. Unfortunately, the hierarchical nature of this relationship means that beyond a certain point it becomes pathological: *any further growth of the material economy can be purchased only at the expense of the dissipative destruction of the ecosphere.* This point occurs when consumption by the economy exceeds production in nature, or pollution exceeds assimilative capacity. It would be signalled by developments such as reduced biodiversity, deforestation, desertification, soil erosion, fisheries collapse, falling water tables, ozone depletion, acid rain, chronic pollution of air and water, atmospheric change or 'wobbly' climate; in other words, the stuff of environmental headlines today. The real-world empirical evidence supports the conclusions of eco-footprint and similar analyses: aggregate human demand already exceeds, and is steadily eroding, the very carrying capacity upon which continued human existence depends. From this perspective, ignorance of the second law by those working within the mainstream economic paradigm is a near-sufficient proximal explanation for the 'ecological crisis' and the material dimensions of the sustainability conundrum. Moving the argument one stage further, catastrophe theory suggests that as systems integrity is lost, we face the threat of unpredictable systems restructuring (for example, disruption of the Gulf Stream, or erratic climate change) as various sub-systems of the ecosphere are captured by new and hitherto invisible attractors. Most importantly, there is no reason to expect that any new equilibrium would support an acceptable quality of human existence. At the least, the loss of the particular autopoietic organisation that has produced and nurtured industrial 'man' will lead to resource shortages, increased local strife, and the heightened threat of ecologically induced geo-political instability.

None of the systems behaviours and phenomena described above are possible in, or captured by, prevailing economic models. The later are blind to biophysical structure and function. Thus, as the economy expands with apparently little friction, there is a finite possibility that for all the apparent success of technology in freeing us from the whims of nature, we may actually be 'on the verge of extinction, blissfully unaware that a mathematical fiction in the space of the possible is about to become reality. And the really nasty feature is that it may take only the tiniest of changes to trigger the switch' (Cohen and Stewart 1994: 212).

It seems that the very resilience of ecosystems has led us into a potentially fatal trap. Their self-organising and self-producing properties enable them to adapt to a broad range of exploitation rates without losing their fundamental character or productivity. In other words, autopoietic systems have strong attractors. Unfortunately, the absence of feedback that exploitation is pushing the system towards a bifurcation point merely reinforces present behaviour and fuels the fire of human hubris. The population increases and demand rises until, finally and with little warning, the catastrophic shift takes place. This is not just theory, but explains, among other things: the irreversible collapse of fisheries (Regier and Baskerville 1986; Cook, Sinclair and Stefánsson 1997); the eutrophication process in freshwater lakes, the human-induced climate change and desertification process in the Sahel (Mann 1987); and the failure of many large forest blocks in western North America to recover, even after several re-plantings, following extensive clear-cut logging (Perry *et al.* 1989). It may also help explain the collapse of many ancient civilisations.

SCALE, GOVERNANCE AND SUSTAINABILITY

The globalisation of the economy has resulted in an upward shift in the centre of economic power in recent decades. At the same time, both the intensity and spatial scale of so-called environmental problems have increased markedly. On one level these two trends are compatible. The geography of ecological change and economic policy and decision-making authority should coincide. However, there is a major problem with present trends. As the scale of the economy has increased, the conceptual models and institutional arrangements for managing it have become increasingly simplified, uniform and centralised. By contrast, as the size of the biophysical system(s) we are trying to 'manage' increases, so does the number of potentially interacting components. More importantly, the number of possible interactions rises even faster: the number of connections between members of pairs of components is nearly one-half the square of the number of components and, in biological systems, there are several types of possible interactions between members of a pair.[6] In short, potential systems complexity can very quickly exceed our capacity to deal with it, whatever our management model.

The divergence in complexity between our economic models and biophysical reality produces a violation of Ashby's law of Requisite Variety: the internal variety (diversity, organisational complexity) of a management system must correspond to the variety of the system being managed if the manager is to maintain control. In other words, 'we cannot regulate our interaction with any aspect of reality that our model of reality does not include' (Beer 1981). Ashby's law is applicable even to relatively simple mechanical systems: the pilot of a 747 is unlikely to be able to keep his aircraft in the air if he ignores all the controls but the throttle. It is all the more relevant when we are dealing with spatially diverse, far-from-equilibrium, autopoietic systems characterised by multiple invisible attractors. How can we hope to regulate our complex interactions with a chaotic ecosphere, or to maintain civil society, if our major management institutions focus mainly on maximising the efficiency of material growth?

This is not an argument against global institutions. Rather, it hints at an appropriate rule for structuring any hierarchy of institutional arrangements for the governance of the ecosphere. There should be a close correspondence between the spatial scale of a management level, the powers it can exercise, and the likelihood of its positively contributing to the sustainable behaviour of the system it is attempting to manage. International institutions and agreements are therefore essential to set out the ground rules for the behaviour of other entities – for instance, transnational corporations, nation-states and urban regions – further down the hierarchy. It is the role of national governments, albeit often through existing international agencies such as the UN, to negotiate international environmental treaties. There is a long history of international and even global treaties in the period since 1945, some more successful than others, dealing with specific problems in the management of the global commons (Sebenius 1984; Benedict 1991; Vogler 1995). Vogler (1995) lists twenty such agreements ranging from the general UN declaration on the human environment (from the Stockholm conference of 1972) through more specific treaties focusing on the oceans, Antarctica, the atmosphere, and even outer space. Among the best known of these is the UN Convention on the Law of the Sea of 1982. Sebenius (1984) identifies three critical factors which contributed to recognition of the need to clarify and revise the law of the sea: the vastly increased use of the oceans, the increase in conflicting ocean claims, and the inadequacy of existing law to deal with these problems. Analogous pressures in their particular focal areas inspired many of the other conventions.

The Montreal protocol on 'Substances That Deplete the Ozone Layer' (16 September 1987) mandated dramatic reductions in the use of chemicals that threatened the integrity of the ozone layer and is perhaps the best known of these transnational accords. Indeed, it is often heralded as a prototype agreement for a wide-ranging set of problems relating to global ecological change. Yet for all the success of this unique accord, it is clear that after ten years even the ozone problem is far from solved. Driven by greed, selfishness, and ignorance, the trade in contraband CFCs (ozone-destroying chemicals) is reported to be second in value only to that of cocaine in some US 'markets'. There are problems of non-compliance with certain provisions by some high-income countries and certain key ozone-depleting substances are not yet covered by the accord. Moreover some of the commonest substitutes for CFCs have now been found to be ozone depleting, although more weakly. Insufficient funds have been made available for the developing countries to meet their obligations under the treaty; thus, the use of CFCs in developing countries is actually increasing and some may not be able to meet their target for a freeze in consumption by 1999 and a total phase-out by 2010. Meanwhile the ozone layer continues to erode, and, even by the most optimistic projections, is unlikely to recover before 2050.

These realities highlight a critical problem with the conventional approach to managing global change. Even the best international agreements may only delay a crisis or buy a little time if it does not address the fundamental values and assumptions that created the problem in the first place. Most international resource and environmental treaties simply set out the rules for the orderly, competitive exploitation of common-pool sources and sinks by an ever-expanding economy. They do not question the growth paradigm itself. On a finite planet, mere reform at the margin risks ultimate failure.

CAN WE RELY ON TECHNOLOGY?

Critics might respond that I am exaggerating the risks. Growth advocates argue that techological efficiency gains can decouple growth from the environment by reducing the energy and material content of goods and services. Even in cases where resource depletion is unavoidable, techno-optimists say we need not be concerned because human ingenuity will find or invent a substitute. As the University of Maryland's famed growth advocate, Julian Simon, recently wrote: 'Technology exists now to produce in virtually inexhaustible quantities just about all the products made by nature', and 'We have in our hands now . . . the technology to feed, clothe, and supply energy to an ever-growing population for the next seven billion years' (Simon 1995).[7] Who is exaggerating now? However encouraging they might seem, such arguments are flawed. Great gains in technological efficiency in the North have been made in recent decades. Yet the most recent studies of resource flows in a selection of high-income countries found that their citizens now require 45–85 metric tons of natural resources *per capita* – including 17–38 metric tons of direct material inputs (excluding air and water) – to produce the goods and services they consume *every year*. Thus, while there has been some reduction in the ratio of resource inputs in these countries per unit GDP since 1975, there has also been 'in most, a gradual rise in *per capita* natural resource use'. We can only conclude that 'meaningful dematerialization, in the sense of an absolute reduction in natural resource use, is not yet taking place' (WRI 1997: 2). With this in mind, it is worth remembering that the bulk of global material growth in the next few decades will take place in the less-developed countries housing 75 per cent of the world's population. This growth starts from a much smaller base, and is even less likely to benefit from efficient technologies than growth in the developed world. It will necessarily produce prodigious increases in material flows.

We must also remember that politically powerful vested interests benefit in various ways from the continued expansion of consumption. In the wealthy countries, in order to ensure that demand remains high, a multi-billion dollar advertising industry is dedicated to exploiting people's natural insecurities. By undermining our sense of self-worth, by creating and emphasising symbols of social status, this industry helps stimulate material consumption far beyond the requirements for a good life. Of course, we never achieve satisfaction because next year's jazzier version of everything is on the store shelves before we have discarded the boxes in which this year's model arrived. If sometimes human wants seem insatiable, much of the blame lies here. Consumerism is a socially-constructed lifestyle. For these and other reasons, it is unlikely that growth will be decoupled from the ecosphere in the foreseeable future. This is no small concern. Based on the results of converging scientific studies (Ekins 1993; Ekins and Jacobs 1994; RMNO 1994), even the Business Council on Sustainable Development (BCSD) concurs that: 'Industrialised world reductions in material throughput, energy use, and environmental degradation of over 90 per cent will be required by 2040 to meet the needs of a growing world population fairly within the planet's ecological means' (BCSD 1993: 10).

As for the potential of technology to substitute for nature's goods and services, there are indeed many examples of the successful substitution of one familiar material or commodity for another: metal for wooden studs in construction, for instance. However, there is considerable debate as to whether such micro-economic successes can be extrapolated to the macro-economic level. The first question is whether we should accept the risk of plunging ahead on the assumption that human ingenuity can find a substitute for any of nature's services likely to be placed in jeopardy. Could we ever hope to replace the ozone layer? In any case, Kaufmann has recently shown that even if technology is able to substitute for certain of nature's services, to assume this capacity would be pointless. Because of the enormous hidden costs of shifting from consumption to investment in the substitutes 'it is not possible to substitute capital for environmental life support and maintain material well-being' (Kaufmann 1995).

These findings suggest that the conventional development path is failing on its own terms to bring society closer to a sustainable state at all spatial scales. It seems that governance for sustainability will have to take a more revolutionary approach in the future. This should start with an international dialogue among nations to re-assess the present situation and come to a more realistic understanding of the biophysics of the problem and its socio-economic implications.

OF CITIES AND URBAN REGIONS

One outcome of such a dialogue might be a better understanding of spatial relations and of the potential role of cities and urban regions in facilitating the transition to sustainability. Perhaps 75 per cent of the population in high-income countries already live in cities and estimates suggest that half of humanity will be urbanised by the year 2000. Approximately 73 per cent of the material consumption and waste production driving global change will therefore soon be taking place in cities. (Recall that ecological footprint analysis reveals cities to be intense nodes of consumption/pollution requiring the biophysical output of an area hundreds of times their geographic areas to sustain themselves.) This implies that cities and urban regions have the potential to make an enormous contribution to achieving sustainability, yet the municipal level is typically the politically weakest level of government. In Canada, for example, cities are the creatures of the provincial governments and are not even mentioned in the country's constitution. Clearly it is time to consider the devolution of adequate powers to cities to enable them to take advantage of their enormous leverage in the quest for sustainability (Rees and Wackernagel 1996; Rees 1998b). The role of international agreements and national laws would shift towards setting out common parameters of sustainability and enabling mechanisms for implementation.

There are many other reasons why cities and urban regions represent the appropriate spatial scale to apply sustainable development policy. Self-reliance, once a noble virtue, has become anathema to the free-trading world of today. However, in an era of real or incipient ecological change, it is time to reconsider the assumptions of the prevailing development model. Cities are increasingly vulnerable to the potentially damaging consequences of overconsumption and global ecological mismanagement. How economically and socially secure can a city of ten million people be if distant sources of food, water, energy or other critical resources are threatened by accelerating ecospheric change, increasing competition and dwindling supplies? Does any development pattern that increases inter-regional dependence on vital (but vulnerable) resource flows make ecological or geo-political sense? The data presented in this chapter suggests that circumstances may already warrant consideration of the potential benefits of greater ecological independence and intra-regional self-reliance.

Achieving significant progress in this area will be difficult for some large urban regions with limited natural capital assets: for example, supplying London alone would require virtually the entire biophysical output of the UK (IIED 1995). An alternative (or supplementary) response is for vulnerable urban regions to negotiate more formal long-term relationships (including international treaties through the facilities of national governments) with producer territories to help ensure reliable supplies of biophysical goods and services. In effect, such agreements acknowledge and formalise portions of the distant ecological footprints of the consumer regions. This is not as far-fetched as it seems. One example – partially in anticipation of global warming – is that Japan currently has nearly 1.5 per cent of Ontario, Canada's cropland under long-term contract to supply a variety of bean crops to the Japanese market.

To reduce their dependence on external flows, more politically powerful urban regions may choose to implement policies to rehabilitate their own natural capital stocks and to promote the use of local fisheries, forests and agricultural land. This makes sense in several ways. First, it would result in a more reasonable and manageable match in scale between the management unit and the ecosystems being managed. Local people, over time, acquire intimate knowledge of local systems and have a better chance of maintaining control over a discrete number of key management variables. Second, people who depend directly on a resource system are more likely to manage it for the long term. Off-shore owners of local resources who are attempting merely to maximise returns on capital have a strong incentive to liquidate natural capital stocks if alternative investments produce a higher return. Everyone is eventually impoverished by this process. Third, a philosophy of locally-based resource management may enable the establishment or re-establishment of effective common-property management regimes at the community level for mobile resources such as fisheries or for community forests. There is now a rich literature describing how small-scale, self-organising and self-managed common property regimes have flourished around the world for decades, providing a model of sustainable management (Berkes 1989; Vogler 1995). In addition to the sustainable management of resource stocks, such regimes build community and a commitment to place. This is clearly lacking in prevailing circumstances in which transnational corporations own and control local resource stocks, and harvests are orientated more towards maximising production and profit than sustaining people and community. Finally, if each significant urban region were to manage its own territorial resources in a sustainable manner, and enter into only ecologically balanced and socially fair exchanges with other regions, then the aggregate effect would be global sustainability.

Policy in support of increased local self-reliance would obviously require violations of existing and planned international agreements to liberalise commodity trade and capital flows. The point, of course, is that as presently conceived, these agreements are the antithesis of sustainability. This is not to say that trade is inherently bad. Indeed, ecological footprint and similar analyses show that many nations could not survive in anything like their current forms without trade. However, not all trade is sustainable (Rees 1994). Sustainable trade would restrict trade to necessary or desirable flows that do not deplete critical natural capital stocks. This will be commerce in true biophysical surpluses. I have elsewhere advocated negotiation of a General Agreement on the Integrity of (Ecological) Assets – a GAIA agreement – to regulate economic activities affecting the global life-support system, including patterns of commercial trade in ecologically signifi-cant commodities (Rees 1994). Such an agreement would set the ecological 'bottom line' for such existing instruments as GATT and the WTO. All of this represents an argument for a restoration of balance between the forces of local cohesion and globalisation. The increase in welfare from enhanced food security, improved environmental quality, greater local control and stronger communities would offset any loss in gross economic product. Increasing the self-reliance of urban regions would also result in significant net savings of energy and material currently used in the global transportation of goods.

In this context, should we not also be reconsidering how we define city systems, both conceptually and spatially? Perhaps it is time to think of cities as whole systems. As such, they comprise not just the node of concentrated activity as presently conceived, but also the entire supportive hinterland. Many city regions could be re-organised formally to incorporate much of their supportive hinter-land into their political realms. Short of so great a conceptual leap, there is much that can be done incrementally to increase the sustainability of our cities. For example, in the domain of land use, planners and politicians should find ways to (from Rees 1997):

- integrate planning for city size/form, urban density, and settlement (nodal) patterns in ways that minimise the energy, material, and land use require-ments of cities and their inhabitants;
- capitalise on the multifunctionality of green areas (for example, aesthetic, carbon sink, climate modification, food production functions) both within and outside the city;
- integrate open space planning with other policies to increase local self-reliance as regards food production, forest products, water supply, carbon sinks, and so on (for example, domestic waste systems should be designed to enable the recycling of compost back on to regional agricultural and forest lands);
- protect the integrity and productivity of local ecosystems to reduce the eco-logical load imposed on distant systems and the global common pool;
- strive for zero-impact development. The destruction of ecosystems and related biophysical services due to urban growth in one area should be com-pensated for by equivalent ecosystem rehabilitation in another.

All such measures bring us closer to recognising 'the city' as the central place in a spatially extended human ecosystem (the total human patch) and therefore as the appropriate locus for the implementation of materially significant sustainability initiatives.

EPILOGUE

> Progress means getting nearer the place you want to be. And if you take a wrong
> turning, then to go forward does not get you any nearer. If you are on the wrong
> road, progress means doing an about face and walking back to the right road, and
> in that case the man who turns back the soonest is the most progressive man.
>
> C. S. Lewis in *Mere Christianity*

In this chapter I have argued that the prevailing international development paradigm is unsustainable. For the most part, the global growth model ignores biophysical reality, the behavioural quirks of complex systems, and the social context
of development. Where problems are recognised they are treated as temporary
aberrations amenable to technical quick fixes. Otherwise, sheer growth is perceived as containing the solution to every socio-economic problem. A more
biophysically realistic approach would require acknowledgement that present
levels of material consumption already exceed the long-term carrying capacity of
the Earth and that the consumer lifestyles of high income countries cannot be
extended sustainably to the entire human population with prevailing technology.
It would also recognise that all new development should be zero-impact development (that is, it should not result in net natural capital depletion). At the least this
would shift the emphasis in sustainability planning from quantitative growth
towards qualitative development.

There is, of course, room for compromise between these perspectives but even
compromise requires a 90 per cent reduction in the energy and material content
of industrial production. This efficiency goal is clearly beyond attainment under
prevailing market conditions, yet vested interests and sheer political inertia inhibit
the implementation of ecological fiscal reforms that might stimulate the private
sector to achieve it. In these circumstances, it is foolish and dangerous for society
to rely on technological and economic solutions alone to 'handle' the sustainability problem. In the final analysis, it seems that achieving sustainability may not
be as much about technology as it is about meaning, values and behaviour.
Indeed, focusing on behavioural change may be the most effective strategy to
address the sustainability conundrum, particularly in the so-called 'advanced
economies': 'It is also the most ethically responsible strategy in many cases, since it
demands that solutions to problems be located in their source: humans, their
behaviour, and their institutions' (Jamieson 1996). The point is that people can
learn to live more materially simple lives and be the better for it. It seems that
from the 'dialectic of denial' springs an opportunity for people to explore what it
means to be more fully human. While accepting that this argument requires a
dramatic about-turn in global development patterns, it is actually consistent with
much economic and social theory. Welfare is based on much more than rising
incomes. Certainly there is a need for income growth in less developed countries,
but this is not the whole story. An ecologically and socially sound approach to
sustainability would restore balance to the sustainable development of human

beings. A whole person needs a sense of belonging, of community, and of person-hood in addition to material security. Getting serious about sustainability also requires reconciling tensions across spatial scales. Complexity theory suggests we are unlikely ever to be able to 'manage' the world safely as a unit. A higher prob-ability of maintaining control – or at least of staying within the desired domain of systems stability – resides at the community and bio-regional levels. Paradoxically, it seems that if we concentrate on the welfare of individuals and the sustainability of their local communities, global sustainability may take care of itself.

Notes

1 Predictably, with the exception of a passing reference to modern humans as 'primary agents of environmental change', people are not included in this special issue of the journal on 'How Animals Shape Their Ecosystems'.
2 The food category includes both a terrestrial (crop- and grazing land) and a marine component, the latter based on seafood consumption. The fossil energy component is based on the area of dedicated carbon sink forest that would be required to assimilate carbon dioxide emissions.
3 Contrast this with the usual economic perspective on cities as productive centres of civilisation and the engines of national growth.
4 The sustainability conundrum is clearly largely a product of so-called First World lifestyles.
5 Kay (1991) refers to the stable domain and its attractor as a 'thermodynamic branch' and 'optimum operating point' respectively.
6 For example, the minimum number of possible interactions among pairs of just 100 objects is 4950.
7 Professor Simon later corrected this statement to read 'for seven million years', but as physicist Albert Bartlett (1996) has shown, even 1 per cent annual growth over this much reduced time frame would result in a human population 30,000 orders of magnitude larger than the estimated number of atoms in the known universe!

References

Ayres, R. (1994) *Information, Entropy and Progress: A New Evolutionary Paradigm*, Woodbury, NY: AIP Press.
Bartlett, A. (1996) 'The Exponential Function XI: The New Flat Earth Society' *The Physics Teacher* 34: 342–3.
BCSD (1993) *Getting Eco-Efficient*, Report of the BCSD First Antwerp Eco-Efficiency Workshop, November 1993, Geneva: Business Council for Sustainable Development.
Beer, S. (1981) 'I said, you are gods', *Tielhard Review* 15: 1–33.
Benedict, R. (1991) *Ozone Diplomacy: New Directions in Safeguarding the Planet*, Cambridge, Mass.: Harvard University Press.
Berkes, F. (ed.) (1989) *Common Property Resources: Ecology and Community-Based Sustainable Development*, London: Belhaven Press.
BioScience (1988) 38, 11 – special issue on 'How Animals Shape their Ecosystems'.
Capra, F. (1996) *The Web of Life*, New York: Anchor Books.
Christensen, P. (1991) 'Driving forces, increasing returns, and ecological sustainability', in A.-M. Jansson, M. Hammer, C. Folke, and R. Costanza (eds) *Investing in Natural Capital: The Ecological Economics Approach to Sustainability*, Washington, DC: Island Press.

Cohen, J. and Stewart, I. (1994) *The Collapse of Chaos*, New York: Penguin Books.

Cook, R., Sinclair, A. and Stefánsson, G. (1997) 'Potential collapse of North Sea cod stocks', *Nature*, 385: 521–2.

Daly, H. (1992) 'The concept of a steady-state economy', in *Steady-State Economics*, Washington, DC: Island Press.

Daly, H. and Cobb. J. (1989) *For the Common Good*, Boston, Mass.: Beacon Press.

Diamond, J. (1992) *The Third Chimpanzee*, New York: HarperCollins.

Drengson, A. (1989) 'Protecting the environment, protecting ourselves: reflections on the philosophical dimension', in R. Bradley and S. Duguid (eds), *Environmental Ethics: Volume Two*, Vancouver: Simon Fraser University.

Ekins, P. (1993) '"Limits to growth" and "sustainable development": grappling with ecological realities', *Ecological Economics* 8: 269–88.

Ekins, P. and Jacobs, M. (1994) 'Are environmental sustainability and economic growth compatible?', in *Energy-Environment-Economy Modelling Discussion Paper No. 7*, Cambridge: Department of Applied Economics, University of Cambridge.

Folke, C., Jansson, A., Larsson, J. and Costanza, R. (1997) 'Ecosystem Appropriation by Cities', *Ambio* 26: 167–72.

Goodland, R. (1991) 'The case that the world has reached limits', in R. Goodland, H. Daly, S. El Serafy and B. Von Droste (eds), *Environmentally Sustainable Economic Development: Building on Brundtland*, Paris: UNESCO.

Heuting, R. (1996) 'Three persistent myths in the environmental debate', *Ecological Economics* 18: 81–8.

Hunt, S. (1989) 'The alternative economics movement', *Interculture* XXII, 1: Issue No.102.

IIED (1995) *Citizen Action to Lighten Britain's Ecological Footprint*, Report prepared by the IIED for the UK Department of the Environment, London: IIED.

Jamieson, D. (1996) 'Ethics and intentional climate change', *Climatic Change* 33: 323–36.

Kaufmann, R. (1995) 'The economic multiplier of environmental life support: can capital substitute for a degraded environment?' *Ecological Economics* 12: 67–79.

Kay, J. (1991) 'A nonequilibrium thermodynamic framework for discussing ecosystem integrity', *Environmental Management* 15: 483–95.

Kay, J. and Schneider, E. (1994) 'Embracing complexity: the challenge of the ecosystem approach', *Alternatives* 20: 32–9.

Logan, J. (1996) 'Patch disturbance and the human niche', Manuscript at <http://csf.Colorado.EDU/authors/hanson/page78.htm >. (also, pers. comm. 1997, and e-mail exchanges with the author on patch disturbance).

Mann, R. (1987) 'Development and the Sahel disaster: the case of the Gambia', *The Ecologist* 17: 84–90.

Margulis, L. and Sagan, D. (1986) *What is Life?*, New York: Simon & Schuster.

Maturana, H. (1980) 'Biology of cognition', in Maturana and Varela (1980).

Maturana, H. and Varela, F. (1980) *Autopoiesis and Cognition*, Dordrecht, Netherlands: D. Reidel.

Maturana, H. and Varela, F. (1987) *The Tree of Knowledge*, Boston, Mass.: Shambala.

Naiman, R.J. (1988) 'Animal influences on ecosystem dynamics', *BioScience*, 38: 750–2.

Perry, D., Amaranthus, M., Borchers, J., Borchers, S. and Brainerd, R. (1989) 'Bootstrapping In Ecosystems', *BioScience* 39: 230–7.

Ponting, C. (1991) *A Green History of the World*, London: Sinclair-Stevenson.

Rees, W. (1990) 'The Ecology of Sustainable Development', *The Ecologist* 20: 18–23.

Rees, W. (1994) 'Pressing Global Limits: Trade as the Appropriation of Carrying

Capacity', in T. Schrecker and J. Dalgleish (eds), *Growth, Trade and Environmental Values*, London, Ontario: Westminster Institute for Ethics and Human Values.

Rees, W. (1995) 'Achieving sustainability: reform or transformation?', *Journal of Planning Literature* 9: 343–61.

Rees, W. (1996) 'Revisiting carrying capacity: Area-based indicators of sustainability', *Population and Environment* 17: 195–215.

Rees, W. (1997) 'Is "sustainable city" an oxymoron?', *Local Environment* 2: 303–10.

Rees, W. (1998) 'Consuming the earth: The biophysics of sustainability', *Ecological Economics*.

Rees, W. and Wackernagel, M. (1994) 'Ecological footprints and appropriated carrying capacity: measuring the natural capital requirements of the human economy', in A.-M. Jansson, M. Hammer, C. Folke and R. Costanza (eds), *Investing in Natural Capital: The Ecological Economics Approach to Sustainability*, Washington, DC: Island Press.

Rees, W. and Wackernagel, M. (1996) 'Urban ecological footprints: why cities cannot be sustainable and why they are a key to sustainability', *Environmental Impact Assessment Review* 16: 223–48.

Regier, H. and Baskerville, G. (1986) 'Sustainable redevelopment of regional ecosystems degraded by exploitive development', in W. Clark and R. Munn (eds), *Sustainable Development of the Biosphere*, Cambridge: Cambridge University Press.

RMNO (1994) *Sustainable Resource Management and Resource Use: Policy Questions and Research Needs*. Publication No. 97, Rijswijk, The Netherlands: Advisory Council for Research on Nature and Environment (RMNO).

Sachs, W. (1990) 'The archeology of the development idea', *Interculture* XXIII, 4: Issue 109.

Schafer, D. (1994) 'Cultures and economies: irresistable forces encounter immovable objects', *Futures* 26: 830–45.

Schneider, E. and Kay, J. (1992) 'Life as a manifestation of the second law of thermo-dynamics', Waterloo, Ontario: University of Waterloo Faculty of Environmental Studies, Working Paper Series.

Sebenius, J.K. (1984) *Negotiating the Law of the Sea*, Cambridge, Mass.: Harvard University Press.

Simon, J. (1995) 'The State of Humanity: Steadily Improving', *Cato Policy Report* 17:5, Washington, DC: The Cato Institute.

Sismondi, J. Simonde de. (1991) *New Principles of Political Economy: Of Wealth in its Relation to Population*, London: Transaction (1st edn 1827).

Stewart, I. (1989) *Does God Play Dice?*, Cambridge, Mass.: Blackwell.

Tainter, J. (1988) *The Collapse of Complex Societies*, Cambridge: Cambridge University Press.

UNDP (United Nations Development Programme) (1992) *Human Development Report*, New York: Oxford University Press.

Viederman, S. (1994) 'Public policy: Challenge to ecological economics', in A-M. Jansson, M. Hammer, C. Folke and R. Costanza (eds), *Investing in Natural Capital: The Ecological Economics Approach to Sustainability*, Washington, DC: Island Press.

Vogler, J. (1995) *The Global Commons: A Regime Analysis*, Chichester: John Wiley.

Wackernagel, M. and Rees, W. (1996) *Our Ecological Footprint: Reducing Human Impact on the Earth*, Gabriola Island, BC, and Philadelphia, PA: New Society Publishers.

Wackernagel, M., Onisto, L., Linares, A., Lalfán, I., Garcia, J., Guerro, A., and Guerrero, M. (1997) *Ecological Footprints of Nations*, Report to the Earth Council, Costa Rica.

WCED (World Commission on Environment and Development) (1987) *Our Common Future*, Oxford: Oxford University Press for the UN World Commission on Economy and Environment.

Wilson, E.O. (1988) 'The current state of biological diversity', in E.O.Wilson (ed.), *Biodiversity*, Washington, DC: National Academy Press.

WRI (World Resources Institute) (1997) *Resource Flows: The Material Basis of Industrial Economies* (WRI/Wuppertal Institute/Netherlands Ministry of Housing/National Institute for Environmental Studies), Washington, DC: WRI.

6 From sustainability to basic income

Wouter Achterberg

In this chapter I will argue that planning for sustainability should include planning for a basic income, which is an 'income unconditionally paid to all on an individual basis, without means test or work requirement' (Van Parijs 1992: 3). The process of planning for sustainability should be comprehensive, but also democratic and iterative. Yet sustainability is an 'essentially contested' (Gallie 1956) concept just like the ideas of democracy and justice. Some discussion of the concept is therefore unavoidable. On the basis of a brief analysis, I argue for a conception of strong sustainability. I also make clear in a preliminary way why planning for a basic income is important if one wants to plan for sustainability. In the second section I try to show why the introduction of a basic income is ideally suited to overcome the dysfunctions of present welfare states and why that is important to our collective project of making patterns of production and consumption sustainable. The argument in this section is empirical and pragmatic: existing welfare state regimes do not seem very successful in providing social security for enough people at a sufficient level. What reforms are required to realise this goal more effectively, especially if one also wants a 'greening' of the welfare state? I shall argue that the introduction of a basic income might be an important part of the answer. If correct, my arguments identify and justify an important element in a 'win-win' solution for the problems of the welfare state on the way to sustainable patterns of production and consumption. In the last section of this chapter I will show how a basic income and strong sustainability can be ethically justified in a mutually coherent way, arguing that planning for a basic income and planning for sustainability are both legitimate in terms of a moral starting point which can be acceptable to all. In fact, appreciating the legitimacy of each institution may facilitate planning for both.

After having summarised the content of the chapter by sections, it may be helpful to sketch out its rather complex argument. Essentially, the argument consists of three strands. The *first* strand (mostly in the first section on sustainability) connects (strong) sustainability and basic income. What a basic income means to sustainability is explained in instrumental terms. It will be pointed out that, given the potentially far-reaching consequences of establishing sustainable patterns of production and consumption, democratic planning for sustainability requires the broadest possible participation of all concerned (see the sections starting on pp. 130 and 132). This is especially important in view of the social process of learning to live and consume sustainably. For in this case 'all concerned' includes the unemployed, involuntary or not, partially or fully, and so on (see the sections starting on pp. 130 and 138). At the very least, a basic income facilitates, and it is to be hoped encourages, broad social participation. The *second* strand (anticipated on p. 132, and developed in the sections starting on pp. 136 and 137) highlights an important aspect of the social context of planning for sustainability (in the developed countries): ailing welfare states in a resurgent capitalism. The proposed remedy, a basic income, looks promising. The suitability of a basic income as an instrument of planning is briefly discussed in the section on p. 137. This second strand is not a sidetrack, but basic to the objective of finding 'win-win' solutions in planning for sustainability. In other words, a no-regret strategy is proposed. The *third* strand concerns the ethical justification (see p. 134, the beginning of the section starting on p. 135, and also the section starting on p. 140). It will be argued that the effort to pursue sustainability, the commitment to maintain a welfare state regime (in a capitalist context, that is, the relevant context for sustainability planning in developed countries today), and the introduction of a basic income are ultimately a matter of *justice*, inter-generational and intra-generational (social) justice. Presumably, though, the ethical argument for a basic income in the strict sense may not be able to do without considerations of efficiency. For those who find this third part of the argument rough going, the more pragmatic and empirical parts of the exposition should make the essential thrust of the case being made sufficiently clear.

SUSTAINABILITY

To begin with, some discussion of the idea of sustainability is necessary before we can go on to explore what taking sustainability seriously implies for the institutions of the welfare state.

Although the concept of sustainability has been in use since the beginning of the 1970s (and precursor ideas such as that of a 'stationary state' go back even further), it has been since the report of the WCED in 1987 that sustainability has come to dominate our thinking about environmental problems and policy. Yet it remains doubtful whether our use of nature and the environment has become quite so sustainable as the frequent invocation of this protean concept in public policy circles might suggest.

A convenient point, then, from which to start the discussion is the concept of sustainability as used by the WCED in the context of their idea of sustainable development. This is a development constrained by a sustainable use of finite resources: that is, a use such that not only the present but also future generations can have the potential to meet their needs. However, sustainable use must not be at the expense of the legitimate aspirations of the poorer countries to meet the vital needs of their current populations. Thus, a process of development has to take place in these countries, a process which includes much more than just economic growth. A main preoccupation of the WCED was that without more just relations today – within and particularly between nation-states, especially between rich and poor countries – the prospect of reaching a more sustainable world would remain slim. To sum up, in the words of the WCED:

> Sustainable development is development that meets the needs of the present generation without compromising the ability of future generations to meet their own needs. It contains within it two key concepts:
> – the concept of 'needs', in particular the essential needs of the world's poor, to which overriding priority should be given; and
> – the idea of limitations imposed by the state of technology and social organization on the environment's ability to meet present and future needs.
>
> (WCED 1987: 43)

The perspective of the WCED raises a number of questions concerning sustainability that must be answered to establish the normative constraints which should govern the process of making society more environmentally benign.

The meaning of sustainability

What exactly is it that is supposed to be sustainable, or to become (more) sustainable? Although reference is often made to a 'sustainable society', this is actually a derived usage of the concept of sustainability. Above all sustainability relates to the consumption of natural resources in the broad sense of 'environmental utilization' (Opschoor 1995). And such use must be maintained for at least fifty, or seventy-five or even one hundred years into the future. Next, sustainable environmental consumption has to be embodied in sustainable patterns of production and consumption (one of the main themes of Agenda 21). Furthermore, it appears that establishing such patterns will take some doing, and may profoundly alter the structure of present-day industrial society. In other words, the emergence of a sustainable society would seem the only way to get sustainable patterns of production and consumption. Some aspects of these structural changes are raised by WCED when it conceives of sustainable development as a 'process of change in which the exploitation of resources, the direction of investments, the orientation of technological development and institutional change are all in harmony and enhance both current and future potential to meet human needs and aspirations' (WCED 1987: 9, 46).

Some institutional patterns merit special attention here because deep tensions between their current mode of operation and the pursuit of sustainability are evident: especially the market economy, the political institutions of democracy in a market-dominated society, and existing property relations (Achterberg 1994). The call for institutional reform should not be seen as an invitation for utopian engineering or planning, or as an encouragement to limit ourselves just to 'piecemeal' engineering. If we compare the institutional order to a house, we might suggest that in this case we do not need a completely new house (yet), and yet leaving the house essentially intact by making just a few changes will not work either. According to de Geus (1996), from whom I have borrowed this metaphor, what we need is something in between: 'a "restructuring" ' – rebuilding the house where 'the existing house is more or less thoroughly altered, rebuilt, reconstructed, to comply with the newly formulated demands'. Thus in 'large part the house stays the same, yet simultaneously it undergoes a structural change'. During the rebuilding one goes on living in the house, and 'plans can be re-adjusted' and one can learn from one's mistakes (de Geus 1996: 199–200).

Thus, planning for sustainable development can be comprehensive, but not in the manner of erstwhile communist command planning, or in the traditional social democratic manner of the Keynesian welfare state. It includes sectoral environmental planning (modest or advanced). But if one defines 'planning for sustainable development' as a 'conscious process of social choice to select and realise a preferred, and sustainable, development trajectory' (Meadowcroft 1997: 172), one of the important problems is how to conceive such a conscious process of social choice. As I emphasise below, it must include a process of social learning, a process in which one discovers collectively how to produce and consume sustainably, and how to institutionalise such patterns. On the one hand governments at different levels can and should initiate, stimulate and channel the learning process and the social debates involved in it, without steering them in directions they or powerful social interests prefer. On the other hand, in view of the social support necessary for *democratic* planning, it is essential that as many citizens as possible can participate in this learning process. Citizens should have the time and resources to participate if they so wish, and they should also have adequate information. Furthermore the results of this process should be taken seriously, especially if it points to the need for institutional reform. The process of planning involved has been called an 'iterative rather than linear planning process. That is, it involves repeated cycles of learning (often by trial and error) and reconsideration, which gradually move people's beliefs and transform community concerns into action' (Wackernagel and Rees 1996: 137).

I believe that a basic income provides the financial security which facilitates a broad participation in the social process of learning to live sustainably. The importance of a basic income is not simply restricted to facilitating broader participation. Another aspect deserves particular emphasis here: how to move to sustainable patterns of consumption and lifestyles. This requires the broadest possible participation, not only by those who have acquired paid work via the labour market. The voluntary, and especially those who are not voluntary, unemployed need some minimal social independence and financial security to be able to find out, alone or together, what a sustainable lifestyle involves. As I try to make clear in the section starting on p. 134 below, a basic income offers all its beneficiaries the opportunity to explore a variety of sustainable lifestyles.

Futhermore, a basic income is a suitable instrument in the context of planning for sustainable development because, as I also point out in the section on sustainability, the welfare state and basic income, it can be introduced flexibly, at a pace and level dependent on the state of other sectors of society. Additionally, it can be funded in a way which contributes to making our patterns of production and consumption less unsustainable: that is, from one or another kind of ecotax. Obviously, the meaning of a basic income is not exhausted by this instrumental view of it, as will become clear in later sections of this chapter.

Thus the most important institutional change discussed here will be the introduction of a basic income, in connection with a restructuring of the welfare state, as a concrete context of planning for sustainability. To anticipate what will be elaborated below, I will here indicate in a general way what I understand as the decisive significance of a basic income to our collective efforts to pursue sustainability.

The first thing to note is that in the rich countries there has been a substantial increase in social inequality since the 1970s. Additionally, involuntary unemployment (masked and unmasked) has become high (about 10 per cent) and seems set to remain high. Partly as a result of this there has been a strong tendency in all welfare states to cut back on the existing systems of social security, although one would have thought that in this situation the moral weight of the claims of social justice should increase. Of great importance also is the fact that nation-states have increasingly less control over the national economy given their involvement in an as yet untamed capitalistic world market. In this situation the introduction of an unconditional basic income for all adult citizens may well be an essential step towards maintaining the valuable arrangements of the welfare state and thereby honouring the demands of social justice. The weight of these demands increases if we focus on the relations between rich and poor countries, and all the more so if we see them in the context of the pursuit of global sustainability and its prospects for limitations on the growth of material production. The introduction of a basic income may also help to bring about the broad public participation required to keep the process of planning for sustainability democratic throughout. This is especially important if sustainable patterns of consumption and sustainable lifestyles are to be established which people accept voluntarily and with understanding. To sum up, in the given circumstances of the rich countries, the introduction of a basic income may well be the most important means to create a situation which is ecologically and socially sustainable without endangering democracy.

Sustainability as a constraint

Sustainability itself is supposed to function as a constraint. But on what exactly? On our use of resources, apparently; but which resources and in what way?

The WCED implies that the total resources available to the next generation should be not less than the total with which the present generation started. The 'capital' left to them does not only include man-made goods like equipment and technological knowledge, but also natural resources or 'natural capital' (WCED 1987: 52 ff., 57 ff.). This raises the question of whether only the aggregated capital should be sustainable or whether the separate categories (in the simplest case: man-made and natural), or even specific parts of these categories, should be too.

Possible answers to this question vary from (very) strong to (very) weak forms of sustainability.[1] In strong forms of sustainability many (or in the absurdly strong version even all) natural resources are conceived to be somehow special with respect to production or consumption. They cannot or should not be substituted by man-made capital; they are complementary to it. Therefore they have to be transferred as such to the next generation. The WCED views sustainability in a weak sense: the aim of environmental policy should be to maintain opportunities for human welfare across generations and the composition of the bundle of resources to be passed on, and by implication the protection of the environment, or of nature, is subordinate to that aim (Norton 1992).

The debate about whether sustainability should be conceived as strong or weak is a bit curious if El Serafy is right. As he points out (1996: 75–81), weak sustainability inherently has nothing to do with environmental concerns. It is based on the economist's idea of income, with natural resources added in as a type of (natural) capital. Specifically, it is based on John Hick's definition of income: 'we ought to define a man's income as the maximum value which he can consume during a week, and still expect to be as well off at the end of the week as he was at the beginning' (Hicks 1946: 172). The point of this very sensible definition is to gauge income and growth of income in the given period, and in order to do that, 'capital, *including natural capital*, must be kept intact,' as El Serafy makes clear. Weak sustainability generalises, so to speak, Hicksian income across generations (at least this generation and the next). But, again, this has nothing yet to do with environmental concerns. These come into their own only in the concept of strong sustainability. Using that concept we express our belief that (some) natural resources have become the limiting factor in our use of the environment and should be considered as complementary to, and not substitutable by, other categories of capital. It should be clear from this explanation that the concept of strong sustainability does not replace the concept of weak sustainability but builds upon it. But because the concept of weak sustainability has inherently nothing particular to do with environmental considerations, I will not discuss it any more. For the purpose of this chapter, sustainability should be taken to mean strong sustainability.

The adoption of a strong conception of sustainability will lead to some simple and practical rules which can function as more specific sustainability constraints: for example, Daly's 'output rule' and 'input rules'. According to these rules projects 'should be designed (constrained) so that':

Output rule: waste outputs are within the natural absorptive capacities of the environment (i.e., nondepletion of the sink services of natural capital);
Input rules: (a) For renewable inputs, harvest rates should not exceed regeneration rates (nondepletion of the source services of natural capital). (b) For nonrenewable inputs the rate of depletion should be equal to the rate at which renewable substitutes can be developed. If a renewable stock is consciously divested (i.e. exploited nonrenewably), it should be subject to the rule for nonrenewables (Daly 1995: 50).[2]

Of course, these rules do not imply any 'hard' or objective constraints. It is misguided to expect a purely scientific specification of these rules. As Weterings and Opschoor put it: the 'most fundamental reason is that making pre-scientific choices and introducing value judgments are inevitable regarding several issues such as: which biospheric elements to preserve and at what levels, which degrees of risk can be taken, and how to handle uncertainties and lack of knowledge' (Weterings and Opschoor 1994: 227; WRR 1995). To be more specific, changing scientific knowledge, statistical uncertainties, more fundamental uncertainties in the face of competing causal explanations, estimations of reserves of resources, expectations of technological developments, attitudes towards risk and even values make it difficult to determine the hard empirical limits required if the output and input rules are to generate clear, unambiguous and precise action guides. There is nothing we can do about that, for *all* parties to the debate on planning for sustainability have to live with this; something we should not forget when debating with those who disagree with us about the implications of sustainability. Obviously this does not mean that anything goes in the debate on the normative and policy implications of sustainability.[3] Some arguments are still better and some reasons stronger than others.

The impossibility of specifying in a purely scientific or objective way what the goal of (strong) sustainability implies provides a fundamental reason, rather than just one from political expediency, as to why the process of planning for sustainability should be democratic. This process should not be top-down and expert-dominated, but to an important extent bottom-up and based on broad participation in the process of social learning involved in the collective effort to establish sustainable patterns of production and consumption.

The normative basis of sustainability

Why should we adopt the constraints of strong sustainability? What is their normative basis? To judge from the WCED, it seems to be a conception of *justice*, in particular of social or distributive justice, applied inter- and intra-generationally. The essential question is: how to distribute access to, and control over, resources between people of the present generation – living here or in other parts of the globe – and between us and future generations?[4]

To say more about a conception of justice, we need to elaborate it theoretically. There are several choices possible here, of course, but we do not necessarily require a fully-fledged theory of justice. It is sufficient for the purposes of this chapter to invoke a basic normative principle that is strong enough to generate principles of intra- and inter-generational (distributive) justice and, moreover, compatible with a wide range of existing theories of justice. Thus, the moral core of sustainability could be articulated in a way which is acceptable to adherents of a broad spectrum of theories of justice. This is also a boon for a democratic process of planning for sustainability. Let us look briefly at one approach to articulating such a basic principle: a liberal-egalitarian perspective proposed by Dworkin.

Dworkin's point of departure is a principle of abstract equality. Initially formulated in an article on Rawls as the principle that 'individuals have a right to equal concern and respect in the design and administration of the political institutions that govern them' (Dworkin 1977: 180), he offered in the same book a more comprehensive version:

> Government must treat those whom it governs with concern, that is, as human beings who are capable of suffering and frustration, and with respect, that is, as human beings who are capable of forming and acting on intelligent conceptions of how their lives should be lived. Government must not only treat people with concern and respect, but with equal concern and respect.
>
> (Dworkin 1977: 272)

Six years later he proposed a generalised version of this principle, called the 'abstract egalitarian thesis', which states that from 'the standpoint of politics, the interests of the members of the community matter, and matter equally' (Dworkin 1983: 24). This means that the members of the community should treat each other as equals, and that all of them, taken one by one, are entitled to equal consideration; it does not necessarily mean that they are entitled to equal treatment. Dworkin considers this principle of abstract or fundamental equality as the 'egalitarian plateau' (Dworkin 1983: 25) on which all serious modern political theories find themselves and from which they have to derive the political, social and economic conditions under which the members of the community must be treated as equals (see also Kymlicka 1990: 4–5). This plateau, from which many different destinations can be reached, might seem too abstract to generate specific conclusions. But the distribution of natural resources is the main subject to be treated in terms of the egalitarian plateau and I will show in the section entitled 'Sustainability and Basic Income: Normative Connections' that, starting from it, sufficiently specific conclusions can be generated concerning basic income and inter-generational justice. First, however, we should discuss the more empirical and pragmatic connections between sustainability, the welfare state and basic income.

SUSTAINABILITY, WELFARE STATE AND BASIC INCOME

My focus throughout this section will be on rich and capitalistic societies. The obvious objection to this is that sustainable patterns of production and consumption will have to be established worldwide, including the poor countries. Sustainability in one country or region is not possible, even if it were morally acceptable. None the less a special responsibility in promoting and adopting these patterns, especially sustainable patterns of consumption, rests with the rich countries. Moreover, they have perhaps not yet the will but at least the means and the knowledge to make the transition to a sustainable society. But are they institutionally equal to this task? The WCED envisaged a comprehensive programme of institutional reform in order to negotiate the transition to a sustainable develop-ment. A part of this programme, a very important part given the emphasis for rich countries of a shift to more sustainable lifestyles, concerns the system of social security.

The basic question in this section, then, is what institutional changes to the welfare state (which rests on 'state responsibility for securing some basis modicum of welfare for its citizens': Esping-Andersen 1990: 19), are required to support collective efforts to make these societies less unsustainable? In other words, what type of welfare state is congenial to a green market economy: that is, a capitalist market economy constrained by the rules of strong sustainability? Putting the question in this way, I presuppose that capitalism in one form or another is going to stay, at least for the foreseeable future, whether we like it or not. I also assume that a capitalist economy requires a complementary system of social security to be viable in the long run (Dryzek 1996: 29–31) and to be morally acceptable (Goodin 1988), from the point of view of social justice, for example. Some qualification of this is perhaps necessary. The element of viability in the long run should be restricted to viability in a liberal democratic context. In an authoritarian political context capitalism might survive for some time even without a robust social safety-net. Fortunately, we do not have to contemplate seriously this undesirable con-figuration given the current situation in the rich countries. Also, to be morally acceptable a capitalist economy requires at least minimal welfare arrangements because otherwise it may very well lead, and in the past has led, to objectionable inequality in the distribution of resources to meet basic needs. I should add that there are different systems of social security and, by implication, different forms of 'welfare capitalism' (Esping-Andersen 1990), both as ideal types (dominated by social assistance or social insurance or solidaristic principles) and in terms of a variety of welfare regimes ('liberal' or corporatist or social democratic). While the welfare state has been in trouble since the 1970s, the different varieties of welfare capitalism are unequally affected. Should they allow the introduction of a basic income, then presumably they would do so in varying degrees and with different results. This is a big and complicated subject and I can do no more here than briefly discuss some of the problems involved and the expected or putative advan-tages of a basic income for the solution of these problems in general and the 'greening' of the welfare state in particular.

Problems of welfare states

Welfare states, but particularly most continental European welfare states (Esping-Andersen 1996), have not yet managed to find a creative policy response to a number of important economic and social changes which have become ever more conspicuous since the 1970s. To begin with, there are economic changes: high unemployment (which now seems to have become endemic); jobless economic growth; a shift from an industrial economy to a service economy; a drastic increase in the flexibility of work (a rising number of casual and part-time jobs, mostly low-skilled and low-paid); globalisation (increasing competition in more or less deregulated global markets and the shifting of production to low wage countries). Next, there are social and cultural changes: the increasingly strong tendencies to individualisation and mobility within national societies (Offe 1992; Standing 1992; Pierson 1995); and the growing diversity of lifestyles and the increasing number of women who want to have paid employment. Then there are technological changes leading to an increasing productivity of labour. Finally, there are demographic changes: for example, in the age distribution of the population (relatively more older people and so on).

The consequences of these developments have been the abandonment of policies of full employment (typical for the Keynesian welfare state); rising costs of maintaining social security, imposing an increasing burden on those active in gainful employment (this last effect in turn leading to jobless growth); harm to the competitive position on international markets; a substantially decreased capacity of national governments to regulate the national economy autonomously and to intervene on behalf of employment or public provision (Pierson 1995: 51); and an increasing inequality in rich Western countries (Standing 1992: 54).

What might basic income contribute to the solution of these problems?

One can agree with Offe that in these economic and social circumstances it is important not to advocate basic income as a kind of panacea, but 'to argue for basic income in terms of a defensive measure to preserve and expand notions of social justice against a welfare backlash that has already started and must be expected to continue' (Offe 1992: 74). The great advantage of a basic income is that it can 'facilitate labour flexibility through providing income security' (Standing 1992: 59). Some other reasons for introducing a basic income are worth mentioning.

1 Simplification of systems of social security.
2 A less unequal distribution of incomes.
3 Redistribution of labour, in at least two respects: between categories of labour (between paid labour and voluntary labour, unpaid but indispensable to fulfil important social tasks like caring for dependants); and between men and women.
4 Enlarging the freedom of the individual.
5 Its contribution to the emancipation of men and women from the roles of lifelong breadwinner and lifelong housewife.
6 Its contribution to finding and maintaining environmentally benign patterns of consumption and sustainable lifestyles.

Most of these reasons speak for themselves and are not dependent upon a specific welfare state regime. Of course, we are not yet in a position to assess the effectiveness of a basic income in achieving the admirable goals specified, either in its own terms or in comparison to alternative efforts to reconstruct the welfare state. Before saying a bit more about the last reason mentioned above, I need to indicate the main sources from which a basic income could be financed and the forms it can take. I do this here from a practical point of view and postpone what may be said on the basis of normative-ethical theory.

A basic income can take the form of monthly direct payments by the government to citizens or an indirect payment by means of a negative income tax. It can be partial or full: that is, it does not necessarily suffice to meet basic needs; it may be lower, at least at the time of introduction, but it might also become higher eventually. It can be introduced, whether partial or full: at once or in steps. This implies that in planning for the introduction of a basic income considerable fine-tuning is possible depending on the state of the economy, the nature of the welfare regime already in place and, of course, political support. A basic income could be financed by: (a) the reallocation of funds from which benefits replaced by the basic income were paid; and (b) a variety of tax measures. One of the tax measures proposed (Steiner 1992; Van Parijs 1992; Davidson 1995) is particularly interesting: an (eco)tax on natural resources, energy and capital goods, to be paid by employers. Because the factor labour is taxed less and the material factors of production more, a shift in the direction of sustainable patterns of production may be the result.

Basic income and sustainability

The circumstances which put the reconstruction of the welfare state on the political agenda also raise the moral demand to make our patterns of production and consumption sustainable; a demand which, as we have seen, is also a requirement of social justice. Arguably, in place of the present system of social security – still oriented to full personal employment and heavily dependent on economic growth – a system that acknowledges basic income for all as a (citizen) right may well function better from this point of view. After all, the transition to this system requires disconnecting, as far as possible, social security and economic growth, particularly unsustainable growth. Otherwise, most people will go on, as beneficiaries of social welfare services, to prefer jobs and growth above the environment. As Offe observed:

> Economic growth, . . . whether or (more likely) not it is accompanied by the attainment of full employment, has in all its currently visible varieties and paths an unequivocally disruptive impact upon the natural environment. The continued dependency of social security upon economic growth conditions the immediate interests of employees in ways which will favour growth even at the expense of environmentally and ecologically sound policies. The productivist link that ties social security to economic growth and budgetary growth dividends operates as an effective brake upon more stringent varieties of policies aiming at environmental protection, as the clients of this type of welfare state will naturally be inclined to prefer economic growth over the preservation of natural resources.
>
> (Offe 1992: 71)

Whatever else establishing sustainable patterns of production and consumption might involve, at the very least they should reduce the environmental impact of our industrial way of life, especially the overconsumption in rich countries. Such a reduction will be achieved not only by increasing technological efficiency in the use of material resources and energy (the environmental efficiency of material production), but also by stabilising material production and consumption, and perhaps reducing resource use. This stabilisation or reduction will have to take place mainly in the rich countries, if we agree that the poor countries must have the opportunity to meet at least the basic needs of their citizens, but preferably to reach a level of welfare or a quality of life that comes somewhere near to the average level enjoyed in the rich countries. The relations between rich and poor, between nations and within nations, should not become another zero-sum game (now on account of the environmental problematique), which means that the rich are rich because others are or become poor and remain so (Heilbroner 1991: 101–2). As Wackernagel and Rees point out forcefully:

> we wealthy members of the human family – the *average* residents of the industrial world – face a discomforting moral dilemma: while we consume on average three times our fair share of sustainable global output, the basic needs of the world's billion plus chronically poor are not being met even today. Meanwhile, just satisfying current aggregate demand is undermining nature's capacity to meet the needs of future generations. If we rely on conventional economic strategies and technologies to fix these problems, the additional material growth, particularly in the high-income countries, would appropriate even more carrying capacity for the rich, thus reducing the ecological space available to the poor. It seems that conventional strategies are both ecologically dangerous and morally questionable. To the extent that we can create room for growth, it should be allocated to the Third World.
>
> (Wackernagel and Rees 1996: 125)

A broad social support, in the rich countries, for sustainable patterns of consumption is not to be expected, though, unless all can share a level of welfare above the social minimum and if the choice for a less materialistic way of life is voluntary and open to all.

What is not so clear in advance, however, as a matter of daily life and of lifestyle, is what sustainable patterns of consumption involve. We need to find out, in a collective learning process, how to lead a life that leaves a shallower ecological footprint on the planet (Wackernagel and Rees 1996); especially if we want to leave the world's poor enough resources for a decent and sustainable lifestyle. There have to be opportunities to experiment with other, 'softer', less material- and energy-intensive lifestyles. Less emphasis on paid labour – made possible by a basic income – may create these opportunities for all. The process of collective learning requires appropriate institutional support and channelling, and also a revitalisation and democratisation of civil society. On the one hand, experimentation with more radical forms of democracy will be made easier for those interested if they enjoy some security of income by way of a basic income. On the other hand democracy outside the traditional political sphere may be necessary if the results of all this experimentation are going to be taken seriously and be consolidated in fitting institutional forms.[5]

SUSTAINABILITY AND BASIC INCOME: NORMATIVE CONNECTIONS

The crisis which the welfare state has experienced since the 1970s has occasioned a variety of proposals for introducing a basic income, which reflect the complete spectrum of political ideologies (Van Parijs 1992: 3–43). A basic income is also frequently discussed in part of the green movement (Dobson 1995: 108–11). Here I am interested only in one issue: arguing for a basic income and strong sustainability on the basis of the 'egalitarian plateau' described earlier. Let us look first at the arguments for a basic income.

Arguing for a basic income

To begin with, some requirements have to be specified which arguments for a basic income should meet. In the first place, arguing for a basic income from the principle of abstract equality should be compatible with an argument for the normative core of strong sustainablity based on the same principle. A second requirement is that a deeply felt moral objection to basic income is defused. This is the objection that a basic income, in the strict sense, allows parasitism or exploitation, because it allows some individuals to benefit from the efforts of others without doing something in return, whether paid labour or other kinds of labour (informal, voluntary, in the household, caring for dependents, and so on), and are therefore better off than the others, while these become worse off than those who benefit from their efforts. It is not quite clear that the arguments for basic income which have been elaborated so far – and some of them are very sophisticated and complex indeed, especially those of Van Parijs (1995b) – satisfy these requirements. It is not even clear whether the philosophers concerned give these requirements, especially the objection of parasitism, the same weight, moral or otherwise, or take them seriously at all. Anyway, what I will try to do in this section is to outline arguments which have been developed by a number of philosophers active in this area (Steiner 1992; Van Parijs 1992; Davidson 1995; den Hartogh 1995). A problem with the argument is that it is vulnerable to the objection of parasitism. As suggested, the moral weight of this argument is by no means clear and it will not do simply to assume, as van Donselaar and others do, that its moral significance is overriding. Anyway, I am going to use another argument in addition, one elaborated by Goodin (1992), that succeeds, I believe, in closing any remaining justificatory gap.[6] Of course, we still have the more pragmatic arguments for a basic income developed in the section starting on p. 135, although these on their own do not point unambiguously in the direction of a basic income in the strong unconditional sense (unless supplemented, again, by a Goodin-style argument).

The basic premise of the argument is due to Thomas Paine and appears in his 'Agrarian Justice' (1797). It is, he says:

> a position not to be controverted that the earth, in its natural uncultivated state, was, and ever would have continued to be, the *common property of the human race*. In that state every man would have been born to property. He would have been a joint life-proprietor with the rest in the property of the soil, and in all its natural productions, vegetable and animal.
>
> (Paine 1995: 417)

From the environmental point of view one would like to add not only its mineral parts but also the functions of the environment such as waste assimilation. What does follow from the thought that natural resources in this broad sense are the common property of humankind? Intuitively, that they should be, if possible (that is insofar as they can be individually appropriated), distributed equally or made equally accessible to use and appropriation by the members of the human race. This intuition is confirmed if we invoke the egalitarian plateau: nobody has, to begin with,[7] a legitimate ground to claim a greater part of the resources of this planet than anybody else.

How do we move on from here, particularly if almost all natural resources in the broad sense have become scarce and are becoming continuously scarcer (which is one very important aspect of what the environmental crisis is all about)? It is hard to see because, apart from the 'collective good' aspects of the environment already mentioned, it is often not physically possible or practicable to distribute the remaining natural resources equally. It is not even clear what an equal part is, as it is not clear what counts as a resource and for whom, given changes in technology, culture and population.

Therefore, an equal part must imply an equal part of the *value* of the relevant natural resources. It is attractive to conceive this value in terms of market prices but these reflect actual markets and a given distribution of property, which is usually not an expression of an equal distribution of (natural) resources. At any rate, if we hold on to the equal part of the value of natural resources for all concerned (and as yet we have seen no theoretical reason to abandon it) it has to be expressed, somehow, in an equal part of their overall and, presumaby, differential purchasing power: that is, in a basic income for all. But how do we fund it?

The obvious way to finance a basic income is from taxes. But which taxes? Three taxes have been proposed as fitting: a tax on the use of natural resources in the broad sense (Steiner 1992; Van Parijs 1992; den Hartogh 1995); a tax on the estates of the deceased (Steiner 1992; Van Parijs 1992); and a tax on jobs (Van Parijs 1992; den Hartogh 1995). The tax proceeds should be distributed equally to all concerned. I will restrict myself to the relevant case of a tax on the use and appropriation of natural resources.

The (part of) basic income financed from the proceeds of this tax can be conceived, as indicated above, as a compensation for being excluded from the use of natural resources which can be appropriated on an individual basis. One's enjoyment of those parts of the environment which have the character of a public good, such as the air, is to be considered a part of the basic income paid, so to speak, in kind. The tax itself can take the form of some kind of ecotax (see p. 138 above) but the proceeds can also be (partially) collected from the selling, by a central authority, of tradable emission permits. Those liable to pay the tax are considered to pay a rent for their use of natural resources in the broad sense.[8]

Is the result an unconditional income? The problem is that the natural resources need labour to deliver most of the goods desired. Labour does not have value without natural resources and natural resources do not have value without labour, so one might correct Locke's theory (1988) that the value from the products of labour is for the most part derived from the labour involved. This means, as den Hartogh suggests (1995: 142–3), that the income derived from the ecotax or from the selling of rights to use the natural resources should be conceived as a rise of income derived *from labour*. Not necessarily paid labour, of course; informal labour, such as voluntary removal of trash from the local environment or caring for dependent members of the family, will do too. So, we do not have a strictly unconditional income here.[9]

Not all is lost again for the basic income, though; consider the problems inherent in trying to determine who is eligible for the income rise drawn from proceeds of the tax. Are only those willing to work eligible? But how do we know who is willing to work if she has not got a paid job but is – busy? Doing what? Inside the house or strolling in the park occasionally picking up a disgarded cigarette butt? Imagine the universal control and incessant prying necessary to find out who and where the people are, and who is not willing to work! It would not be practicable; it would be demeaning and morally objectionable. We may still have reason, then, to pay a basic income to all on an individual basis, if we could also be reasonably sure that most people want to work and consider it, whether paid or not, important in their life. Apart from what empirical research would reveal about people's considered preferences concerning work, we can spell out this argument for a basic income a bit more. It has been elaborated by Goodin (1992).

Goodin argues that the introduction of an unconditional basic income is preferable as a social welfare policy because it is minimally presumptuous. All welfare policy presuppose facts about the particular people or distinctive categories of people which are eligible for specific benefits or types of benefit for the right (type of) reasons. The problem with these presumptions is that they are vulnerable to 'factual error', 'to social change', and 'to errors in emphasis' (Goodin 1992: 204–5), in a world where the relevant sociological facts are 'uncertain, highly variable and, in any case, constantly changing' (Goodin 1992: 210). Because of this the 'target efficiency' of more traditional welfare programmes decreases, the target efficiency being 'concerned strictly with how well a programme achieves its own goal' (Goodin 1992: 196). An unconditional basic income approach to social security makes minimal presumptions: 'it takes no notice of why a person's income is low – or, indeed, of how high or low their income is. Whether a person is unable to work or merely unwilling to do so is of no consequence' (Goodin 1992: 207). Therefore this approach is maximally target-efficient. Efficiency is valued here, as Goodin reminds us, as a means; its value is derived from the other goals we pursue: we want to pursue these efficiently, in order to realise more of them and as many as possible. 'So, at root, the reason we should cherish the target efficiency of basic income strategies is simply that it guarantees that we will, through them, be able to relieve human suffering as best as we can' (Goodin 1992: 210). Needless to say, the egalitarian plateau enables one to argue for Goodin's position without any difficulty. Thus qualified by considerations of efficiency, the case for an unconditional basic income still stands.

Arguing for strong sustainability

It is interesting to note that on the same Painean premise an argument can be based leading to the constraints of strong sustainability as mentioned above. This has been formulated by Luper-Foy and I will briefly summarise it here, reconstructing it slightly as regards its starting-point.

We have already seen that the Painean premise of the argument for basic income can be interpreted as the principle that people should be treated as equal in the distribution of natural resources. Nobody can claim beforehand a preferential right to a greater share of natural resources than anybody else, although most people would prefer to have as much of them as possible because they are 'critical' for almost every way of life. Present natural resources are not the property of anyone in particular, wherever or whenever they may live. And 'anyone' in the previous sentence includes groups or collectives. So the natural resources on this planet, inluding the land, are not the special property of nations or generations either. Therefore, the resources should be distributed equally, intra-generationally and inter-generationally, unless an unequal distribution would be justified. Thus we are led to accept a principle of intra-generational and inter-generational equity. This is precisely the principle Luper-Foy argues for[10] under the name of the '*resource-equity principle*: resources are to be handled in a way that is equitable both across the globe and across the generations' (Luper-Foy 1995: 96). He infers from it that inter-generational equity 'reduces to the demand for indefinite sustainability in the areas of both pollution and consumption' of natural resources (Luper-Foy 1995: 96). The rate at which people reproduce makes a difference, though. The rate of reproduction should also be indefinitely sustainable. Therefore the 'resource-equity principle' has to be generalised to the 'sustainable consumption-reproduction principle': 'each generation may consume natural resources, pollute, and reproduce at given rates only if it could reasonably expect that each successive generation could do likewise' (Luper-Foy 1995: 98). Intra-generational distributive justice is constrained by inter-generational justice in the following way: by 'setting the ceiling on the resources that are available to each generation, and by delineating *how* resources may be consumed, the sustainable consumption-reproduction principle specifies what resources are available to us as a generation' (Luper-Foy 1995: 100). Luper-Foy concludes with a short discussion of a plan to make the transition from the present order of nation-states to an order of global justice. The most important part of it is that nation-states begin to perform the tasks within their territory, which had been assigned earlier to the World Bank in his proposal discussed above (see note 8).

When Luper-Foy specifies in some more detail to what extent pollution and consumption are allowed to be indefinitely sustainable (Luper-Foy 1995: 96–9), it turns out that he in fact accepts a version of strong sustainability comparable to the one outlined above (pp. 132–4).

We may summarise the result of the normative exercise in this section by saying that both a basic income and strong sustainability can be ethically justified, and that there is substantial ethical convergence between their justifications. Therefore the effort to plan for sustainability by planning for a basic income receives additional legitimacy (that is, above and beyond that based upon the more pragmatic and empirical arguments in the first two sections).

CONCLUSION

The result of the analysis in this chapter is that, generally speaking, there are strong reasons of both a pragmatic and an ethical nature for accepting the thesis that planning for strong sustainability implies planning for a basic income. Pragmatically, the implication has been spelled out by an analysis of the problems of present welfare states and of the manner in which a basic income might offer relief. In this same context it turned out that the introduction of a basic income would also contribute substantially to 'greening' the welfare state. Ethically, it was shown that the justification of a basic income and of strong sustainability invoked ultimately the same fundamental principle of political philosophy: the principle that people, wherever and whenever they live, should be treated equally.

Notes

1 See the debate between Beckerman, Daly and Jacobs in *Environmental Values* 1994–5; also in van Dieren (1995: 99–123).
2 See van Dieren (1995: 105) for alternative formulations drawn from Serageldin.
3 In Achterberg (1997) I argue that the ideal forum for this and similar debates should be structured by the principles of deliberative democracy.
4 In order to avoid the closing of moral options by conceptual decisions, more needs to be said here about nature in relation to sustainability. For example, in a non-anthropocentric (for example, ecocentric) argument for sustainability, some natural entities are not to be considered simply as resources for humans or others, but as beings with a moral standing of their own; *prima facie* they should not be harmed. If we accept that some natural entities are such that they deserve moral consideration and if we also agree that this – perhaps not widely shared – moral intuition can be spelled out in terms of justice, we must also agree that sustainability subsists in a moral field of force generated by three forms of justice: intra-generational, inter-generational and ecological. This is not to deny that, for example, claims derived from inter-generational justice and from ecological justice may converge, at least in the long run (see Norton's

hypothesis of convergence (1991: 240)). In any case, theoretically at least there is a moral case for a non-anthropocentric conception of sustainability; in rather more practical terms this case has been made by *Caring for the Earth* (IUCN, UNEP and WWF 1991). In this chapter I will limit myself to purely anthropocentric considerations.

5 I have argued (Achterberg 1996a and 1996b) for the importance of associative democracy in this context.

6 To make my argument here I have been forced to set aside a number of complex issues. For example, I will not pay any attention to the thorny problems of differential psychical and bodily endowments, which, of course, should be taken into account in a complete argument. On the force of the objection of parasitism to a basic income I have learned most from van Donselaar (1997), who has urged this objection (in the precise sense derived from Gauthier 1986: 205–6) with great ingenuity and tenacity against, especially, Van Parijs' equally ingenious arguments for a basic income. For theoretical purposes one of the conclusions drawn by van Donselaar is that an equal distribution of natural resources is only permitted if parasitism can be excluded.

7 It would make a difference here if the simplification mentioned by way of example in the previous footnote was rectified.

8 Particularly radical is the arrangement proposed by Luper-Foy (1995). However, it is not clear whether he would accept a basic income, let alone an unconditional basic income, on the basis of his premises. The similarity of his arguments to those who do is striking, though. Luper-Foy's proposal is radical because it does not recognise the present order of nation-states as legitimate (but he envisages a transition regime). He conceives of a 'World Bank' which sells 'on the open market the right to recover resources that, unlike land and air, require recovery' (Luper-Foy 1995: 100). The Bank will sell these rights, and lease rights for land as well, but only for limited periods and 'always with an eye to maximising its revenues'. After subtracting from these its operating costs it distributes the remainder equally among the 'members of the generation at hand' . Of course, the 'World Bank' can sell the rights and lease the land under conditions regulating how, where and when to use the resources. In this way we reach not just a basic income, but even a sustainable income!

9 Moreover, I believe an element of parasitism seems to be involved. For the explanation of this see van Donselaar (1997: ch. 4).

10 Albeit in a somewhat different way. He makes use of the Rawlsian apparatus of the original position and the veil of ignorance, but he conceives the deliberating parties behind the veil as representatives of everyone in the world, wherever and whenever they may live (Luper-Foy 1995: 93–4), in contrast to Rawls' original interpretation in the *Theory of Justice*.

References

Achterberg, W. (1994) *Samenleving, Natuur en Duurzaamheid*, Assen: Van Gorcum.

Achterberg, W. (1996a) 'Sustainability, Community and Democracy' in Doherty and de Geus (1996).

Achterberg, W. (1996b) 'Sustainability and associative democracy', in Lafferty and Meadowcroft (1996).

Achterberg, W. (1997) 'Duurzaamheid en Reciprociteit', in M. Davidson (ed.), *In debat de toekomst*, The Hague: Ministry of Housing, Physical Planning and Environmental Management. Publikatiereeks Milieustrategie no. 8: 85–95.

Beckerman, W. (1994) 'Sustainable Development: Is it a Useful Concept?', *Environmental Values* 3: 191–209.

Daly, H. (1995), 'On Wilfred Beckerman's Critique of Sustainable Development', *Environmental Values* 4: 49–55.

Davidson, M. (1995) 'Liberale grondrechten en milieu. Het recht op milieugebruiksruimte als grondslag van een basisinkomen', *Milieu* 10: 246–9.

De-Shalit, A. (1995) *Why Posterity Matters*, London: Routledge.

Dieren, W. van (ed.) (1995) *Taking Nature into Account*, New York: Copernicus.

Dobson, A. (1995) *Green Political Thought*, London: Unwin Hyman (2nd edn).

Doherty, B. and de Geus, M. (eds) (1996) *Democracy and Green Political Thought*, London: Routledge.

Donselaar, G. van (1997) 'The Benefits of Another's Pain: Parasitism, Scarcity, Basic Income', Ph.D. Thesis, University of Amsterdam.

Dryzek, J. (1996) *Democracy in Capitalist Times*, New York: Oxford University Press.

Dworkin, R. (1977) *Taking Rights Seriously*, London: Duckworth.

Dworkin, R. (1983) 'In Defense of Equality', *Social Philosophy and Policy* 1: 24–40.

El Serafy, S. (1996) 'In Defence of Weak Sustainability: A Response to Beckerman', *Environmental Values* 5: 75–81.

Esping-Andersen, G. (1990) *The Three Worlds of Welfare Capitalism*, Cambridge: Polity Press.

Esping-Andersen, G. (1996) 'Welfare states without work. The impasse of labour shedding and familianism in continental European welfare states', in G. Esping-Andersen (ed.), *Welfare States in Transition*, London: Sage.

Gallie, W. (1956), 'Essentially contested concepts', *Proceedings of the Aristotelian Society* 56: 167–98.

Gauthier, D. (1986) *Morals by Agreement*, Oxford: Oxford University Press.

Geus, M. de (1996) 'The Ecological Restructuring of the State', in Doherty and de Geus (1996).

Goodin, R. (1988) *Reasons for Welfare: The Political Theory of the Welfare State*, Princeton, NJ: Princeton University Press.

Goodin, R. (1992) 'Towards a Minimally Presumptuous Social Welfare Policy', in P. Van Parijs (ed.), *Arguing for Basic Income*, London: Verso.

Hartogh, G. den (1995) 'Het Basisinkomen als Grondrecht', in van der Veen and Pels (1995).

Heilbroner, R. (1991) *An Inquiry into The Human Prospect*, New York: Norton.

Hicks, J. (1946) *Value and Capital.* Oxford: Oxford University Press (2nd edn).

IUCN, UNEP and WWF (1991), *Caring for the Earth*, Switzerland: Gland.

Jacobs, M. (1995), 'Sustainable Development, Capital Substitution and Economic Humility: A Response to Beckerman', *Environmental Values* 4: 57–68.

Kymlicka, W. (1990) *Modern Political Philosophy*, Oxford: Clarendon Press.

Lafferty, W. and Meadowcroft, J. (eds) (1996) *Democracy and the Environment*, Cheltenham: Edward Elgar.

Locke, J. (1988) *Two Treatises of Government*, Cambridge: Cambridge University Press.

Luper-Foy, St. (1995) 'International justice and the environment', in D. Cooper and J. Palmer (eds), *Just Environments*, London: Routledge.

Meadowcroft, J. (1997) 'Planning, democracy and the challenge of sustainable development', *International Political Science Review* 18: 167–90.

Norton, B. (1991) *Toward Unity Among Environmentalists*, New York: Oxford University Press.

Norton, B. (1992) 'Sustainability, Human Welfare and Ecosystem Health', *Environmental Values* 1: 97–111.

Offe, C. (1992) 'A Non-Productivist Design for Social Policies', in P. Van Parijs (ed.), *Arguing for Basic Income*, London: Verso.

Offe, C. (1996) 'Precarious and the Labour Market. A Medium Term Review of Available Policy Responses', Unpublished MS.

Opschoor, J. (1995) 'Ecospace and the fall and rise of throughput intensity', *Ecological Economics* 15: 137–40.

Opschoor, J. and Weterings, R. (1994) 'Environmental utilisation space: an introduction', *Milieu* 9: 198–205.

Paine, T. (1995) 'Agrarian Justice', in *Rights of Man, Common Sense and Other Political Writings*, Oxford: Oxford University Press.

Pierson, C. (1995) *Socialism After Communism, The New Market Socialism*, Cambridge: Polity Press.

Standing, G. (1992) 'The Need for a New Social Consensus', in P. Van Parijs (ed.), *Arguing for Basic Income*, London: Verso.

Steiner, H. (1992) 'Three Just Taxes', in P. Van Parijs (ed.), *Arguing for Basic Income*, London: Verso.

Van Parijs, P. (1992) 'Competing Justifications of Basic Income', in P. Van Parijs (ed.) *Arguing for Basic Income*, London: Verso.

Van Parijs, P. (1995a) 'De solidariteit voorbij. Over de ethische transformatie van de verzorgingsstaat', in van der Veen and Pels (1995).

Van Parijs, P. (1995b) *Real Freedom for All: What (if anything) can justify capitalism?*, Oxford: Clarendon Press.

Veen, R. van der and Pels, D. (eds) (1995) *Het Basisinkomen. Sluitstuk van de Verzorgingsstaat*, Amsterdam: Van Gennep.

Wackernagel, M. and Rees, W. (1996) *Our Ecological Footprint*, Gabriola Island, BC, Canada: New Society Publishers.

WCED (1987) *Our Common Future*, Oxford: Oxford University Press.

Weterings, R. and Opschoor, J. (1994) 'Environmental utilization space and reference values for performance evaluation', *Milieu* 9: 221–8.

WRR (Netherlands Scientific Council for Government Policy) (1995) *Sustained Risks; A Lasting Phenomenon* (Reports to the Government 44), The Hague: WRR.

7 Three decades of environmental planning: what have we really learned?

Paul Selman

INTRODUCTION

This chapter considers some of the principal factors which have influenced the development of environmental planning during the relatively recent past. It represents environmental planning as a rather diffuse activity, operating in a complex milieu, yet generally retaining a reasonable coherence of purpose and approach. Although its emphasis is on the 'environment' rather than the broader concept of 'sustainable development', it inevitably encroaches on the latter as the two are now seamlessly connected. Planning is viewed here in two ways: as a formal process of land management, guiding and controlling the built environment, civil engineering operations and certain changes of use; and as a generic activity, involving provision for the future and the strategic and tactical allocation of human and physical resources. Thus it encompasses both statutory town planning and the wider process of public sector engagement with environmental change. The environment is perceived to be similarly varied, as an entity which can be constructed in biophysical, built, economic-political or socio-cultural terms.

INTRODUCING ENVIRONMENTAL PLANNING

Environmental planning is thus a diverse activity, comprising multiple approaches, and based on a range of options for direct action and indirect influence. Its theory and practice can be related to four broad spectra. One represents the continuum of degrees of compulsion over environmental modification, ranging from land purchase, through 'command-and-control' legislative powers and economic incentives and disincentives, to advice and exhortation. Another reflects the inclusion of local opinion and expertise, both through a system of elected members and via mechanisms of public participation, ranging from virtual exclusion, through token involvement, to citizen control. A third entails the production of technical knowledge, enabling environmental problems to be conceptualised and viable solutions to be proposed. Finally, there is a concern to make environmental governance less sectoral and more integrated, seldom by major legislative or institutional reforms, but more commonly through the creation of partnerships to facilitate multi-disciplinarity. Considerable controversy surrounds all these issues.

Environmental planning should be understood as a rational human activity aimed at taking decisions which optimise welfare both presently and at some time in the future. This approach raises questions about rationality, technocracy, patriarchy and equity; it also tends to detach planning analyses from the main engines of change in state and economy. Limitations of space mean that only a passing acknowledgement of these wider issues is possible. It should be clear that rational choice is the theory appropriate to the generic activity of planning, which is a diagnostic human characteristic and which we practise at all scales from the personal to the transnational. But pragmatic planning tends to absorb many ideas originating from political economy or post-modern schools, for instance, simply because they tend to lead to better results on the ground. Similarly, 'rationalist' models in principle give way to 'realist' models in practice, as the latter represent more accurately the non-linear and interactive nature of actual planning decisions.

Consequently, the present account is somewhat positivist and procedural in tenor, not because these characteristics are considered especially desirable, but because they provide a manageable analytical framework for policy and practice, which is capable of extension to wider issues. Very simply, a classic positivistic interpretation of planning incorporates rational choice theory, and implies a smooth, cyclical sequence of survey, consultation, design, implementation, monitoring and review. One study of environmental planning (DTA/CAG 1994) portrays it as an idealised process which is reminiscent of the early positivist models (Figure 7.1). Even so, brief reflection on this diagram will readily suggest points at which it may articulate with wider debates about structure and agency, and with the more post-modern subtleties of transactive and communicative processes. Indeed, critics of positivist-rationalist models concede that similar sequences emerge regardless of ontological framework. Healey (1997), for example, acknowledges the following generic stages: review of issues (survey); sorting through findings (analysis); exploring impacts in relation to values (evaluation); inventing and developing new ideas (choice of strategy); and continuous review (monitoring).

The Tyldesley Report (DTA/CAG 1994) argues, in terms of the above model, that the long-established planning cycle remains substantially unaffected, and that adopting environmentally sensitive practices will not prove disruptive. The depiction of environmental planning in this manner suggests two possibilities which, in a sense, provide a reflexive framework for this review: environmental planning is either a gradual, modernising, reformist extension of established managerial approaches to land, air and water quality; or it is a more disruptive paradigm shift in planning practices, designed to propel society towards a fundamentally sustainable future.

Whilst our focus is on the major influences of approximately the last thirty-year period, it is worth marking the more historical mainstays of environmental planning which, perhaps subconsciously, still mould policy and practice. One has been the notion of 'amenity' encapsulated by Abercrombie's pursuit, in the 1930s and

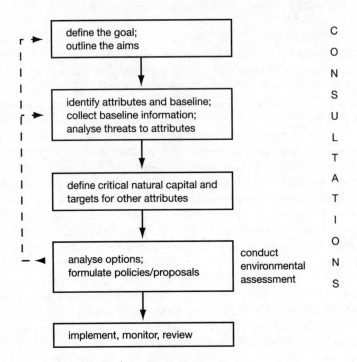

Figure 7.1 The basic environmental planning process

Source: DTA/CAG (1994)

1940s, of 'beauty, health and convenience' (Abercrombie 1933). Another is that of 'containment', most comprehensively chronicled in Peter Hall's (1973) exposition of the post-1947 British regime. This is founded on urban containment, protection of rural resources and the creation of balanced communities, with secondary importance attached to the prevention of scattered development and the selective reinforcement of service centres. In general, twenty years of environmental planning from the late 1960s to the late 1980s has supplanted this very physical conception and its associated expert-led blueprint rationale, with a more ecologically-grounded, integrated, adaptive and transactive approach, placing increased emphasis on assessment, implementation and monitoring. From the late 1980s, there has been further acknowledgement of the need for a strong defence of 'critical' environmental capital, confronting the demons of traffic congestion and energy-inefficient settlements, and taking a more holistic approach to agency reform, citizen involvement and virtuous development. This said, much routine practice still reflects, often with good reason, the philosophy of the 1940s.

The highly heterogeneous nature of environmental planning has thus led to different interpretations of its character. The more conservative interpretations still extol restraint over development and the protection of rural resources, and these are stances not to be jettisoned lightly. More ambitious analyses seek to achieve 'ecological gain' in new development (Boucher and Whatmore 1993; Healey, Purdue and Ennis 1995), whilst the most radical ones advocate low impact communities achieving order of magnitude reductions in their ecological footprint (Wackernagel and Rees 1996; O'Riordan and Voisey 1997). Many official policies now identify options for more compact settlements, reductions in car journeys, energy reductions in the home and workplace, and keeping tourist and recreation impacts within the 'limits of acceptable change'.

A key factor in creating the possibility of a sea change in environmental planning practice has been the impact of economic explanations of sustainable development. These pivot around the disaggregation of environmental resources into critical and constant capital (Pearce 1993; Tate 1994). This distinction between irreplaceable assets, and assets which can, relatively easily, be re-created or re-located, has provided an elegant basis on which to re-conceptualise core planning policies. It has been especially useful in decisions relating to key land-scapes, habitats, water resources and minerals and is starting to permeate policies and practices underpinning contemporary environmental planning (Winter 1994; Rowan-Robinson, Ross and Walton 1995; Jackson and Roberts 1997).

It is important to consider the principal social forces which shape environmental planning, namely, the state, professions, citizens and science. Again, only a few passing observations can be made about each, with the purpose of helping to clarify subsequent arguments.

First, *the state* must be understood not simply as government, but also as the cognate apparatus of organised activities affecting the 'public interest', and it holds fundamental significance for planning as, essentially, it determines the rules of transference which legitimise environmental change. It also acts at various 'scales' (from 'supra-state' activities to the 'local patch'), and the degree of policy specificity applied to each scale is seen increasingly to be a major influence on objectives and styles of planning. The role of the central state in environmental planning has been a contentious issue, especially as the post-1945 consensus about welfarist and collectivist programmes, within which most land-use planning systems were conceived, has started to fracture. Thus approaches based on blueprints, collectivism and regulation have tended to conflict with powerful trends towards post-Fordist administrative and political liberalisation, which view the state as a facilitator able to accommodate individualistic solutions and wider choice (Amin 1994). A leftward political swing in the 1990s in the character of some western governments has done little to arrest this general trend. Hence, even though official pronouncements still laud the merits of planning and pollution control, and environmental regulatory frameworks continue to be buttressed, emphasis recently has been placed on economic instruments such as green taxes and incentive-based agri-environment schemes. This more 'hands-off' approach nationally, following a 'rolling back' of the frontiers of the state, has been reflected in the partial transition of local government from being a direct provider to a contractor of services (Snape 1995).

The role of the state at the local level has been the focus of considerable recent interest. Britain has experienced the diminishing of the powers of the democratically accountable elements of local government, and this has been accompanied by the growing influence of single issue pressure groups, often by-passing the formal democratic niceties of the local state. A blurring of the domains of central and local state has occurred, not only via the imposition of more central direction on local government, but also by the administrative devolution of central government departments, quangos and agencies. This latter process has taken place in the name of 'bringing government closer to the people' but, whilst this may be true in terms of physical propinquity, it does not necessarily imply greater local democratic influence or public awareness. In mainland Europe we can see trends towards enhancing the powers and potential of local councils, whilst a notable international trend has been towards devolving significant responsibilities in a climate of fiscal restraint, so that public expenditure cuts are effected by bodies closest to the clients.

Second, *the skills* of environmental professionals have had to change accordingly. The most striking shift has been from the rational, quantitative training of the 1960s to the more humanistic competencies in the 1990s. It is easy to simplify this trend though. Whilst rational, decision-optimising and forecasting techniques have become less prominent in planning generally, the environmental movement has – almost as a means of asserting its professional credentials – adapted and extended the quantitative foundation of planning. Indeed, there has been the emergence of new professional groupings and institutes, which place an even stronger emphasis on scientific analysis. Nevertheless, part of the armoury of the emerging environmental planner is an awareness of new methods of citizen and community involvement in the decision-making process, such as 'planning-for-real', citizens' juries and focus groups, and this represents part of a broadening concern for conflict mediation and consensus-building. Equally, across the whole sustainability spectrum, there is a need for extending 'citizen science', facilitating the role of lay knowledge in minimising environmental risks and hazards (Irwin 1995). However, whilst modern environmental practice increasingly acknowledges the role of the laity, it has simultaneously been characterised by the emergence of new professional groupings, whose members are finding new opportunities to assert their chartered status in fields complementary to traditional planning and public health.

Third, whereas the former British style of environmental regulation tended to be discretionary, collaborative and secretive (O'Riordan and Wynne 1987), sustainability planning has seen the explicit inclusion of *citizens* as agents of indigenous development and conservation. As part of a wider rediscovery of the role of citizenship, many countries are invoking specific 'environmental citizenship' programmes. Citizens are imagined in two main ways, perhaps creating a duality of irreconcilable tension: both as 'passive' consumers of high quality environmental goods and services and/or as 'active' catalysts who (hopefully, from the government's point of view) channel their energies into local projects rather than protest and civil disobedience. The 'heretic' active citizen is, nevertheless, starting to exert a considerable influence on environmental planning, especially by hampering major transport proposals. Notions of citizenship and citizen participation are also being reappraised in relation to the empowerment of traditionally disempowered groups, and even to non-human species (van Steenbergen 1994; Dobson 1995), and this brokerage of influence is a key element in the transition from environmental to sustainability planning. A regrettable aspect of the increased attention given to modes of participatory democracy has been the relative neglect of local representative democracy, and the two need to be spliced together to establish a more legitimate basis for environmental and sustainability planning.

Finally, the role of *science* is complex, and its myriad contributions may be seen as benign or hazardous. Two aspects are of particular significance. One is the huge influence of management information (or decision support) systems – especially geographic information systems – which permit real-time manipulation and the sophisticated display of multiple natural and social science datasets. Far from being an obscure technicality, information technology is a powerful engine driving sustainability planning, and opening up novel possibilities in terms of holistic design, adaptive environmental management, the communication of 'virtual' futures, and comprehension of fuzzy problems. The second view of science is that it is largely the handmaiden of technology, thus conspiring to expose society to risks and hazards which are intrinsically unmanageable. Boehmer-Christiansen (1994), for instance, argues that science is an unreliable ally of environmental protection policy as the role of directly relevant knowledge tends to be that of defending the status quo. The current context of environmental planning is now inescapably that of the 'risk society' (Beck 1992), in which people are alert to the omnipresence of anonymous and uncontrollable risks – for instance in food, energy and manufacturing chains, and transport and distribution systems – which exceed scientists' moral or epistemological competence. This interpretation potentially provides a framework for future political change, as new class fractions organise themselves around the need to confront ecological doom, and some see in this a basis for a process of reflexive modernisation towards an ecological society. This may require planners to distance themselves from the corporate interests of science, technology and development if they are to facilitate public discourse about quality of life. Several implications of this analysis will be touched upon in due course, but a personal perception is that the emergent generation is strongly influenced by ideas associated with notions of risk, chaos and catastrophe, which may seriously undermine the rationale of environmental planning as a future-oriented activity.

PROBLEMS WITH ENVIRONMENTAL PLANNING

The need to plan is often driven by the existence of dilemmas, and so the activity is typically problem-focused. It is also future-oriented, and is thus associated with a climate of uncertainty. At the same time, it often has a retrospective element whereby we seek to audit past performance to help us learn from experience. Whilst planning is a universal activity, its expression in statute, which has occurred mainly within the latter part of the twentieth century, has generally been associated with the 'environment'. Town and country planning has focused even more narrowly upon 'land', only being able to exert indirect and often very tenuous influence over other aspects of environment, society and economy. Despite this legal-administrative focus, the generic enterprise of environmental planning has tackled characteristically complex problems associated with a multiplicity of interest groups and environmental and cultural systems. Our understanding of the 'environment' has also broadened from a predominantly reductionist account of bio-physico-chemical phenomena, via a recognition of the social forces which impinge on environmental change, to a somewhat incohesive cluster of 'quality of life' issues. This recognition of the inseparability of human and scientific issues has led to a progression from 'expert' mono-disciplinary solutions, through multi-disciplinarity, to integrated approaches involving both a range of agencies and affected parties. Many now refer to holistic solutions, entailing seamless analysis of and response to problems, and the merging of top-down and bottom-up strategies.

Alongside this must be considered the well-known spectrum of ecocentric and technocentric environmentalist philosophies (O'Riordan 1989; Turner, Pearce and Bateman 1994), reflecting a spectrum from very strong to very weak sustainability, and which with slight variations typically covers deep ecology, communal lifestyles, 'accommodating' approaches, and cornucopianism. The ecologically modernising planning profession has tended to find its approach to environmental stewardship located slightly to the 'technocentric' side of the mid-point, though individual planners may, of course, adopt very different stances. This positions environmental planning within a dominant meta-narrative, which sees the environment as an organising framework for human quality of life within constraints set by our understanding of bio-rights. In the 1980s, a notion of equity and fairness in the use of environmental resources was probably dominant, whilst, prior to that, the environment was perceived more as 'neutral stuff' from which a growing population could derive an existence. Conservation and development were traded off, though this polarisation is now generally seen to be a false dichotomy. Nevertheless, although there is an increasingly convergent purpose to environmental planning, we should note the warning of Dryzek (1996) that too complicitous a relationship 'may leave public policies unchanged (whilst) the administrative state would still grind out policies completely insensitive to the play of civil society'. His advocacy of a strong role for civil society in protest and policy pressure reinforces the need for transactive planning and citizen science as the basis for confronting technological risk, and a planning profession which is constantly forcing the agenda on 'strong sustainability' options.

After nearly three decades of studying, practising, teaching and researching environmental and planning issues, I find that the sum total of my knowledge can be represented in something like the simple diagram in Figure 7.2. This holds broadly true for environmental planning as practised in various legislatures and by various corporations, and at various geographical and administrative scales.

Where problems are clearly defined, possess only one or two aspects, and are associated with a straightforward solution, there is scarcely a need to plan. Planning is thus, by definition, typically associated with *wicked problems*. These are

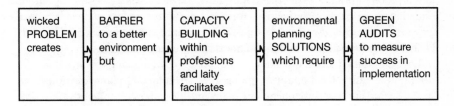

Figure 7.2 A simple problematisation of environmental planning

dilemmas which have no definitive formulation and are too complex to be broken down and solved individually (Rittel and Webber 1973). Colloquially, they have been likened to bars of soap, slipping out of one's grasp at the crucial moment. One aspect of this is the 'multi-actor' problem, in which conflicting viewpoints are reconciled slowly and tortuously, if at all. However, genuinely 'wicked' problems comprise many more facets than simply their actor network. Planners often find themselves 'between a rock and a hard place', trying to provide a workable outcome to an impossible puzzle and reaching a decision which may alienate some and please no-one very much. Over the years, environmental planners have sought to limit the difficulties posed by wicked problems by improving the reliability and accessibility of information, working in inter-disciplinary groups, and including a greater number of viewpoints in analyses. In so doing, however, they have faced a number of barriers.

Barriers to effective environmental decision-making have classically been defined as: agreement (lack of consensus over problem formulation); knowledge (inadequate or conflicting information); technology (lack of effective solutions); economics (costly or unattractive options); society (public unacceptability); and politics (lack of will: see Trudgill 1990). Moore (1994) has identified a similar set of perceptual-behavioural, institutional-structural and economic-financial barriers, whilst Paehlke (1996) has added problems of incrementalism and uncertainty over responsibilities. Lafferty and Meadowcroft (1996) note that environmental dilemmas revolve around knowledge deficits, complex geographical patterns of impact and causation, difficulties of re-distributing losses and gains between affected parties, and time scale effects (some very short-term, others way beyond electoral cycles).

Agenda 21, which arose from the 1992 Earth Summit (UNCED 1992), popularised the notion of *capacity building* as a means of raising the capacities of countries (especially developing ones) to cope with the challenges of sustainable development. This was interpreted as creating research facilities, education programmes, appropriate administrations and effective legislation. In reality, the notion is equally applicable to 'advanced' economies, where planning systems have developed incrementally or to address isolated issues, and which may no longer have these capacities to deal with contemporary 'wicked' problems. Capacity-building requires a receptive administrative-political framework, an open information and participation system, institutions for long-term planning, and a problem-oriented scientific community. To these, it may be appropriate to add the presence of resourceful actors and a culture of active environmental citizenship. It is salutary to note that new environmental agencies and laws are likely to have little impact in the absence of these wider conditions.

Environmental planning produces many outputs which can be viewed as *solutions*. These range from statutory plans, through informal plans and indicative strategies, to site-based management plans and design/development briefs. The instruments used to implement these solutions include acquisition of land or its associated rights, 'command and control' legal regulations (often based on licences and permits), economic incentives and penalties, and persuasion and education. Specific theories have also been developed to explain the successful implementation or failure of particular planning solutions (Greed 1996).

The missing link in most models of 'rational' planning has too often been that of monitoring/review, and a welcome feature of environmental planning has been its association with state of environment (SoE) reports and environmental indicators. Green audits comprise a range of monitoring and measuring methods, from SoE reporting to specific environmental assessments, and are frequently associated with performance indicators (Barton and Bruder 1995). They have involved a variety of techniques for information capture, processing and communication. Whilst SoE surveys were initially regarded as ends in themselves, they are now seen as only an early stage in a series of steps to be undertaken in the course of local authority 'greening'. Environmental assessments have been associated mainly with the decision-making end of planning and pollution control, although they are starting to spread to the production of plans and policies, despite the extraordinary difficulties of estimating impacts at a strategic scale (Thérivel 1995; Byron and Sheate 1997).

It may well be that the essential purpose of environmental planning is to help us cross the 'sustainability transition', so that this becomes the ultimate barrier to holistic planning, which cannot be crossed by business-as-usual (or perhaps even by incremental reformist) lifestyles, institutions or planning instruments. We must consider our achievements realistically in relation to this fundamental objective. One possibility is that environmental planning has moved on little in real terms over the past thirty years: we have merely, at roughly ten-year intervals, been relabelling familiar activities. Alternatively, if there has been some measurable change in the substance of environmental planning such that it is actually delivering elements of sustainable development, or even merely acclimatising citizens, businesses and governments to the prospect of drastic change in the future, then this will have been a highly significant achievement.

A BRIEF SURVEY OF ACTUAL ENVIRONMENTAL PLANNING

The activity of environmental planning could be characterised in numerous ways, but a simple four-fold framework has been adopted for the present discussion:

- planning socio-economic systems;
- planning life-support systems;
- social learning; and
- environmental modernisation and the sustainability transition.

Planning socio-economic systems

Environmental planning of the built environment has emphasised principles such as low-rise/high-density development, innovative detailed design principles and the creation of more energy-efficient patterns of urban form. However, each of these remains controversial, and too prescriptive an approach to urban space could be unrealistic and damaging. The concept of urban environmental 'robustness' in relation to urban design is thus seen to cohere around: flexible forms and structures for maximised lifespan and energy-efficiency, yet with a high quality living space; construction methods and materials that minimise waste, undue obsolescence and embodied energy; and efficient systems and services that reduce the overall consumption of fuels and other renewable resources in day-to-day use (Goodchild, 1994). Notwithstanding the risks of prescription, the approach of the UK Building Research Establishment Environmental Assessment Method, based on auditing the environmental performance of the design and specification of certain building types, has proved highly influential (Guise *et al.* 1994). More formally, building regulations have been refined progressively in Britain since 1952. At the time of writing, the most recent ones demonstrated how builders could achieve ambitious targets for CO_2 reduction via a Standard Assessment Procedure (SAP) based on energy labelling (Barlow and Bhatti 1997).

Various studies have also demonstrated that alternative urban forms are at least theoretically conducive to energy conservation (Owens 1992), though these are obviously difficult to design retrospectively, and options based on densification and re-use of brownfield sites are difficult to achieve. Alternative options for future growth comprise urban infill, peripheral urban extensions, key villages, multiple village extensions and new settlements. Debate still rages about the alternative merits of these and, given the force of NIMBY-ism (the acronym stands for 'Not in my back yard!'), there is a danger by default of incremental diminution of undeveloped land. A study of alternative settlement forms (Breheny, Gent and Lock 1993) demonstrated that their performance could be related to social, economic and environmental criteria, such as loss of land or natural habitats, energy consumption, pollution levels and town cramming effects. Whatever the respective merits of different layouts, the fundamental conclusion was that 'unless much tougher containment policies are introduced . . . it is inevitable that significant greenfield/village development will take place'. Such conclusions add fuel to the debate about new countryside settlements, which increasingly are being viewed as environmental showpieces within a 'sustainable social city region' (Breheny and Rookwood 1993) and, as such, could be viewed as a potential means of ecological modernisation. At a much more ambitious scale, the concept of the Japanese designer city has been exported to Australia in the form of the multi-function polis (MFP: Carter and Brine 1995). Focused on Adelaide, but linked to activities elsewhere in Australia and overseas, it sought to create business investment and employment in relatively 'clean' growth industries (environmental management, education and training, and information technology and telecommunications), and its 'smart' design is intended to ensure high levels of efficiency in resource use and recycling. In practice, results on the ground have been much more modest and limited than originally intended, though the initial design remains a striking contribution to the concept of ecological modernisation.

Perhaps the 'wickedest' problem of all facing developed countries (and metropolitan regions in many developing countries) at the close of the twentieth century is transport. Massive traffic growth is related broadly to affluence, demographic change and the redistribution of human activity patterns. The combination of an ageing population coupled with growth in early retirement is creating a vast new travel market, at a time when more flexible and uncertain work activities are complicating patterns of commuting and inter-urban travel. Coupled with the changes in housing structure (many smaller units) and re-location of retail units to peripheral sites, a vicious circle of increased car dependency is becoming entrenched (Bannister 1995). Options for future traffic planning include letting congestion find its own level, providing for growth by constructing new roads, altering personal lifestyles, charging for the use of certain road space, and relying on technology to produce lower impact forms of movement. Although many policies genuflect in the direction of reducing travel, or at least the need to travel (by the provision of more convenient facilities), there is, in reality, little that local authorities can do in the absence of concerted central government action.

Planning life-support systems

Environmental 'life-support systems' relate to the air, water and biotic resources which sustain life on earth. Indirectly, they also include scenic landscapes as places of beauty and recreation. Air quality has been a marginal consideration in most planning jurisdictions, though one of central significance to the realm of public health. The historical trend has been one of substantial achievement in many areas of lowering 'visible' air pollutants (especially particulates) but of patchier success in reducing gaseous emissions, and certainly of limiting long-range transport of air pollutants or complex synergistic chemical reactions between emitted gaseous compounds. Also, as inferred in the previous section, planning jurisdictions have made some attempt to promote more efficient transport and settlement patterns in the interests of reducing thermal, aural and air pollution.

Air quality

The difficulties of strategic planning of air quality have been recounted in a review of the 'Clouds of Change' programme in Vancouver (Moore 1994). This city council-endorsed report defined a framework to protect public health, phase out the use of ozone-depleting chemicals, reduce emissions of sulphur dioxide and methane, and address the challenge of carbon dioxide reduction. It included a range of ambitious proposals for transportation and land-use planning, energy conservation, and various political strategies involving leadership, lobbying and networking. However, implementation proved to be slow and incomplete, and a survey of officials, elected members and citizens identified numerous barriers, operating in a mutually reinforcing way. It was argued that they were unlikely to be overcome unless a diverse assault on the problems was agreed, focusing on realistic targets and combining public, political, expert, legislative and financial resources. Patterns of individual and corporate behaviour affecting atmospheric quality are, though, notoriously resistant to change. For example, a study of three key sectors – domestic space heating, domestic appliances and personal transport – indicated that neither economic instruments nor regulatory controls would, in themselves, be sufficient to bring about the necessary investment in energy efficient products and processes. Underlying disincentives to change included the price-sensitive nature of markets for consumer durables and the pervasive influence of short-termism on business calculations (Neale 1994).

Water quality

Water quality has again been of marginal interest to planners, but is gaining prominence with increased concerns about the variability of weather patterns (leading to droughts or floods), the potential need for the 'managed retreat' of coastlines, regional deterioration of seas and their fisheries, depleting ground-water resources and the multiple roles of rivers and lakes in rural and urban landscapes. Water resources have frequently been less well demarcated, or less susceptible to public intervention than land resources, and attempts at integrated management have often relied on consensual approaches. For instance, Mormont (1996) has described the role of 'river contracts' in Belgium, facilitated by a respected non-governmental 'trust', to forge agreements between riparian inter-ests over collective management decisions. A promising level of adherence to the (non-binding) contracts is attributed to the esteem in which the trust is held, and its ability to act as a broker at the highest levels. In a similar example in Scotland, Edwards-Jones (1997) reports on a 'River Valleys Project' (in the former Lothian Region), reflecting a catchment management approach based on voluntary co-operation between stakeholders. The situation is more favourable in England and Wales, where the Environment Agency's LEAPs (Local Environment Agency Plans, formerly known as Catchment Management Plans) are enabling a formal resolution of the conflicts among water management, developmental, conser-vation and agricultural interests. Regrettably, there is as yet little critical evi-dence of the value of these in practice, though those involved in their production would attest at least to the benefits of the consultative process during the initial stages. Increasingly, the river catchment is regarded as the most appropriate geographical unit for integrated planning, and the LEAP process is thus of widespread interest.

Coastlines

The increasing deterioration of coastlines, inshore waters and enclosed seas has led to numerous reports and some localised actions on concerted management. Ideally, given the highly complex and multi-partite interests affecting coastal policy, an integrated approach is invariably necessary. Lawrence and Nelson (1994) argue for planning to be based on ecosystem and watershed principles, with explicit inclusion of human perceptions of and responses to coastal hazards, and interactive and adaptive methods of research and management. This ideal situation rarely exists, though, and non-statutory consensus-based or partnership arrangements are the norm. Kidd (1995), for example, describes the case of English Nature's Estuaries Initiative, supporting the preparation of estuarine management plans. She refers specifically to the Mersey, where an advisory framework amongst the many existing interests (thirty agencies, eight local authorities, and a mix of land ownership and tenure) aims to develop the potential of the estuary as a natural resource. The Vision Statement addresses estuary resources, economic development, recreation and implementation, whilst strategic objectives relate to the integrity of the associated land and water systems. Once more, there is little critical evidence of the long-term success of such approaches.

Biodiversity

Biodiversity has, especially since the Rio summit, established itself relatively firmly as a key environmental issue, though its significant influence on aspects of strategic and site planning has a far longer pedigree. Various schools of landscape ecological planning have emerged over the past twenty years, based on assumptions about the behaviour of species in relation to corridors, habitat patches (biotopes) and inhospitable 'matrix' areas (Selman 1996b). The most notable adoption of these principles has been in the Czech and Slovak Republics, where landscape ecology serves as a mapping and planning framework, partly to try to 're-stabilise' landscapes damaged by industrialisation and intensive agriculture, and to recognise the countries' function as an ecological corridor within a strategic area of central Europe. More recently, Dutch planners have used landscape ecological techniques to devise strategies for the 'green structure' of the Randstad and for creating attractive countryside in reclaimed polders. Similar approaches are also increasingly widespread in continental Europe and North America, where they have been influential in planning for greenways, forests, reconstructed agricultural holdings (*remembrements*) and nature reserves. More generally, the influence of 'landscape scale' analyses has been important in raising the horizons of planners and conservationists above the site level. In view of the continuing attrition of biodiversity, it is anticipated that a more strategic treatment of ecological resources in the wider countryside will address the shortcomings of traditional site-based approaches. These assumptions underlie, for example, the networking provisions in the European Community Habitats Directive (92/43/EEC) and European Ecological Network (EECONET).

Countryside protection

The traditional tenets of countryside protection may be summarised as: safe-guarding places of outstanding ecology, beauty and cultural significance; maintaining the life-supporting diversity of ecosystems (species, genetic variation and ecological processes); protecting the cultural qualities and local environmental benefits of traditionally managed landscapes; and providing for the scientific, educational, recreational and spiritual needs of societies (Bishop, Phillips and Warren 1997). Whilst these purposes are still widely accepted, they do have increasingly apparent deficiencies related to the treatment of protected areas as 'islands' set apart from their surroundings, poor integration into cognate policy sectors such as agriculture and transport, and inadequate recognition of the needs and skills of local people. Consequently, recent trends have involved greater planning and policy integration, stronger definition of international programmes, and the elevation of biodiversity (rather than various scientific and aesthetic qualities) as the key criterion. Despite this increasing rationalisation of purpose, however, there is still a complex and confusing proliferation of conservation designations, with twenty-nine different types of protected area in the UK alone. This panoply of protected areas reflects differences of spatial importance (from local to global significance), objective (purpose for which established), responsible authority, type of protective device (whether regulatory, management, promotional or consultative), legal status, and optional or compulsory participation (Bishop, Phillips and Warren 1997).

The post-Rio focus on biodiversity action plans, at both national and sub-national levels, may at least provide a framework in which differing purposes and actions can be reconciled. Conservation agencies reflect these differences to an extent, most notably in the level of separation between landscape and wildlife organisations. In Britain, there has been a measure of *rapprochement* between the two (recently combined agencies in Scotland and Wales, and a joint mapping focus in England), and clauses in countryside legislation since the mid-1980s requiring conservation, agricultural, rural development and forestry activities to have regard to a 'balance' of interests when pursuing their objectives. Nevertheless, it has been argued that the central roles and philosophies of the rural planning agencies established in the 1940s have changed little despite significant agency restructuring, and it was contended that much of the change has been cosmetic (Hodge, Adams and Bourn 1994). Conservation of the wider countryside matrix within which special areas are set has only recently become an established policy area, and no agency has specific sole responsibility.

Landscape conservation has always tended to be the poor relation to nature conservation and, in land-use plans, has typically reflected 'cosmetics' rather than 'critical constraints' (Punter and Carmona 1997). A more dynamic approach is possible, though, incorporating established principles of architecturally 'responsive environments' – variety, vitality, permeability, legibility and robustness (Bentley *et al.* 1985) – whilst adding the principles of energy efficiency, wildlife support and cleanliness. Although Punter and Carmona's (1997) study of landscape elements in British plans did reveal a wide range of strategic, local and sustainability considerations, they perceived a need for a much clearer 'strategic greenspace frame for development' and saw the multi-scale and legally robust German approach to landscape appraisal as a promising model. Gradually, though, shifts are taking place in landscape conservation practice, changing from an almost exclusive concern with the protection of the 'best' towards interests in whole-landscape diversity and local distinctiveness. These are coupled with moves from protection towards creative conservation and from an essentially aesthetic approach towards a deeper appreciation of the ecological, historical and cultural values of landscape and the way in which these are interwoven (Bishop, Phillips and Warren 1997).

Geographic information systems

The advent of geographic information systems (GIS) as a major element of environmental decision-support systems (DSS) has had a profound impact on the practice of natural environmental planning, especially in relation to climate flux, hydrological systems and ecological change. Whilst spatial modelling has made signal contributions to urban management, its ability to help environmental planners undertake real-time monitoring and analysis of dynamic natural systems has been even more profound. In particular, GIS can help decision-makers confront poorly structured (wicked) problems, through direct interaction with data and models. A sophisticated but user-friendly model has been developed for the north of England (NELUP) to aid the management of complex land-use changes deriving from many separate interest groups with potentially conflicting rights, duties and objectives (McClean *et al.* 1995). The system is based on two broad levels of abstraction, the lower ones containing general inventory information and displaying incidences of land use and socio-economic phenomena, and the higher ones supporting models of agricultural economic, ecological and hydrological activities. The DSS are characterised by the relative ease with which non-expert users can interact with the database and models, so that they provide support throughout the decision-making process rather than simply computing definitive answers to individually structured questions. The wider significance of this approach is that it enables us to address environmental problems where the tasks involved are not fully defined, and only an estimate of the required functionality can be supplied by users and developers.

Social learning

Much of the contemporary debate in environmental planning concerns the extent to which, and mechanisms whereby, the lay public can engage in decision-making, other than in a highly intermittent or reactive fashion (Selman and Parker 1997). Despite a more tortuous process and unpredictable outcome, decisions reached on an inclusive basis are generally deemed to be more stable and liable to long-term success. More participatory, or less adversarial, approaches to environmental planning may be sorted into a spectrum spanning environmental diplomacy (national and international negotiation of settlements), policy-focused consensus-building dialogues, and case-specific 'environmental mediation' or 'dispute resolution' structures. Though very fashionable, it should be noted that non-adversarial approaches have been much hyped but remain relatively untested in practice. Foucauldian influenced critics also argue that they take a naive view of the control exerted by external sources of power. Moreover, a move towards more consensual modes of environmental planning needs to be achieved without undermining the properly constituted processes of local democracy and roles of elected members.

This debate is reviewed here under the heading of 'social learning', which implies not only active citizenship and participatory democracy but also that opinions and skills are developed during the process of engagement. Thus, Glasbergen (1996) argues that continuous reflection on failures and their aversion can aid the efficacy of the environmental policy process by organising it as a learning process. He advocates a shift from cognitive to social learning. Whilst this process certainly facilitates a better formulation of problems, it does not automatically yield easier or more effective solutions, as increasingly stubborn problems tend to emerge. It is argued that conceptual learning is good for many policy areas, but that social learning (which approximates to network management) is better for the environment, and is characterised by structural openness, participatory roles and responsibility for implementation. For various reasons, though, it is not a panacea, and thus serves as an enrichment of, rather than a replacement for, traditional models.

The process of social learning implies fairly high levels of citizen activity, strongly advocated by communitarians, but difficult to reconcile with contemporary social trends. Hill (1994), for example, notes that we now value the city as a site of hotels and shopping centres, but are losing a sense of the city as polity. She notes in particular the reduced ability of local authorities to provide authoritative governance, and queries what impact this may have on the exercise of citizenship and the effectiveness of the municipality as a location of significant decisions. Healey (1996) offers a more positive perspective on the incorporation of citizen views, even where governance is fragmented and interests are diverse and conflictual. An advocate of collaborative, communicative practices, she argues that we should build 'institutional capacity' to foster the social and intellectual capital which is generated (and currently often dissipated) during interactive working. Thus improving the supportiveness of institutional cultures could involve a deeper awareness of the identity of stakeholders, arenas for and styles of discussion, policy discourses and modes of agreement.

Evidence from the early stages of Local Agenda 21 processes confirms that, despite some encouraging innovations, even relatively positive local authorities may find it difficult to relinquish control, either because of an innate aversion or because they are inescapably committed to environmentally damaging projects (Freeman, Littlewood and Whitney 1996; Carter and Darlow 1997). Exclusion of citizens from critical nodes of decision-making precipitates the NIMBY syndrome. Despite its stereotypical portrayal, this may deserve sympathetic treatment, and it may be possible for appropriately re-skilled planners to turn it to positive effect (Grundy and Memon 1994; Gleeson and Memon 1997). The experience of listening to many NIMBY views suggests that they are based on fundamental misunderstandings, and reflect a desire to simplify the problem and apportion blame, a failure to be self-critical, and a reluctance to change procedures. Community involvement in environmental decision-making tends to succeed or fail in proportion to the adequacy of time for proper discussion (prior to pre-emptive decisions) and the willingness of affected parties to treat others as equals and modify their opinions (Wilcox 1994). In this context, the use of an active Community Advisory Forum to review an energy-from-waste facility in Hampshire, England, was observed to lead to improvements in representativeness, effectiveness, heightened awareness and influence on the decision process (Petts 1995). Similar benefits were realised by a citizens' jury on waste disposal alternatives in Hertfordshire (Kuper 1997).

A specific medium of social learning has been the use in various legislatures of public registers of environmental information. Historically, concern has been expressed that these are tantamount to 'busybodies' charters', on the grounds that: the public are not competent to interpret environmental data; data may be misinterpreted and create unwarranted alarm; disclosure may confer a commercial advantage on competitors; and administrative costs would be disproportionate to the likely level of usage (Ross and Rowan-Robinson 1994). However, the commitment in the EC fourth Environmental Action Programme towards openness, and the Directive on Freedom of Access to Information on the Environment (90/313/EC), gave an impetus to the use of registers, and the UK government supports their use on the grounds of public reassurance, agency accountability, industrial responsibility and public participation (DoE 1990). Actual use of registers is highly variable (planning application registers are consulted quite frequently, for instance, but discharge consents only rarely) but pressure groups advocate raising levels of awareness and accessibility. More positive approaches to public register management may promote wider participation, and a pertinent example is the Canadian Environmental Assessment Registry which includes a variety of electronic and locally based facilities whereby the public can consult environmental assessment information (LeBlanc and Ray 1996).

Ecological modernisation and the sustainability transition

In many areas of environmental degradation, a combination of environmental fragility, economic dependency, human poverty and political defensiveness has created a 'vicious circle' of deteriorating resource quality. The mirror image of this is the 'virtuous cycle' of development in which inclusive, reflexive and adaptive decisions lead to patterns of social investment and technological innovation which have neutral or positive environmental impact. The obvious conclusion is one of 'convergence', based on an increasing harmony of developmental and conservation objectives. Marshall (1993) reviews the tensions between environmental quality and capital accumulation, but anticipates the possibility that in the 'social and ecological market economy' (arguably, emergent in Germany) this disjuncture may lessen. From this, we might expect that processes of ecological modernisation will confer mutually reinforcing solutions, based on devices such as green taxes, planning gain and compensation of 'constant' environmental capital. Convergence though, as previously noted, is not always wholly desirable, as it may normalise outlooks and ensure that alternative conceptions (both more and less green) are not tolerated.

A key element of ecological modernisation is integration, as reflected in green plans, environmental assessment, and the creation of multi-purpose environmental agencies. One view of integration is that it involves co-ordinated direction or influence over the range of human activities within a particular environmental system to reconcile and implement the broadest possible spectrum of short- and long-term objectives (Cairns and Crawford 1991), whilst Margerum and Born (1995) argue that integrated environmental management hinges on inclusivity, interconnectedness, and shared goals and problem formulations. In practice, integration may never truly be reached, as stakeholders constantly adapt to new knowledge. The strategic aspect of integration is now attested to by an increasing range of multi-functional (though often non-statutory) plans such as catchment plans, indicative forestry strategies, biodiversity action plans, waste management plans, environmental charters and Local Agenda 21s. A more generic Strategic Services Planning Framework is advocated by the International Council for Local Environmental Initiatives (ICLEI 1996), and this has been tested through an action research process within their Model Communities Programme. Examples of national green plans include Canada's Green Plan (Government of Canada 1990) and the Dutch National Environmental Policy Plan (VROM 1993). The former included a range of actions concerning individual citizenship, public expenditure commitments and legislation. These have been partly fulfilled and, whilst the plan received criticism for its limited implementation and ambition, most observers acknowledge that it was an important step in developing the notion of governmental green planning (Selman 1994; Darier 1996). The Dutch plan reflects a highly developed national environmental policy, based upon serious attempts to deal with pollution and energy issues, linked to other national plans and policies, and negotiated with each industrial sector.

At the project and site level, the most salient innovation has been environmental assessment, which has now become established internationally, either as an add-on to an existing system of strategic and site planning, or as a 'fast-track' solution to local environmental decision-making in the absence of a mature land use regulatory framework. However, practice still leaves much to be desired, and a study of nearly two hundred UK environmental statements concluded that the ecological information was often so limited or of such poor quality that it was not possible to assess the ecological implications of proposed schemes (Thompson, Treweek and Thurling 1997). Although impacts were considered to be probable in 93 per cent of statements, only 9 per cent made any attempt to quantify them, and less than half the statements based their findings on new ecological surveys, whilst substantially fewer proposed detailed mitigation measures or monitoring arrangements. Strategic environmental assessment is even less well developed, and even one of the UK's more imaginative and diligent strategic EAs used mathematically 'fallacious aggregations' so that claims about the plan's progress towards sustainability or comparative evaluation of options were difficult to justify (Merrett 1994).

The reformist approach to environmental law has sought the improved integration and sometimes wholesale revision of statutes. A main plank of this strategy has been to ensure that countries should 'practise integrated pollution prevention and control, taking into account the effects of activities and substances on the environment as a whole and the . . . commercial and environmental life cycles of substances' (OECD 1991: Article 1(a)). This view is based on a recognition that substances can move among different environmental media as they travel along pathways from sources to receptors, and that controls over releases of a substance to one environmental medium can result in shifting the substance to another. Thus European action on Integrated Pollution Prevention and Control has promoted the use of single permits covering all releases and processes, and has sought closer links between land-use planning, transport regulation, economic instruments, cleaner technologies and industrial life-cycle management. A key expression of this has been the BATNEEC principle (Best Available Technology Not Entailing Excessive Cost) in the 1990 UK Environmental Protection Act. It has been suggested that possible future developments may focus on 'source based' approaches, through the use of mass balances and life-cycle analyses (Emmott and Haigh 1996). Nevertheless, whilst the 1990 Act implied an integrated approach to pollution control, Jordan (1993: 1) averred that its introduction had been 'haphazard, incremental and protracted'.

The Environment Act passed in Britain in 1995, which set up 'integrated' agencies (the Environment Agency in England and Wales, and the Scottish Environmental Protection Agency), is also a notable advance. The Act gave statutory recognition, for the first time, to 'sustainable development' as the 'new principal aim' of domestic environmental law and policy (Jewell and Steele 1996), and its adoption was complemented by the use of cost-benefit and risk-assessment techniques. These agencies approximate to 'one stop shops' for the largest industrial polluters, and this combination of apparently sound environmental aspirations with commercial convenience is a key feature of sustainable development as it has been elaborated by UK policy-makers. Nevertheless, the image of shopping for pollution licences from a trusted monopoly supplier raises questions about the relationship between agencies and the regulated sector, and between the environmental and commercial purposes of the new regulatory structure. The agencies, though, did not receive conservation functions – thus limiting the potential for comprehensive integration – as this was perceived to be inconsistent with the role of issuing licences. Thus, although instructed to pay attention to various 'environmental' principles (such as the need for a long-term 'holistic' approach and the desirability of maintaining biodiversity), specific functions mostly relate to a reconciliation of the needs of the environment and those of development, and the focus is on the adoption of improved technologies and the provision of authoritative advice. In legal practice, it seems that the new priority of 'sustainable development', despite its supposed potential for revising wealth-creating activities, in fact implies the dominance of one set of perceptions – that of the regulated constituency (that is, the polluter) – in defining environmental problems and their solutions (Jewell and Steele 1996). Green taxes as an expression of 'Best Practical Environmental Option' are still at the teething stage. The UK Landfill Tax, for example, seeks to charge premia for solid waste disposal, to shift solutions higher up the waste hierarchy, though in practice it possibly serves to augment local taxes, deflect disposal to less well controlled sites, penalise small businesses and exacerbate illegal tipping. Nevertheless, it is a genuine innovation which has been greeted with some optimism, and will no doubt inform subsequent policy initiatives.

A notable example of radical reform of environmental law has been New Zealand's Resource Management Act of 1991, which swept aside the country's inherited town and country planning system, replacing it with an integrated framework for resource management based on efficiency, sustainability and public participation. The Act replaced the plethora of policies and regulations evolved since the 1940s and, with the exception of Crown-owned mineral reserves and fisheries, encompassed all natural and environmental resources (Furuseth and Cocklin 1995; Morgan 1995; Gleeson and Grundy 1997). The Act established sustainable management as the guiding principle for decisions over resource use and adopted a sustainability-based standard for public policy. Planners are required to examine alternative mechanisms for achieving desired outcomes (such as land acquisition, tax incentives, ordinances and standards), with the underlying purpose of moving policy towards an environmental bottom line, so that policy decisions are linked to 'the establishment of clear environmental outcomes and a range of possible approaches and instruments for achieving the outcomes' (Brash 1993: 1). Environmental impact assessment is a core process, and is incorporated not only in development appraisals, but also policy analysis of plans and water resource consents. Even this radical and widely acclaimed legislation, though, reflects the neo-liberal philosophy of a 'new right' political administration, and the Act seeks an uneasy compromise between two potentially contradictory (that is, green and productivist) socio-political forces. Further, it appears in practice that councils are still attached to traditional ideas of zoning, whilst the vague wording of compensation and notification provisions has allegedly led to a situation where big business can virtually 'buy' consent. Although the Act set out a comprehensive sustainable management strategy, and is still watched with hope and interest, its anticipated innovations appear to have been limited.

Summarising this section, we may note that the character of environmental planning has been forged by complex forces, and there is some evidence that these may now be promoting a more responsive professionalism which can help twenty-first century society to make the sustainability transition (Table 7.1). Indeed, many planners would argue that ecological concerns have given new purpose to their

Table 7.1 Towards the sustainability transition? An idealised classification of the evolution of environmental planning

	1970s+	*1980s+*	*1990s+*
Level of integration	fragmented/ reductionist	integrative	holistic
Role of expertise	top-down	consultative	mixed-mode (merging top-down and bottom-up)
Importance of nature	cosmetic site treatment	striking a 'balance' between development and conservation	respecting limits imposed by life support systems
Eco-philosophy	technocentrism	ecological modernisation	sustainability planning
Level of systems control	controlling nature	accommodating nature	managing risk
Characteristic techniques	based on mapping and limited problem conceptualisations	based on environmental assessment and optimisation of trade-offs	based on responsive and inclusive management of ill-defined problems

enterprise, and have created exciting developments in terms of technical expertise and lay involvement (Selman 1996a). However, two associated risks should be borne in mind. One is that it is the rhetoric, rather than the substance, of planning policy which has changed, and that planners will be unable to spearhead transforming mechanisms in the face of ever-increasing developmental pressures. The second is that the scope of 'green planning' has enlarged to the point of decomposition. However desirable it may be to address the spectrum of 'quality of life' issues on a widely participatory basis, this may create an ill-focused and self-defeating agenda. Provided these dangers can be averted, though, there is a strong prospect that planning can regain the vigour of its early years as a purposeful activity focused both on improving local quality of life, and on recognising the effects of that quality of life on 'distant elsewheres'.

CONCLUSIONS

The consolidation of environmental planning as a core activity of the central and local state over the past generation has, even on a cautious assessment, been impressive. Official government statements and the conclusions of the more optimistic commentators give an impression of mature and effective legislatures, integrated and accountable agencies, and skilled professionals. In practice, despite enormous amounts of dedication and inspiration, environmental planning only ever achieves partial success. This is due to the 'wickedness' of environmental issues, deriving not only from their technical complexity, but also from the

Table 7.2 Some problems and potentials in environmental planning

Wicked problems	Barriers	Capacity-building	Solutions	Audits
multiple and complex – grounded in scientific disagreement, political indifference and vested interest, complicated by corporatist relationships, patchy and ageing legislation, crisis management and retro-fitting . . .	confrontation and protest; lack of urgency/ understanding/ knowledge/ resources/ skills/electoral relevance; planners more interested in social and economic issues; pseudo-integration of agencies, with field staff not 'buying in' to corporate objectives . . .	research, new legislation, experimentation, lay involvement (citizen science), new institutional and financial resources, social learning; new skills for public participation and evaluation of environmental performance; improved quality and quantity of environmental information . . .	transnational, national and sub-national/ federal reform; neighbourhood design; integrated plans for land and water management; sustainable settlements; pursuit of environmental bottom-line . . .	state of environment indicators, ecological footprints, measuring and monitoring for environmental assessment; networked assessments utilising lay knowledge . . .

multiple arenas where they are contested and debated. As capacities are built to overcome one barrier, another one arises; as progress is made towards sustainability, so the finishing line recedes. One heartening feature is a shift to an apparent consensus position over key environmental problems, and the recognition of the need for a modernised or even radical response based on a blend of mandatory and persuasive instruments. This 'convergence interpretation', though, is perhaps too convenient, and it may lead to a degree of normalisation which is intolerant of alternative conceptions (whether more or less green). We have still not yet learned any definitive lessons from three decades of environmental planning and, if we are not to be eco-authoritarians, we must be prepared to engage in debate about the proper influence of ecological imperatives on the planning process.

Looking back at our earlier characterisation of environmental planning, we can observe numerous problematic attributes, as well as some opportunities for overcoming barriers (Table 7.2). The primary lesson from thirty years' experience is that such a complex problem domain creates tremendous technical, bureaucratic and political difficulties for concerted action. International best practice has rolled forward the frontiers of integrated planning and management although, as much of this has only emerged during the 1990s, there is still a paucity of evidence on which to judge implementational success. Yet, understandably, many observers would argue that we cannot afford the luxury of procrastination.

Whilst the environment is a 'holistic' concept *par excellence*, 'planning' (in its generic sense) seems destined to be sundered between different legal frameworks and administrative agencies. Perhaps this is a necessary inconvenience, as the tendency for the green agenda and its policy responses to become ever more encompassing and labyrinthine requires the setting of boundaries to render problems manageable. What is more important is that flexibility of policy instruments and team-working become more habitual in the pursuit of an environmental bottom line. This benchmark must itself be based on the notion of environmental limits rather than the balancing of objectives.

This chapter has been written in the wake of the 'Rio+5' negotiations, which have generally been viewed as a considerable disappointment, diminishing further the likelihood of sacrificial national action on behalf of the environment. Nevertheless, there is some evidence that 'planners' working in some sectors are starting to grasp the importance of ecological limits, are seeking the best environmental options, and are becoming skilled in new scientific and humanistic techniques to aid transparent and adaptive decision-making. 'Virtuous' development may never wholly vanquish 'wicked' problems, but the human spirit will always seek such a possibility.

References

Abercrombie, P. (1933) *Town and Country Planning*, London: Butterworth.

Amin, A. (ed.) (1994) *Post-Fordism: a reader*, Oxford: Blackwell.

Bannister, C. (1995) 'Transport and the Environment', *Town Planning Review* 66: 453–8.

Barlow, J. and Bhatti, M. (1997) 'Environmental performance as a competitive strategy? British speculative house builders in the 1990s', *Planning Practice and Research* 12: 33–44.

Barton, H. and Bruder, N. (1995) *A Guide to Local Authority Auditing*, London: Earthscan.

Beck, U. (1992) *Risk Society: Towards a New Modernity*, London: Sage.

Bentley, I., Alcock, A., Murrain, P., McGlynn, S. and Smith, G. (1985) *Responsive Environments: A Manual for Designers*, London: Architectural Press.

Bishop K., Phillips, A. and Warren, L. (1997) 'Protected areas for the future: models from the past', *Journal of Environmental Planning and Management* 40: 81–110.

Boehmer-Christiansen, S. (1994) 'Politics and environmental management', *Journal of Environmental Planning and Management* 37: 69–86.

Boucher, S. and Whatmore, S. (1993) 'Green gains? Planning by agreement and nature conservation', *Journal of Environmental Planning and Management* 36: 33–50.

Brash, D. (1993) *Sustainable Environmental Management and the Environmental Bottom Line: Resource Management Ideas No. 2*, Wellington, New Zealand: Ministry for the Environment.

Breheny, M., Gent, T. and Lock, D. (1993) *Alternative Development Patterns: New Settlements*, DoE Planning Research Project, London: HMSO.

Breheny, M. and Rookwood, R. (1993) 'Planning the sustainable city region', in A. Blowers (ed.), *Planning for a Sustainable Environment: A Report by the Town and Country Planning Association*, London: Earthscan.

Byron, H. and Sheate, W. (1997) 'Strategic environmental assessment: current status in the water and electricity sectors in England and Wales', *Environmental Policy and Practice* 6: 155–66.

Cairns, J. and Crawford, T. (eds) (1991) *Integrated Environmental Management*, Chelsea Mich.: Lewis.

Carter, N. and Brine, J. (1995) 'MFP Australia: a vision of sustainable development for a post-industrial society', *Planning Practice and Research* 10: 25–44.

Carter, N. and Darlow, A. (1997) 'Local Agenda 21 and planners: are we better equipped to build a consensus in the 1990s?', *Planning Practice and Research* 12: 45–58.

Darier, E. (1996) 'Environmental governability: the case of Canada's Green Plan', *Environmental Politics* 5: 585–606.

DoE (Department of Environment) (1990) *This Common Inheritance*, Cmnd 1200, London: HMSO.

Dobson, A. (1995) 'Biocentrism and genetic engineering', *Environmental Values*, 4: 227–40.

Dryzek, J. (1996) 'Strategies of ecological democratization', in W. Lafferty and J. Meadowcroft (eds), *Democracy and the Environment: Problems and Prospects*, Cheltenham: Edward Elgar.

DTA/CAG (1994) *Planning for Environmental Sustainability*, David Tyldesley Associates with CAG Consultants, Peterborough: English Nature.

Edwards-Jones, E. (1997) 'The River Valleys Project: a participatory approach to integrated catchment planning and management in Scotland', *Journal of Environmental Planning and Management* 40: 125–42.

Emmott, N. and Haigh, N. (1996) 'Integrated Pollution Prevention and Control: UK and EC approaches and possible next steps', *Journal of Environmental Law* 8: 301–11.

Freeman, C., Littlewood, S. and Whitney, D. (1996) 'Local government and emerging models of participation in the Local Agenda 21 process', *Journal of Environmental Planning and Management* 39: 65–78.

Furuseth, O. and Cocklin, C. (1995) 'Regional perspectives on resource policy: implementing sustainable management in New Zealand', *Journal of Environmental Planning and Management* 38: 181–200.

Glasbergen, P. (1996) 'Learning to manage the environment', in W. Lafferty and J. Meadowcroft (eds), *Democracy and the Environment: Problems and Prospects*, Cheltenham: Edward Elgar.

Gleeson, B. and Grundy, K. (1997) 'New Zealand's planning revolution five years on: a preliminary assessment', *Journal of Environmental Planning and Management* 40: 293–314.

Gleeson, B. and Memon, P. (1997) 'Community care: implications for urban planning from the New Zealand experience', *Planning Practice and Research* 12: 119–32.

Goodchild, B. (1994) 'Housing design, urban form and sustainable development', *Town Planning Review* 65: 143–58.

Government of Canada (1990) *Canada's Green Plan*, Ottawa: Government of Canada.

Greed, C. (ed.) (1996) *Implementing Town Planning: The Role of Town Planning in the Development Process*, Harlow: Longman.

Grundy, K. and Memon, P. (1994) 'The NIMBY syndrome and community care facilities: a research agenda for planning', *Planning Practice and Research* 9: 105–18.

Guise, R., Barton, H., Davis, G. and Stead, D. (1994) 'Design and sustainable development', *Planning Practice and Research*, 9: 221–39.

Hall, P. (ed.) (1973) *The Containment of Urban England, Vol. one and two*, London and Beverly Hills, Ca.: Allen & Unwin/Sage.

Healey, P. (1996) 'Consensus-building across difficult divisions: new approaches to collaborative strategy making', *Planning Practice and Research* 11: 207–16.

Healey, P. (1997) *Collaborative Planning: Shaping Places in Fragmented Societies*, London: Macmillan.

Healey, P., Purdue, M. and Ennis, F. (1995) *Negotiating Development: Rationales and Practice for Development Obligations and Planning Gain*, London: Spon.

Hill, D. (1994) *Citizens and Cities: Urban Policy in the 1990s*, Hemel Hempstead: Harvester Wheatsheaf.

Hodge, I., Adams, W. and Bourn, N. (1994) 'Conservation policy in the wider countryside: agency competition and innovation', *Journal of Environmental Planning and Management* 37: 199–214.

ICLEI (1996) *The Local Agenda 21 Planning Guide: An Introduction to Sustainable Development Planning*, Toronto: ICLEI.

Irwin, A. (1995) *Citizen Science: A Study of People, Expertise and Sustainable Development*, London: Routledge.

Jackson, T. and Roberts, P. (1997) 'Greening the Fife economy: ecological modernisation as a pathway for local economic development', *Journal of Environmental Planning and Management* 40: 615–29.

Jewell, T. and Steele, J. (1996) 'UK regulatory reform and the pursuit of "sustainable development": the Environment Act 1995', *Journal of Environmental Law* 8: 283–300.

Jordan, A. (1993) 'Integrated Pollution Control and the evolving style and structure of environmental regulation in the UK', *Environmental Politics* 2: 405–27.

Kidd, S. (1995) 'Planning for estuary resources: the Mersey Estuary Management Plan', *Journal of Environmental Planning and Management* 38: 435–42.

Kuper, R. (1997) 'Deliberating waste: the Hertfordshire Citizens' Jury', *Local Environment* 2: 139–54.

Lafferty, W. and Meadowcroft, J. (1996) 'Democracy and the environment: congruence and conflict – preliminary reflections', in W. Lafferty and J. Meadowcroft (eds) *Democracy and the Environment: Problems and Prospects*, Cheltenham: Edward Elgar.

Lawrence, P. and Nelson, J. (1994) 'Flooding and erosion hazards on the Ontario Great Lakes shoreline: a human ecological approach to planning and management', *Journal of Environmental Planning and Management* 37: 289–304.

LeBlanc, P. and Ray, A. (1996) 'The Canadian Environmental Assessment Act's public registry system', *Journal of Environmental Planning and Management* 39: 419–28.

McClean, C., Watson, P., Wadsworth, R., Blaiklock, J. and O'Callaghan, J. (1995) 'Land use planning: a decision support system', *Journal of Environmental Planning and Management* 38: 77–92.

Margerum, R. and Born, S. (1995) 'Integrated environmental management: moving from theory to practice', *Journal of Environmental Planning and Management* 38: 371–92.

Marshall, T. (1993) 'Regional environmental planning: progress and possibilities in Western Europe', *European Planning Studies* 1: 69–90.

Merrett, S. (1994) 'Ticks and crosses: strategic environmental assessment and the Kent structure plan', *Planning Practice and Research* 9: 147–50.

Moore, J. (1994) 'What's stopping sustainability? Examining the barriers to the implementation of "Clouds of Change"', Master's Thesis, School of Community and Regional Planning, University of British Columbia.

Morgan, R. (1995) 'Progress with implementing the environmental assessment requirements of the Resource Management Act in New Zealand', *Journal of Environmental Planning and Management* 38: 333–48.

Mormont, M. (1996) 'Towards concerted river management in Belgium', *Journal of Environmental Planning and Management* 39: 131–42.

Neale, A. (1994) 'Climate stability and behavioural change: the limitations of economic and regulatory instruments', *Journal of Environmental Planning and Management* 37: 335–48.

OECD (1991) *Integrated Pollution Prevention and Control*, Environment Monograph No. 37, Paris: OECD.

O'Riordan, T. (1989) 'The challenge for environmentalism', in R. Peet and N. Thrift (eds), *New Models in Geography*, London: Hyman Unwin, 77–102.

O'Riordan, T., and Wynne, B. (1987) 'Regulating environmental risks', in P. Keindorfer and H. Kunreuther (eds), *Insuring and Managing Hazardous Risks*: Berlin: Springer-Verlag.

O'Riordan, T. and Voisey, H. (1997) 'The political economy of sustainable development', *Environmental Politics*, 6: 1–23.

Owens, S. (1992) 'Energy, environmental sustainability and land use planning', in M. Breheny (ed.) *Sustainable Development and Urban Form: European Research in Regional Science*, No. 2, London: Pion.

Paehlke, R. (1996) 'Environmental challenges to democratic practice', in W. Lafferty and J. Meadowcroft (eds), *Democracy and the Environment: Problems and Prospects*, Cheltenham: Edward Elgar.

Pearce, D. (1993) *Blueprint Three: Measuring Sustainable Development*, London: Earthscan.

Petts, J. (1995) 'Waste management strategy development: a case study of community involvement and consensus-building in Hampshire', *Journal of Environmental Planning and Management* 38: 519–36.

Punter, J. and Carmona, M. (1997) 'Cosmetics or critical constraints? The role of landscape in design policies in English development plans', *Journal of Environmental Planning and Management* 40: 173–98.

Rittel, H. and Webber, M. (1973) 'Dilemmas in a general theory of planning', *Policy Sciences* 4: 155–69.

Ross, A. and Rowan-Robinson, J. (1994) 'Public registers of environmental information', *Journal of Environmental Planning and Management* 37: 249–360.

Rowan-Robinson, J., Ross, A. and Walton, W. (1995) 'Sustainable development and the development control process', *Town Planning Review*, 66: 269–86.

Selman, P. (1994) 'Systematic environmental reporting and planning: some lessons from Canada', *Journal of Environmental Planning and Management* 37: 461–76.

Selman, P. (1996a) *Local Sustainability: Managing and Planning Ecologically Sound Places*, London: Paul Chapman.

Selman, P. (1996b) 'The contribution of landscape ecology', in F. Aalen (ed.), *Landscape Study and Management*, Dublin: Boole Press.

Selman, P. and Parker, J. (1997) 'Citizenship, civicness and social capital in Local Agenda 21', *Local Environment* 2: 171–84.

Snape, S. (1995) 'Contracting out local government services in Western Europe', *Local Government Studies* 21: 642–58.

Steenbergen, B. van (1994) 'Towards a global environmental citizen', in B. van Steenbergen (ed.), *The Condition of Citizenship*, London: Sage, 141–52.

Tate, J. (1994) 'Sustainability: a case of back to basics?', *Planning Practice and Research* 9: 367–80.

Thérivel, R. (1995) 'Environmental appraisal of development plans: current status', *Planning Practice and Research* 10: 223–34.

Thompson, S., Treweek, J. and Thurling, D. (1997) 'The ecological component of environmental impact assessment: a critical review of British environmental statements', *Journal of Environmental Planning and Management* 40: 157–72.

Trudgill, S. (1990) *Barriers to a Better Environment: What Stops Us Solving Environmental Problems?*, London: Belhaven.

Turner, R., Pearce, D. and Bateman, I. (1994) *Environmental Economics: An Elementary Introduction*, Hemel Hempstead: Harvester Wheatsheaf.

UNCED (1992) *Agenda 21 – Action Plan for the Next Century*, Rio de Janeiro: UNCED.

VROM (1993) *National Environmental Policy Plan 2*, The Hague: Ministry of Housing, Spatial Planning and the Environment.

Wackernagel, M. and Rees, W. (1996) *Our Ecological Footprint: Reducing Human Impact on the Earth*, Gabriola Island, BC: New Society Publishers.

Wilcox, D. (1994) *A Guide to Effective Participation*, Brighton: Partnership Books.

Winter, P. (1994) 'Planning and sustainability: an examination of the role of the planning system as an instrument for the delivery of sustainable development', *Journal of Planning and Environmental Law*: 883–900.

8 National environmental policy planning in the face of uncertainty

Martin Jänicke and Helge Jörgens[1]

INTRODUCTION

Uncertainty is often regarded as a distinctive issue facing environmental policy-makers and ecological issues are frequently described as 'wicked' or 'messy' in kind (Lafferty and Meadowcroft 1996: 4; Bressers 1997: 289; OECD 1995a: 12–13). This chapter explores the potential of long-term environmental planning as a better basis for dealing with issues *characterised* by extreme uncertainty.

Four aspects of uncertainty that environmental policy has to take into account, if it is to be successful, can be distinguished.

1 *Uncertainty of prognosis about environmental changes and their possible negative impacts.*[2] This first dimension concerns uncertainty about the future of environmental circumstances and the possible negative consequences of these. This stems from a lack of understanding of environmental processes as bio-physical systems and also of social processes both as drivers of environmental change and as receivers of a changed environment (Lafferty and Meadowcroft 1996: 4). This uncertainty may lead to the overestimation as well as underestimation of environmental problems. Paradoxically, the potential danger of over-estimating environmental problems has received most attention within polit-ical and scientific debates while the dangers of underestimating the negative effects of environmental degradation have largely been omitted. Although in the course of more than twenty-five years of modern environmental policy no example of serious overestimation is known (on the contrary, many prog-noses have rather ignored negative environmental effects), the uncertainty of prognosis weakens the position of environmental policy-makers.

2 *Political uncertainty about the need for action regarding long-term problems which are still invisible to the general public.* The reactive mechanisms of parliamentary demo-cracy (and the mass media) are useful for policy learning from bad experi-ences (as in the examples of visible air and water pollution). However, the political perception of long-term, slowly accumulating environmental degra-dation (such as soil and groundwater pollution, loss of species and climate change) is structurally constrained. In this case certainty based on real experience is no political resource. Problems that cannot be directly perceived

and experienced by the public therefore depend heavily on scientific prognosis and a different institutional mechanism of agenda setting and policy formulation. The remarkable accomplishments of environmental policy in areas of highly visible environmental problems have led to a paradox of 'self-defeating environmental policy success': the general impression that environmental problems have been satisfactorily solved weakens the political recognition of the less visible, unsolved problems.

3   *Uncertainty about the environmental, social and economic consequences of policy decisions and non-decisions.* With its central concepts of policy cycles and policy learning, the discipline of public policy generally assumes uncertainty about the impacts of regulation (in contrast to simplistic neo-classical models of top-down governance).[3] This insecurity is stressed even more by environmental policy experts. Bressers, for example, argues that 'despite the omnipresence of uncertainty, there is a sort of "taboo" on decision-making under uncertainty' (1997: 291). Generally, the need to justify action is seen as more important than the need to justify inactivity. Scientific calculations of damage caused by inaction therefore cannot be found too frequently.

4   *Uncertainty of environmental pioneers about the chances and risks of innovative behaviour.* Innovations are the most important source of ecological improvements. Policy innovations can stimulate technological innovations but innovators run a high risk. Proactive environmental policy therefore has to deal with improving the conditions for innovators by providing stable and calculable conditions for investment in better technology. Clear policy goals, time frames or early information about future policy actions are important to reduce such uncertainty. Although, logically, this is a sub-category of the third dimension, its perspective is different. The third dimension focuses on uncertainties about the impacts of policy choices from a government perspective. The fourth dimension, on the other hand, looks at the uncertainties of economic, social and political actors about the general political and legal framework within which they act. It operates from the perspective of potential innovators.

Suggestions about how to deal with uncertainties in public policy-making have thrown up concepts such as 'increased flexibility', 'decentralisation', 'participation' and 'self-regulation', 'applying the precautionary principle' or 'strengthening the role of science' in policy-making (Bressers 1997: 292). Still more important may be the existence of highly legitimised, or broadly accepted long-term policy goals (Jänicke 1996). The central hypothesis of this chapter is that strategic environmental policy planning represents a way of dealing with the uncertainties of environmental policy-making. The following sections give a broad overview of this new and increasingly widespread approach to environmental policy in OECD countries.[4] Three categories of analysis will be introduced in order to analyse the widely differing national approaches to strategic environmental planning. Following this, a preliminary evaluation of three national strategies will be made. The last section draws some tentative conclusions with regard to the central hypothesis.

THE DIFFUSION OF ENVIRONMENTAL POLICY PLANNING

Following the 1992 Rio Conference and the general shift towards sustainable development in environmental policy, a new and more comprehensive approach has become salient in most industrialised countries. The policy innovation resulting from the sustainability debate lies in the emphasis placed on setting long-term goals on a broad political and societal basis, the integration of environmental policy objectives into other policy areas (inter-sectoral integration), a co-operative target group policy and the mobilisation of additional decentralised societal capacities. The most visible expression of this development is the broad diffusion and adoption of strategic and integrative environmental planning at the national level.

Environmental planning of the new Agenda 21 type is not simply another 'instrument' of environmental policy, but a comprehensive strategy; a permanent process of learning, setting goals, formulating and implementing measures. A large number of industrialised countries have already introduced some kind of national environmental policy planning, among them about two-thirds of the OECD countries (OECD 1995b; Dalal-Clayton 1996a, 1996b; Jörgens 1996; REC 1996; Jänicke, Carius and Jörgens 1997; Jänicke and Weidner 1997a; Johnson 1997; see Table 8.1). The same is true of many developing countries (Lampietti and Subramanian 1995). Moreover, this diffusion is paralleled by the rapid spread of general concepts of strategic planning and the new public management (OECD 1993; Berry 1994; Damkowski and Precht 1995).

Among the variety of existing approaches, there is as yet no uniform model for undertaking strategic environmental planning. Nevertheless, some general characteristics can be distinguished. In this chapter we will analyse the following types of long-term strategy: (a) general environmental policy plans (the Netherlands, South Korea, Austria, Japan, Portugal, Canada and France); (b) national strategies for sustainable development (UK, Ireland, Finland, New Zealand and Australia); (c) formalised policy statements with – at least in the medium-term – significant environmental targets, where these are linked to a mechanism for regular environmental reporting (in Sweden and Norway); and (d) strong sectoral and regional plans within a general national environmental framework (in Denmark and Switzerland).

The following section presents an empirical overview of selected environmental policy plans at the national level.

Table 8.1 Green plans in OECD countries.[5]

Country	Green Plan (official name)	Year
Australia	National Strategy for Ecologically Sustainable Development	1992
Austria	National Environmental Plan (Nationaler Umweltplan – NUP)	1995
Canada	Canada's Green Plan for a Healthy Environment	1990
	Environment Action Plan 1996/97–1999/2000	1996
Denmark	Action Plan for Environment and Development;	1988
	Nature and Environment Policy Plan;	1995
	sectoral action plans, e.g. Energy 21 (1990, 1996)	
Finland	Sustainable Development and Finland	1989/90
	Finnish Action for Sustainable Development	1995
France	National Plan for the Environment/Green Plan (Plan Vert)	1990
Ireland	Sustainable Development – A Strategy for Ireland	1997
Japan	The Basic Environment Plan; Action Plan for Greening Government Operations	1995
Luxembourg	National Plan for Sustainable Development (*Plan National pour un Développement Durable*)	planned for 1998
Netherlands	National Environmental Policy Plan (NEPP); NEPP plus; NEPP 2, NEPP 3	1989/90/93/97
New Zealand	Resource Management Act	1991
	Environment 2010 Strategy	1995
Norway	Environmental Policy for a Sustainable Development (Report to the Storting)	1997
Portugal	National Environmental Policy Plan (*Plano Nacional da Política de Ambiente*)	1995
South Korea	Medium-Term Plan	1987/91/97
	Korea's Green Vision 21	1995
Sweden	Enviro '93; Towards Sustainable Development in Sweden (parliamentary environmental goals since 1988)	1993/1994
Switzerland	Strategy for Sustainable Development in Switzerland (Strategie Nachhaltiger Entwicklung in der Schweiz)	1997
UK	This Common Inheritance: Britain's Environmental Strategy;	1990
	Sustainable Development: The UK Strategy	1994

ENVIRONMENTAL POLICY AS STRATEGIC AND CO-OPERATIVE PLANNING: COUNTRY EXPERIENCES

Particular attention has been paid to the description and analysis of the Dutch National Environmental Policy Plan (NEPP). The first environmental policy plan of 1989 included a detailed statistical description of the environmental situation and its foreseeable development. It is unique in its wide range of binding goals and objectives with clear time frames as well as the extent of societal mobilisa-tion which accompanied its development. Its preliminary results were evaluated in the second environmental policy plan and its goals were partly revised. In 1997, the third NEPP was finalised. It proposes, *inter alia*, a package of new green taxes.

The Dutch approach to environmental planning – which has had a legal basis since 1993 – contains an institutionalised mechanism for evaluation and revision. Other important features of the Dutch environmental policy plan are the underlying system of decentralised planning at local and provincial levels and negotiated agreements (covenants) focused on industrial target groups. In particular, the covenants with industry represent a highly developed form of 'social technology' and are one of the central innovations of the new planning approach. In this respect, the Netherlands have clearly been setting the pace in global environmental policy learning (Jänicke and Weidner 1997b). The existing system of negotiated agreements with industry is impressive, even if (as recent evaluations show) the quality of the different agreements varies widely (Tweede Kamer 1995).

The Danish government passed an Action Plan for Environment and Development as early as 1988. In spite of the growing importance of the comprehensive Environmental Protection Report, published in 1995, for integrated environmental planning, the strengths of Danish planning lie at the sectoral level. Most important is the 'Energy 2000' plan, which was introduced in 1990 and revised in 1996 ('Energy 21'). The plan includes targets for a 20 per cent reduction in CO_2 emissions (1988–2005), a 15 per cent decrease in energy consumption by 2030, and an increase in the use of renewable energy, to constitute one-third of the total energy supply by 2030. A broad network of organisations and institutions is responsible for the evaluation of energy savings. Other important sectoral plans include the Environment and Traffic Action Plan, the Aquatic Environment Plan and a system of national land and regional planning which has a strong emphasis on environmental protection and conservation of natural resources. Even the Danish Ministry of Defence has its own environmental action plan (Christiansen and Lundqvist 1996: 343).

The Swedish planning approach since 1988 consists of regular parliamentary target-setting combined with periodic reporting. Particularly relevant is the 'Enviro '93' strategy, which was prepared by the Swedish Environmental Protection Agency. It includes programmes for significant target sectors such as Industry, Energy, Traffic, and Agriculture. More than 100 concrete targets with different time frames have been formulated: for instance, phasing out the use of chlorinated solvents (by 1995), of mercury (by 2000), and of lead (no deadline). Eighteen new objectives have been added recently, including a 20 per cent reduction of CO_2 emissions by the year 2020. Regular reports are published on the implementation of the targets. As in Denmark and the Netherlands, the planning approach is closely connected with a comprehensive green tax reform (1991). At present, the Swedish government is drawing up a more radical strategy for sustainable development which was presented to Parliament in 1998. The government's Eco-Cycle Commission has recently proposed a strategy for cutting resource use to one-tenth of today's levels within the next twenty-five to fifty years. Following a government initiative, all of the 288 Swedish local authorities have started work on a local Agenda 21.

In Canada, a Green Plan for a Healthy Environment was decided upon in 1990. Its centrepiece was the integration of environmental goals into other policy fields and the wide participation of citizens and organisations in the process of goal-setting; more than 10,000 people participated in the (admittedly somewhat hurried) consultation process. The plan provided for six main fields of action, ranging from traditional air pollution control and species protection to promotion of the use of renewable resources. It covered a period of five (later six) years with a total budget of 3 billion Canadian dollars. After a change in government in 1993, the Green Plan lost much of its importance and was abandoned by 1996. However, Canada is trying to maintain a strategic approach to environmental policy. In 1995 the Canadian government published the *Guide to Green Government*, which introduces the drafting of sustainable development strategies – including regular reports – by all federal departments. Furthermore, Environment Canada recently published an Environment Action Plan for the period from 1996/97 to 1999/2000, which sets out general priorities and objectives for government.

The Austrian National Environmental Plan (NUP), published in 1995, is of interest because of its differentiated description of problems, targets and the measures to be taken. Although a number of societal actors participated in its drafting, public awareness of the NUP has been very slight. The groundwork for the plan had been laid in 1992, the year of UNCED in Rio de Janeiro. Its core elements are largely qualitative long-term environmental goals as well as plans for reducing the use of non-renewable resources and for the minimisation of material flows. A 20 per cent reduction of CO_2 emissions by the year 2005 (relative to 1988 levels) is among the most ambitious targets contained in the plan. In 1997, two years after its publication, the NUP was presented to (and adopted by) Parliament.

In 1995, the Japanese government passed its Basic Environment Plan. Following Agenda 21, a broad range of rather vague targets have been formulated and tasks assigned to all relevant organisations and institutions. The plan represents a policy monitoring tool in that it refers in detail to already existing environmental policy targets and measures. Implementation of the Basic Plan will take place mainly at local and company level. By the end of 1995, there were forty-six local environmental and climate protection plans. A special Action Plan for Greening Government Operations has been formulated on the basis of the Basic Environment Plan, and includes thirty-seven targets, eleven of which are quantitative. With this action plan, the Japanese government intends to set a good example to other sectors of society.

South Korea may be one of the most interesting cases. The country has a long tradition of economic planning. This has contributed to enormous industrial growth, but also to equally significant environmental damage. In the course of South Korea's transition to democracy after 1987, planning was extended to include environmental protection. Since 1987 Korea has had medium-term (five year) and long-term (ten year) environmental plans. The first medium-term plan of 1987 was formulated just before the Olympic Games in Seoul in 1988 and already had concrete, budgeted targets. The goals of the second medium-term plan of 1991 included doubling the proportion of effluent water treated, a radical increase in the amount of waste treated, a clear improvement in the air quality in Seoul and an increase to 10 per cent in the proportion of protected areas. During its first two years, costs for the plan were estimated at more than 1 per cent of GNP. The importance of participation is broadly stressed, but does not, in reality, play an important role in the Korean planning process. However, the plan must be agreed by the relevant administrative authorities and the heads of towns and provinces.

The Basic Environmental Policy Act of 1990 formulates clear criteria for the Comprehensive Long-term Plan for the Preservation of the Environment. The present long-term plan – 'Green Vision 21' – contains precise goals for different areas and its costs are budgeted. The slogan 'From a model country of economic growth to a model country of environmental preservation' is at the heart of this apparently ambitious governmental strategy.

SOME EMPIRICAL CHARACTERISTICS OF EXISTING GREEN PLANS

As the description of some of the existing green plans has illustrated, there is no uniform model for environmental planning. National responses to the demand for comprehensive and consensual long-term strategies vary considerably and display a wide range of different characteristics (OECD 1995b; Dalal-Clayton 1996a). Frequently, they represent merely a first step towards a coherent strategy for sustainable development and are limited to the description of problems and options, with general statements of intent.

In order to classify green plans, this chapter proposes three categories for analysis: (a) *the accuracy and relevance of environmental goals*, (b) *the degree of participation in and integration of the planning process*, and (c) *the extent of institutionalisation of the plan*. Recent research at the Environmental Policy Research Unit suggests that these features are important if green plans are to have the positive effects outlined above (Jänicke 1996: 27–8; Jörgens 1996: 105–8). Table 8.2 gives a preliminary overview of green plans in highly developed market economies – also including South Korea – according to these categories.

Accuracy and relevance of environmental goals

With respect to this first category, the following significant questions present themselves. Does the plan include concrete quantitative targets, or do these in fact remain unspecified and vague? Are the designated goals contextually relevant, or does the plan ignore important national environmental problems? Are the goals realistic: that is, are they scientifically based and does the plan take into account the political system's and the target groups' capacity to achieve these goals, or

Table 8.2 National approaches to environmental policy planning

Country	Accuracy and relevance of goals (contents)		Degree of participation and integration (process)			Extent of institutionalisation (stabilisation)				Current status
	Type of plan	Quality of targets	Leading authority	Inter-policy co-ordination	Participation	Legal/legislative basis	Special planning institutions	Reports and evaluations	Financing	
Australia	national strategy for sustainable development	quantitative and qualitative goals divided into 8 sectors and 22 themes	Council of Australian Governments, Dept of Environment	Prime Minister, premier ministers and chief ministers, inter-governmental ESD Steering Committee	9 pluralistic working groups; about 200 draft strategy statements		Steering Committee on Ecologically Sustainable Development	every 2 years, co-ordinated by ESD Steering Committee		active, but gradually losing public support
Austria	environmental policy plan	472 mainly qualitative goals	Ministry of Environment; NUP Committee	all relevant ministries	labour and industrial associations (neo-corporatist actors), later NGOs	parliamentary decision (1997)	NUP Committee	every 4 years		active, but little public interest
Canada	environmental policy plan	about 120, mostly qualitative initiatives divided in 8 thematic sections	Environment Canada	Priorities and Planning Cabinet Committee including all relevant departments; 'green' reporting in other departments	NGOs, industry, other interested social actors through public hearings after presentation of full draft green plan			two reports	$3 billion additional funding over 5 (subsequently 6) years	gradually abandoned
Denmark	strong sectoral and regional plans within national framework	concrete overall goals; sectoral and regional plans, often with quantitative goals	Ministry of the Environment, Government	consultation and negotiation with all relevant ministries and agencies	mostly internal government process without significant participation	parliamentary decision		regular reports		active

Country	Accuracy and relevance of goals (contents)		Degree of participation and integration (process)			Extent of institutionalisation (stabilisation)		Reports and evaluations	Financing	Current status
	Type of plan	Quality of targets	Leading authority	Inter-policy co-ordination	Participation	Legal/legislative basis	Special planning institutions			
Finland	national strategy for sustainable development	mainly qualitative targets	Commission on Environment and Development; government	partly	300 written statements e.g. by local governments		Finnish National Commission on Sustainable Development (1993), chaired by the Prime Minister			
France	environmental policy plan	some quantitative targets, mostly institutional and legislative targets	Ministry of Environment	broad, often negative co-ordination with other ministries	mostly internal process, few public meetings, some written NGO comments	parliamentary decision (1990), without binding character			general assignment of environmental costs	completed
Ireland	national strategy for sustainable development	large number of (mainly quantitative) environmental and institutional goals	Department of Environment, government	'green' reporting by task managers in other ministries	public consultations; submissions of over 50 organisations and individuals		National Sustainable Development Council planned	reporting and revision of the strategy are planned; environmental indicators to be developed by 1998		active
Japan	environmental policy plan	mainly qualitative; references to previous quantitative goals and deadlines	government; Central Environmental Council; Environment Agency	consultation of ministries and agencies	yes	legal basis in Basic Environment Law (1993)		monitoring and reporting every year by Central Environment Council; revision within 5 years	vague	active

Table 8.2 – contd

Country	Accuracy and relevance of goals (contents)		Degree of participation and integration (process)			Extent of institutionalisation (stabilisation)		Reports and evaluations	Financing	Current status
	Type of plan	Quality of targets	Leading authority	Inter-policy co-ordination	Participation	Legal/legislative basis	Special planning institutions			
Netherlands	environmental policy plan	50 strategic objectives and over 200 specific quantitative goals and time frames arranged in 8 themes and directed at 9 defined target groups	Ministry of Environment, Prime Minister	direct integration of ministries of industry, transport and agriculture; consultation with other ministries	high levels of public attention before and during preparation of NEPP; about 600 participants (science, government, target groups, NGOs) during NEPP 2	parliamentary decision (1990); legal basis (1993)		yearly reports; operational plans every four years; annual rolling programmes	concrete budgeting	active
New Zealand	law; national strategy for sustainable development	qualitative targets, divided in 11 thematic sections	Ministry of the Environment, government	only with Ministry of Finance	participation of NGOs, economic interest groups, Maori	RMA constitutes basis in law (1991)	no	*Environment 2010*: reviews and revisions every 4 years	no	active
Norway	formalised policy statements	qualitative and quantitative goals	Ministry of Environment, government	'green' reporting by all ministries	some written contributions	parliamentary basis		yearly reporting		active
Portugal	environmental policy plan	qualitative and quantitative goals with time frames	Ministry of Environment; National Environmental Agency; government	consultation of Economic and Social Council	public debate with NGOs, industrial associations, other societal actors, towns and districts, but few alterations to the plan	legal basis (1987) in Basic Environmental Act		revision after 2 years was initially intended	general assignment of financial needs to actors (EU, central and local administration, other sectors, industry)	losing importance

Country	Accuracy and relevance of goals (contents)		Degree of participation and integration (process)			Extent of institutionalisation (stabilisation)				Current status
	Type of plan	Quality of targets	Leading authority	Inter-policy co-ordination	Participation	Legal/legislative basis	Special planning institutions	Reports and evaluations	Financing	
South Korea	long- and medium-term environmental policy plan	over 30 quantitative targets	government; Ministry of Environment	consultation of departments and cities	weak	legal basis (1990)	planning bureau of the Ministry of Environment	reporting with a basis in law	detailed budgeting	active
Sweden	formalised policy statement	numerous goals, often quantitative and with clear time frames	Environmental Protection Agency (SEPA); parliament	other government agencies, experts from municipalities and countries	mainly internal government process; general written comments before preparation	parliamentary decision		intended, but without concrete time frames		active
Switzerland	sectoral and regional plans within national framework	some qualitative goals are intended	inter-departmental commission (IDARio); Government	20 federal authorities represented in IDARio, including relevant ministries			IDARio, Council for Sustainable Development	no		relatively weak
UK	national strategy for sustainable development	350 mostly general commitments; few quantitative targets and time frames; institutional commitments	Department of Environment, government	Consultation with all government departments in 2 Ministerial Committees, signed by most departments; 'Green Ministers'	consultation of NGOs in the 1994 strategy; only informal consultation of NGOs in 1990 White Paper		Ministerial Committee on the Environment (EDE, 1992); Government's Panel on SD (1994); UK Round Table on SD; Citizen's Environmental Initiative	yearly reports, adding new goals; environmental section in annual departmental reports		active

Notes
ESD = ecologically sustainable development
RMA = Resource Management Act
SD = sustainable development

have goals been formulated without regard to existing political and societal capacities for environmental protection?

The majority of green plans in industrialised countries set a wide variety of somewhat general goals, and few concrete quantitative targets. The British White Paper, 'This Common Inheritance', published in 1990, for example, contained some 350 rather vague commitments. Wilkinson (1997: 91) criticises the White Paper thus: '[t]here were few quantitative targets, deadlines, firm commitments or new initiatives – apart from institutional ones. Instead the White Paper was littered with promises to "review", "consider", "examine" and "study further". Most of the 350 commitments it contained reiterated existing policy.' The green plans of Japan, Finland and Austria follow a similar pattern. Quantitative targets combined with accurate time frames and a detailed description of the measures to be taken are rare in these plans. If they appear, they usually refer to existing national or international obligations. This is the case, for example, in the 20 per cent reduction of CO_2 emissions foreseen in the Austrian plan: a target that had already been announced in the previous Austrian government energy reports of 1990 and 1993 (Österreichische Bundesregierung 1995: 20). Similarly, the concrete and quantified targets included in the Japanese plan are all taken from existing national or international laws and agreements. The genuinely new goals introduced by this plan, however, remain largely vague as to the nature of a problem, its causes and the concrete measures to be taken.

There are, however, examples of green plans which contain specific and relevant targets and are committed to implementing concrete measures. Here, the Dutch National Environmental Policy Plan, with over 200 quantitative targets and corresponding measures, such as covenants with the principal polluting industries, is the most prominent example (Weale 1992; Bennett 1997; Bressers and Plettenburg 1997; van Kampen 1997). But with regard to the clarity of its goals and the concrete nature of the scheduled actions, the South Korean Master Plan for the Preservation of the Environment does not lie too far behind (Nam 1997). Some of the main targets of the Dutch and Korean plans are shown in Tables 8.2 and 8.3. The Swedish approach to comprehensive environmental goal-setting is another example of relevant quantitative goals with clear time frames without, however, a central planning document, relying more on parliamentary target-setting within a broad framework.

Canada might be placed somewhere between these two groups of countries. The Green Plan of 1990 offered a mix of quantitative and qualitative goals. It included some significant targets, such as a 50 per cent reduction in Canada's generation of waste by the year 2000, a 50 per cent reduction in SO_2 emissions in Eastern Canada by 1994, phasing-out of CFCs by 1997 and other ozone-depleting substances by the year 2000, as well as eliminating the discharge of persistent toxic substances into the environment (Gale 1997). However, critics have pointed out that most of the proposed measures have only an indirect influence on behaviour and more than half of the initiatives refer to the relatively vague instrument of 'information development' (Gale 1997: 107–8; Hoberg and

Harrison 1994). The Environment Action Plan, successor to the Green Plan, leaves still more room for interpretation of its targets.

A special type of target which figures prominently in the British and French strategies concerns the creation of new institutions for environmental planning and sustainable development. In the course of implementing the French Green Plan, for example, the environmental administration was thoroughly restructured (Müller-Brandeck-Bocquet 1996). In the UK, various new government bodies were established, including the UK Round Table on Sustainable Development as well as a Government Panel on Sustainable Development. Similarly, the Irish strategy of 1997 schedules the creation of a National Sustainable Development Council. These institutional targets are an important element of environmental planning, as they improve the political system's capacity for further strategic environmental policy (Jänicke 1997).

How integrated are these planning processes, and who participates in them?

The second category proposed in this chapter concerns the degree of integration of and participation in the planning process. Integration refers to the degree to which environmental concerns are incorporated into other sectoral policies (inter-policy co-ordination). An indicator of the extent of inter-policy co-ordination can be found in the level and relevance of consultation and co-operation between the relevant sectoral ministries, especially during the drafting stage. In almost all the countries analysed, the leading authority in the planning process has been the Ministry of the Environment. Usually, this ministry produced a draft plan which was then discussed with other government departments, and often changed in accordance with the interest constellations within a particular cabinet. In some cases, however, the relevant ministries were directly and constructively involved in the development of the plan. To some extent, this has been the case in Switzer-land, where an inter-departmental commission (IDARio) has taken a leading role in the drafting of the green plan. The most intense co-operation between government departments has taken place in the Netherlands, where four ministries (environment, industry, transport and agriculture) worked together on the preparation of the NEPP for a period of almost three years (van Kampen 1997: 7–11). In the UK, the White Paper 'This Common Inheritance' was developed by the Department of the Environment in very close co-operation with two inter-ministerial committees, one of which was headed by the Prime Minister. The final plan was signed by eleven ministers, including those for trade and industry, energy, transport and agriculture. The second British plan, the UK Sustain-ability Strategy of 1994, carried the signature of sixteen different ministers (Wilkinson 1997).

Furthermore, a number of countries have, through their green plans, intro-duced some mechanism for 'green' reporting by non-environmental ministries. Norway, for example, which explicitly locates responsibility for external environ-mental effects within the various sectoral ministries, plans to require sectoral environmental action plans combined with an annual progress report entitled 'Environmental Profile of the Government and the Environmental State of the Nation'. In the UK so-called 'green ministers' have been established inside all government departments, each of which is required to dedicate a chapter of its yearly reports to environmental matters within their areas of competence.

The second category of analysis covers the extent of societal participation in the planning process. A claim that broad participation by societal actors will occur can be found in almost all planning documents. However, in reality, participation is usually handled in a restrictive manner, if it is present at all. The Austrian plan, for example, has been criticised for having excluded environmental organisations during the initial drafting process, yet including trades unions and employers' associations. In addition, media coverage has been very low-key, as the environmental administration made little effort to publicise the ongoing process (Payer 1997). In South Korea, the general public has been virtually excluded from the drafting process, and even the Swedish planning process has been characterised as 'an internal government process' (Dalal-Clayton 1996a: 41). In contrast, the drafting of green plans in Australia and Canada, the second Dutch National Environmental Policy Plan (NEPP 2) and New Zealand's Resource Management Act were characterised by a higher level of consultation and participation (Dalal-Clayton 1996a; Johnson 1997).

Institutionalisation of the green plans

The third category introduced in this chapter concerns the extent of institutionalisation of each green plan. With regard to the long-term nature of the goal of sustainable development and respective targets and measures, this may well constitute the most important condition for successful environmental planning. The OECD points out that the question of institutionalisation becomes important as the time frames for planning for sustainable development extend beyond terms of office and legislative periods (OECD 1995b: 19). Strong institutionalisation could make the difference between programmatic declarations issued by one government only to be discarded by its successor, as has been the case with the Canadian or Portuguese green plans, and genuine long-term strategies. Institutionalisation plays an important role not least because of the cyclical nature of public attention to, and mobilisation over, political issues (Downs 1972). Some important questions need to be pursued here. Does the plan have a legal or legislative basis, for instance in a national environmental framework law or through a binding parliamentary decision, or is it merely a cabinet decision or a government statement of intent? Has a responsible (administrative) institution been established or designated to co-ordinate the planning process? Does the plan provide for regular, obligatory reports and evaluation of its progress? And, finally, does it include a finance scheme?

To date, only five green plans have been established on the basis of a national environmental law. This is the case in the Netherlands, Japan, South Korea, New Zealand and Portugal. It is interesting to note that in the Netherlands the legal institutionalisation of the planning process did not take place until four years after the publication of the first NEPP (Bennett 1997). The Danish and Austrian plans, as well as the Swedish and Norwegian approaches, have been given a legislative basis through a binding parliamentary decision. In a large group of countries, including Australia, Canada, Finland and the UK, green plans lack such a legal or legislative basis and are thus more likely to stand and fall along with the particular government in office.

Provisions for regular reports on the progress of the planning process exist in most countries, but there are important differences in the quality of these reports. In the Netherlands, long-term environmental goals are 'achieved through . . . specific measures that are formulated every four years in operational plans and implemented through annual rolling programmes' (Bennett 1997: 78). The process thus provides for strongly institutionalised periodic opportunities to evaluate results and to adapt targets and measures if necessary. A remarkable feature of the UK strategy is that it foresees yearly reports on its implementation. In 1997, the sixth annual report was published, reviewing in detail more than 600 targets and measures (Wilkinson 1997). Furthermore, the aforementioned inclusion of environmental sections in the annual reports of all government departments constitutes an important institutional mechanism. Similar mechanisms for 'green' reporting by other ministries have been introduced in Canada, Norway and Ireland. The British plan, with its strong emphasis on institutional innovation, is also among the few approaches that have established particular national authorities responsible for continuing strategic action. These administrative bodies are the Ministerial Committee on the Environment of 1992 and Government Panel on Sustainable Development of 1994.

EARLY EVALUATIONS OF EXISTING PLANS

Although strategic and comprehensive planning at the national level is a very recent approach in environmental policy, three plans have already been evaluated regarding their implementation and goal-attainment. This section summarises and interprets the results of these evaluations.

The Netherlands

Recent evaluations of the achievements of the Dutch planning approach for 1995 show that while no target was met precisely (which may be due not least to the 'soft' instruments applied), many targets were exceeded (RIVM 1994; van Kampen 1997). Among the targets that have not been reached, CO_2 and NO_x emissions (relating to the issues of climate change and acidification respectively) stand out clearly. However, about half the targets set for 1995 have actually been realised, among them emissions of SO_2 (acidification), phosphor (eutrophication), cadmium and chromium (surface water), and lead or dioxins (air). What seems to be still more important is that – compared to the pre-NEPP period from 1985 to 1990 – nearly all trends have improved and some have even been reversed between 1990 and 1995 (see Table 8.3).

South Korea

The evaluation of the second Korean medium-term plan for 1995 showed that some targets had been too ambitious (for example, the treatment rates for sewage and solid wastes) while others – especially concentrations of SO_2 in the city of Seoul – had already been met by 1996 (see Table 8.4). Although actual developments generally fall short of the targets formulated in the medium-term plan, South Korea (like the Netherlands) is experiencing remarkably positive trends in many areas of environmental protection. Of course, the impact of the acute financial crisis which hit Korea at the end of 1997 and the change of government on the country's environmental performance remain to be seen.

Sweden

In 1996 the Swedish Environmental Protection Agency presented a review of the 167 environmental objectives previously approved by the Riksdag. A hundred of

Table 8.3 Environmental trends in the Netherlands 1985–90, 1990–95, and NEPP targets for 1995

Theme/substance	Trend 1985–90 (%)	Trend 1990–95 (%)	NEPP 1995 target (%)
Climate Change/CO_2:	+13	+6.8	0
Acidification:			
SO_2	−20	−29	−15
NO_x	0	−10	−27
NH_3	−16	−28	−18
Eutrophication:			
Nitrogen	−3	−26	−50
Phosphorus	−24	−65	−50
Diffusion surface waters:			
Copper	+7	−13	−50
Lead	−19	−47	−70
Zinc	−3	−21	−50
Cadmium	−33	−90	−70
Chromium	−3	−77	−50
Diffusion air:			
Copper	+7	−3	−50
Cadmium	−25	−25	−33
Chromium	0	−18	−50
Fluorides	+12	−18	−50
Lead	−75	−89	−70

Sources: van Kampen (1997); RIVM (1994).

Table 8.4 Targets and budget of the second Korean Master Plan

Programme	1991	1996	Achievement 1995[a]
Improving the quality of drinking water resources			
Proportion of 1st-rate drawing posts for drinking water (to total drawing posts)	34%	70%	53.4%
Recovery of water quality in rivers treatment rate of sewage	33%	65%	45%
Sanitary treatment of solid wastes proportion of sanitary treatment of wastes from everyday life (to total treatment)	27%[b]	90%	66%
Maintenance of clean air concentration of SO_2 (Seoul City)	0.043 ppm	0.033 ppm[c]	0.017 ppm
Enlargement of green areas for rest and recreation			
proportion of natural park area (to total land area)	7.5%	10%	7.5%
area of parks in the cities	680 km^2	800 km^2	885.8 km^2

Budget of the master plan (unit: trillion won)	1992	1993	1994	1995	1996
GNP	226.4	256.7	288.4	320.9	357.1
Budget of master plan	2.38	2.79	2.82	2.62	1.58
Proportion to GNP	(1.05%)	(1.08%)	(1.00%)	(0.82%)	(0.44%)

Source: Ministry of Environment (1994).

Notes
a Actual goal attainment in 1995.
b Later revised to 19.9%.
c Later revised to 0.018 ppm.

them were difficult to assess or have not been evaluated in detail. Nonetheless, of the sixty-seven clearly formulated objectives, forty-six have been achieved or will be achieved within the stated time frame, while twenty-one targets will probably not be realised (SEPA press release, 4 September 1997). As in the Netherlands and South Korea, the SO_2 target was met earlier than planned, while the NO_x target was only partially achieved. The 50 per cent reduction target for pesticide use was reached in 1990, but the additional reduction of 50 per cent could not be fully achieved in 1995. In September 1997, the SEPA proposed eighteen new objectives. Some of the former targets (for instance, for CO_2 and NO_x emissions) have now have been more stringently formulated.

The experience of planning initiatives in these countries might be summarised as follows.

1　No target has been met precisely, but fine-tuning in public policy has scarcely ever been a realistic goal. Indicative environmental planning, therefore, should not be evaluated according to perfectionist criteria. On the one hand, there may be restrictions that have been ignored to date. On the other hand, dynamic processes may conceivably be stimulated by unexpected success.

2　In the Netherlands, where trends can be compared before and after the plan, a clear improvement can be observed, even where the target itself was not met (as in the case of CO_2 emissions).

3　In all three countries, failure was clearly reported and led (at least in Sweden and the Netherlands) to the reformulation of policy, which usually resulted in stricter measures.

4　A precise evaluation of the immediate effects of environmental policy plans is difficult. In fact it is impossible in cases where 'soft' implementation measures predominate, as in the Netherlands. The role of information, networking and voluntary agreements cannot easily be evaluated because they usually result in complex, dynamic communication processes. The effects of these may only become visible in the long term. This methodological problem, however, is a general difficulty arising from a causal interpretation of policy outcomes and is not unique to environmental policy plans.

SUMMARY: MAIN SHORTCOMINGS OF EXISTING GREEN PLANS

Most of the green plans examined here could be characterised as pilot strategies, which display a number of weaknesses. The character of their goals is often inadequate. Targets are predominantly qualitative and frequently somewhat vague. Time frames and operational measures for reaching targets are the exception rather than the rule. Furthermore, in most cases, traditional environmental protection prevails. National resource or materials auditing hardly ever constitute the starting point for the goal-setting process. Exceptions are the Dutch and Austrian plans. In many cases green plans remain rather non-committal as they lack a strong basis in law, an institutionalised obligation for regular progress reports, or mechanisms for evaluating and reformulating the proposed targets and measures.

The first steps towards integration of environmental concerns into other policy fields have been taken, but the early experience of some plans reveals the difficulty of maintaining some form of sectoral environmental responsibility over a longer period of time. This is especially the case with regard to highly polluting sectors such as traffic and transport, energy, building or agriculture. Most of the plans should thus be considered as a first step towards important inter-sectoral communication. Furthermore, a number of plans are either suffering from insufficient participation (France and South Korea) or rely too heavily on voluntary action (Canada and Japan), with the implicit danger of a more or less rapid 'exhaustion'. Almost all the plans refrain from making a detailed analysis of obstacles to attaining policy objectives, and thus fail to draw any conclusions from previous policy failures in environmental protection.

This last point is important, because the success of environmental plans depends so heavily on their realism. To make this clear, it is worth briefly considering a scheme for handling obstacles to policy implementation presented by Cohen and Kamieniecki (1991) that seems highly realistic in comparison to the great number of idealistic approaches in the field of environmental policy. In a seven-step model for strategic regulatory planning, the authors propose to analyse systematically the involvement of actors as targets are formulated. The main question is: what are the motivations, goals, positions and resources of each party to either comply with, ignore, or resist the desired behavioural changes? The most appropriate devices for influencing the target group's behaviour should then be chosen on this basis (Cohen and Kamieniecki 1991: 31). Voluntary agreements are seen as the best solution, but coercion is not excluded as a last resort (or threat). The Dutch NEPP, with its thorough and scientifically based target-group policy, is the most remarkable empirical example of such an approach.

CONCLUSIONS

How does this new type of strategic environmental planning reduce the uncertainties outlined at the start of this chapter?

First, *uncertainty of prognosis about environmental changes and their possible negative impacts*. The most advanced environmental policy plans are connected with an increase in diagnostic capacities, including the capacity to communicate this new knowledge base. The scientific description and analysis of environmental changes has been given great weight in many of the plans. Furthermore, the comprehensive approach to environmental protection (which covers all sectors where environmental degradation can occur) followed in these plans and strategies reduces the danger of underestimating or ignoring significant, but not highly visible, environmental problems.

Another promising way to deal with prognostic uncertainties is to give a high priority to the principle of precaution. This happens in a variety of national environmental policy plans (for example Norway, Ireland and Denmark). The Irish *Strategy for Sustainable Development*, for instance, states that:

> The precautionary principle requires that emphasis should be placed on dealing with the causes rather than the results or environmental damage and that, where significant evidence of environmental risk exists, appropriate precautionary action should be taken even in the absence of conclusive scientific proof of causes.
>
> (Department of the Environment 1997: 27)

Similarly, Denmark's Nature and Environmental Policy argues that: 'The precautionary principle means that the prioritisation of environmental concerns must be based on well-founded documentation, but that nature and the environment should be given the benefit of the doubt' (Ministry of Environment and Energy 1995: 11).

Second, *political uncertainty about the need for action regarding long-term problems which are still invisible to the general public.* Solutions to problems of the type of 'long-term degeneration' – as opposed to the more visible problems of acute danger or (health) risk – cannot rely directly on the resource of political mobilisation. They do not result in immediate public awareness and, therefore, require consensus rather than conflict, a consensus which can best be brought about through anticipatory efforts from highly legitimised and competent political and scientific actors in conjunction with participation by target groups and other societal actors in the process of policy formulation and implementation. Environmental policy plans such as the Dutch NEPP or Swedish Enviro '93, which give great weight to scientific analysis of problems and possible measures, illustrate this potential of strategic planning to supplement direct experience with anticipatory science and policy.

Third, *uncertainty about the environmental, social and economic consequences of policy decisions and non-decisions.* The early evaluation of three medium-term plans confirms the view that there is no exact causal relationship between policy measures and outcomes. However, a general improvement for most targets can be observed in all three cases with positive as well as negative deviations from the actual targets. Taking into account everything we know about policy outcomes, this may be no bad result. Up-to-date, strategic environmental planning with its institutionalised processes of reporting and evaluation seems to be the best available mechanism of environmental policy-learning. In this context of permanent and strongly institutionalised evaluation and revision, initial policy failure can effectively foster learning processes and thus reduce uncertainty about the effects of political decisions.

Moreover, strategic planning approaches, as we have seen, can involve a broad policy dialogue between stakeholders (policy-makers, target groups and proponents of environmental protection) about priorities and necessities in environmental policy. This dialogue may be a relevant contribution to reduce uncertainties about the effects of environmental decisions and non-decisions as it increases the probability of including negative effects that otherwise would be ignored.

Furthermore, fostering a serious dialogue between policy-makers and target groups may reduce the risk of taking decisions that bring about severe economic costs and later turn out to be wrong or ineffective in reducing environmentally harmful emissions ('problem shifting'). Kloepfer (1996: 58) therefore argues that in fields characterised by high environmental insecurity, the softer instruments of dialogue and negotiated agreements may be more adequate than traditional and prescriptive command-and-control measures.

Fourth, *uncertainty of environmental pioneers about the chances and risks of innovative behaviour.* Long-term environmental planning could be an effective mode for handling the dynamic complexity of those conditions supporting innovation. By stressing societal goals, it combines pressure for change with methodological flexibility. It provides long-term orientation and more calculable conditions for innovative investors as it renders environmental policy less dependent on short-term events. In addition, it intensifies communication and the availability of information. Wätzold and Simonis (1997: 11) argue that a policy that encourages integrated technological innovation could be an adequate strategy in situations characterised by high environmental uncertainty. Contrary to end-of-pipe technologies which are aimed at reducing just one specific emission, integrated technologies alter the production process and reduce a wider range of potentially hazardous emissions and material uses. They are therefore more apt to put into practice the principle of precaution. Furthermore, the application of integrated environmental protection measures is less dependent on conclusive knowledge about environmental effects of emissions as it brings about positive effects of its own (reducing energy and material input). Hitherto, it has been difficult to create the conditions that foster technological innovations by traditional top-down government intervention (Wallace 1995).

A similar situation may exist for pioneer countries regarding regulatory competition in the environmental field (Héritier *et al.* 1996; Andersen and Liefferink 1997; Jänicke and Weidner 1997b). The fact that at the international level too, strategic goal-setting has become common practice, increases the security of pioneering countries to find followers at the international level and new markets for their political innovations through processes of international policy harmonisation and policy convergence.

* * *

In conclusion, it is clear that strategic environmental planning as it has been put into practice in a great number of industrialised countries could be an effective mechanism to deal with and possibly reduce some of the uncertainties with which environmental policy-makers are confronted. The greatest potential of strategic planning lies in increasing the political system's capacity to deal with those problems of long-term environmental degradation which, in spite of the past successes of environmental protection, remain largely unsolved. It does so by intensifying the elements of flexibility, participation and self-regulation in environmental policy-making as well as giving more weight to scientific expertise in describing problems and setting priorities. This, as well as the pronounced effort to integrate environmental policy objectives into other policy fields, serves to encourage necessary learning processes at all levels of the political system and society. Furthermore, the strong emphasis on long-term goal-setting makes environmental policy more calculable for economic actors and thus improves the conditions for environmental innovations in products and production processes. A preliminary evaluation of existing strategies supports this cautious optimism regarding their capacity to deal with environmental uncertainties and more effectively solve the less visible problems of long-term environmental degradation.

Notes

1 The authors wish to thank the editors for their valuable comments and suggestions and Alex Sawyer for English editing.
2 See Wätzold and Simonis (1997) for a detailed typology of uncertainties about the effects of environmental changes.
3 Richard Rose (1993: 13–14) argues that

> the uncertainties of policy analysis have much more in common with medical diagnosis than with a mechanically predictable science . . . Applying medical knowledge to individual patients is an art as well as a science. Success is more or less probable, not certain . . . [W]hen a doctor makes a prescription, he or she rarely guarantees success; the intention is to have a better than random chance of removing the causes of a complaint.

4 The chapter focuses on the 'old' OECD countries and – as an especially interesting case of strategic environmental planning – South Korea. The new OECD member states (Poland, Czech Republic, Hungary and Mexico) are not included in the analysis.
5 New member states – except for South Korea – are not included.

References

Andersen, M. and Liefferink, D. (eds) (1997) *European Environmental Policy: The Pioneers*, Manchester/New York: Manchester University Press.

Bennett, G. (1997) 'The Dutch Environmental Policy Plan', in Jänicke, Carius and Jörgens (1997).

Berry, F. (1994) 'Innovation in Public Management: The Adoption of Strategic Planning', *Public Administration Review* 54: 322–30.

Bressers, H. (1997) 'Institutional and Policy Responses to Uncertainty in Environmental Policy', in L. Mez and H. Weidner (eds), *Umweltpolitik und Staatsversagen: Festschrift zum 60. Geburtstag von Martin Jänicke*, Berlin: Edition Sigma.

Bressers, H. and Plettenburg, L. (1997) 'The Netherlands', in Jänicke and Weidner (1997a).

Christiansen, P. and Lundqvist, L. (1996) 'Conclusion: A Nordic Environmental Policy Model?', in P. Christiansen (ed.), *Governing the Environment: Politics, Policy, and Organization in the Nordic Countries*, Aarhus: Nordic Council of Ministers.

Cohen, S. and Kamieniecki, S. (1991) *Environmental Regulation Through Strategic Planning*, Boulder, San Francisco and Oxford: Westview Press.

Dalal-Clayton, B. (1996a) *Getting to Grips with Green Plans: National Level Experience in Industrial Countries*, London: Earthscan.

Dalal-Clayton, B. (1996b) 'Great Expectations? Green Planning in Industrial Countries', Paper presented at the International Conference: The Environment in the 21st Century: Environment, Long-term Governability and Democracy. Abbaye de Fontevraud, France, 8–11 September.

Damkowski, W. and Precht, C. (1995) *Public Management. Neuere Steuerungskonzepte für den öffentlichen Sektor*, Stuttgart: Kohlhammer.

Department of the Environment (1997) *Sustainable Development: A Strategy for Ireland*, Dublin: Department of the Environment.

Downs, A. (1972) 'Up and Down with Ecology – the "Issue-Attention-Cycle"', *Public Interest* 28: 38–50.

Gale, R. (1997) 'Canada's Green Plan', in Jänicke, Carius and Jörgens (1997).

Héritier, A., Knill, C., and Mingers, S. (eds) (1996) *Ringing the Changes in Europe: Regulatory Competition and the Transformation of the State*, Berlin: Walter de Gruyter.

Hoberg, G. and Harrison, K. (1994) 'It's Not Easy Being Green: The Politics of Canada's Green Plan', *Canadian Public Policy* 20: 119–37.

Jänicke, M. (ed.) (1996) *Umweltpolitik der Industrieländer: Entwicklung – Bilanz – Erfolgsbedingungen*, Berlin: Edition Sigma.

Jänicke, M. (1997) 'The Political System's Capacity for Environmental Policy', in Jänicke and Weidner (1997a).

Jänicke, M., Carius, A. and Jörgens, H. (1997) *Nationale Umweltpläne in ausgewählten Industrieländern*, Berlin: Springer.

Jänicke, M. and Weidner, H. (in coll. with Helge Jörgens) (eds) (1997a) *National Environmental Policies – A Comparative Study of Capacity-Building*, Berlin: Springer-Verlag.

Jänicke, M. and Weidner, H. (1997b) 'Summary: Global Environmental Policy Learning', in Jänicke and Weidner (1997a).

Johnson, H. (1997) *Green Plans: Greenprint for Sustainability*, Lincoln and London: University of Nebraska Press (2nd edn).

Jörgens, H. (1996) 'Die Institutionalisierung von Umweltpolitik im internationalen Vergleich', in Jänicke (1996).

Kampen, M. van (1997) 'The Formation and Implementation of the Dutch National Environmental Policy Plan', Leiden: Dr Reinier de Man, Adviesbureau voor Milieubeleid (mimeo).

Kloepfer, M. (1996) 'Umweltschutz zwischen Ordnungsrecht und Anreizpolitik: Konzeption, Ausgestaltung, Vollzug – Erster Teil', in *Zeitschrift für angewandte Umweltforschung* 9: 56–66.

Lafferty, W. and Meadowcroft, J. (1996) 'Democracy and the environment: congruence and conflict – preliminary reflections', in W. Lafferty and J. Meadowcroft (eds), *Democracy and the Environment: Problems and Prospects*, Cheltenham: Edward Elgar.

Lampietti, J. and Subramanian, U. (1995) *Taking Stock of National Environmental Strategies*, Environmental Management Series Paper No. 010, World Bank.

Ministry of Environment (1994) *Environmental Protection in Korea*, Kwacheon: Ministry of Environment.

Ministry of Environment (1996) *Our Environment: Environmental Activities During the Year*, Stockholm: Ministry of Environment.

Ministry of Environment and Energy (1995) *Denmark's Nature and Environmental Policy*, Summary Report, Copenhagen: Ministry of Environment and Energy.

Müller-Brandeck-Bocquet, G. (1996) *Die institutionelle Dimension der Umweltpolitik: Eine vergleichende Untersuchung zu Frankreich, Deutschland und der Europäischen Union*, Baden-Baden: Nomos.

Nam, Y.-S. (1997) 'Korea', in Jänicke and Weidner (1997a).

OECD (1993) *Public Management: OECD Country Profiles*, Paris: OECD.

OECD (1995a) *Developing Environmental Capacity. A Framework for Donor Involvement*, Paris: OECD.

OECD (1995b) *Planning for Sustainable Development. Country Experiences*, Paris: OECD.

Österreichische Bundesregierung (1995) *Österreich – Nationaler Umwelt Plan*, Vienna: Österreichische Bundesregierung.

Payer, H. (1997) 'Der Nationale Umweltplan (NUP) für Österreich', in Jänicke, Carius and Jörgens (1997).

REC (Regional Environmental Center for Central and Eastern Europe) (1996) *Status of National Environmental Action Programs in Central and Eastern Europe*, document available at the WorldWideWeb site of the REC (http://www.rec.hu/).

RIVM (Rijksinstituut voor Volksgezondheid en Milieuhygiene) (1994) *National Environmental Outlook 1993–2015*, Bilthoven: RIVM.

Rose, R. (1993) *Lesson-Drawing in Public Policy: A Guide to Learning across Time and Space*, Chatham and New Jersey: Chatham House Publishers.

SEPA (Swedish Environmental Protection Agency) (1997) 'Press Release: 18 New Objectives for the Environment', 4 September 1997, Stockholm.

Tweede Kamer der Staaten General (1995) *Convenanten van het Rijk met bedrijven en instellingen. Vergaderjaar 1995–1996*, 24, 480, 1–2.

Wallace, D. (1995) *Environmental Policy and Industrial Innovation: Strategies in Europe, the USA and Japan*, London: Earthscan.

Wätzold, F. and Simonis, U. (1997) 'Ökologische Unsicherheit: Über Möglichkeiten und Grenzen von Umweltpolitik', in *Aus Politik und Zeitgeschichte* B 27/97: 3–14.

Weale, A. (1992) *The New Politics of Pollution*, Manchester, New York: Manchester University Press.

Weidner, H. (1996) *Basiselemente einer erfolgreichen Umweltpolitik: Eine Analyse und Evaluation der Instrumente der japanischen Umweltpolitik*, Berlin: Edition Sigma.

Wilkinson, D. (1997) 'The Drafting of National Environmental Plans: The UK Experience', in Jänicke, Carius and Jörgens (1997).

9 Local sustainability in a sea of globalisation? The case of food policy

Tim Lang

Sustainability is a modern notion, vague at times, but intriguing and useful because it provides a critique of contemporary living and captures aspirations in equal amount. In these supposedly centrist, (or perhaps neo-liberal) ideologically dominated times, there is something appealingly utopian about the notion. The assumption behind it is that policies should promote environmental protection, social equity and diversity, putting economic and social activity on a more eco-logically long-lasting footing. Sustainability has an implicit recognition of the local, captured in the often quoted environmental slogan 'think globally, act locally'.

Contemporary food policy debates do fit this global-local dichotomy well; and although it is politically fashionable to celebrate globalisation as unstoppable, in food policy there are powerful arguments for a different perspective. In this chapter I will explore some of the implications that sustainability raises for food policy and consider whether any notion of planning is appropriate.

On the face of it, modern food methods, from farm to home, appear to be extraordinarily successful. These days, a phenomenal range of foods is available to the British and hunger appears to have been banished from this fertile island. But there is another side to the coin. Food poverty has not in fact been banished, merely modernised; there may be no 'kwashiorkor' but there is under- and mal-nutrition (Leather 1996). At the other end of the social scale, while it might be pleasant for the rich consumer to sample fresh foods grown around the world 365 days a year from a display at one's local hypermarket, this is not a sustainable food culture in any meaningful sense of the word (Lang 1997). Besides the extra-ordinary expenditure of non-renewable resources in transport, a neo-colonial relationship can easily ensue (Thrupp 1995).

The products of the cultural industries such as films or music might fly the world, but food probably ought to be as local as is reasonably possible. Much depends, of course, on what is 'reasonable'; it is easier to agree on what is exces-sive, like parsnips being flown in Northern summers from Australia in its winter, but harder to agree on the way forward; planning is never a mechanistic operation but a problem of how to translate what President Clinton used to call 'the vision thing'.[1]

Putting such debates to one side, the arguments within food policy circles which call for a re-localisation of the food system, rather than its further globalisation, could, I believe, herald the emergence of a counter-globalisation vision. In developing countries, it is nonsense to assume that others in the North will feed you, yet that is what we in the North partially expect of the South: green beans in mid-winter from Tanzania, fruit from the Gambia, potatoes from Egypt, all driven by consumer expectations. At a policy level, it is different; debates about food security assume the need to grow as much food nationally or regionally as possible (Lang 1996). Yet the economic reality sends opposite signals. Since the 1994 Uruguay Round of GATT, tariffs on imported foods have been lowered. This has sent a frisson round food policy circles. It might or might not make sense for capital to circulate the globe in pursuit of market opportunities, but does it make ecological or cultural sense for food to follow suit? I think not. It might be profitable for the trader to import (or export) food, but it does not necessarily feed everyone's stomachs. Few in food policy circles are autarkists, and most agree that a food trade can be financially useful to the domestic economy, but concern rises if staple foods are externally sourced, or if land which could grow food for a needy local population is used to grow feed for animals on distant farms or for exotic crops and 'different' foods for rich dining tables.

The argument that re-asserts the need to celebrate the local in food policy sends a shudder down the spine of many economists. Although many political theorists know Keynes' dictum in *National Self-Sufficiency* that ideas, art and culture should circulate freely across borders but that capital and goods should remain national, the currently dominant economic analysis argues that, even if one wanted it, no goods or capital could be constrained within borders. The financial markets are quick to punish aberrant finance ministers, after all. The local, according to this world view, represents the past – quaint, historically understandable perhaps, but impractical and inefficient today – whereas the global is the future, a culture and economy which is already unfolding. Globalisation is in fact a code-word for the primacy of neo-liberal market economics.

It is against this wider political economy that I argue that in the case of food policy the goal of sustainability raises a serious challenge not just about the notion of planning but about what a desirable food system might entail. Who would do the planning? How? Where? In town halls? Private utilities? International fora? To conceive of improving the present food economy by planning implies that we already have an excellent understanding of the forces driving the contemporary food system and that we know what should be planned 'in' and 'out' of the future. We may indeed all have clear notions of what we want as individuals, but to say that society as a whole has such clarity or a consensus is surely not true. Food policy, as we shall see, is a contested arena.

The history of food policy is an epic struggle between forces which seek to exert control through food and those who seek emancipation (Lang 1998c). Disagreement about the goals for any possible planning process peppers food policy history, even in wartime, a reality which raises the uncomfortable fact that current procedures for deciding what the citizenry do or do not want from their food system are somewhat weak. Generally the forces of control have triumphed. So when raising the possibility, nay necessity, that food should be more sustainably produced and distributed, some humility about achieving such a reasonable goal is in order. This is not just a challenge for public policy, but also for intellectuals. Understanding of how the current food system works, what drives it, who gains and loses, is remarkably patchy. Those academics interested in food have tended to work in departments and disciplines tied to powerful interests, notably the state and corporate efficiency. Independent research into supermarket power, for instance, is scant but there is a greater literature on trying to make firms more efficient (Trienekens and Zuurbier 1996).

The problem in food policy has not just been a deficiency of non-partisan academics: it has also been a failure of public institutions. With the demise of the consumer and health-oriented Ministry of Food in Britain in 1955, and its merger, as a rump, into the long-established and industry-friendly Ministry of Agriculture and Fisheries, the channels of communication for health and the public interest have been restricted. Officially, it was assumed that the existing machinery of government represented the sum of the public interest. The persistence of food scandals, beginning with the attempted suppression of a health education report in 1983 and culminating in the mishandling of the bovine spongiform encephalitis (BSE) crisis from 1987, show that radical critics in food policy have not been alone in questioning the adequacy of food governance. The Blair government was elected in 1997 with a commitment to the first radical overhaul of the state food machinery since 1875 when the current Ministry of Agriculture, Fisheries and Food (MAFF) was created as a stand-alone department. This tale is important to any complete understanding of the possible role of planning in achieving sustainability, and there is no doubt that not only the machinery of government requires overhaul, but also its policies and culture (Lang *et al.* 1996).

Recent food scandals – from BSE to food poisoning – have put even European Commission structures on the defensive. Responding to a highly critical report by the European Parliament on the Commission's handling of the BSE débâcle in 1997 (European Parliament 1997), President Jacques Santer admitted serious failures and institutional bias towards productionist elements; it was time, he said, to reassert political control over the current food and farming scene, to assert the primacy of the public health and public desire for better systems of production (Santer 1997). Sustainability is thus a challenge for politics, not just the mechanics of government.

I suggest that the re-localisation of the food economy will have to be a central feature of any food system which claims to move in a more sustainable direction. There may be arguments about what is local – is an apple local if it is grown within five miles or two hundred? – but the drift of policy must surely encourage trends to be more local rather than more global; this is the reverse of today's implicit food policy.

If re-localisation is to be the hallmark of a more sustainable food economy, the issue is: how can it be driven in such a direction? What political changes are required to help make it a reality? Proponents of the status quo inevitably argue that implicit in such an analysis is a more 'dirigiste' state, anything from eco-totalitarianism to a benign environmental dictatorship. But the strong state model, they argue, flies in the face of the contemporary drift of political economy where considerable ingenuity and will are expended on reducing the 'nanny state'. The call to re-invent government has in fact been a call to reduce and privatise it. So to argue for sustainability and localism is folly, say the critics; the clock cannot be turned back. This is a powerful argument and one much rehearsed in international arenas such as negotiations on climate change. This model of the state – replete with the 'old' ideology of commanding heights, levers and five-year plans – is indeed one version which could arguably be invoked to pursue the vision of sustainability in food. There is, however, another.

In this, the role of the state is as a facilitator, rule-setter and educator. If the former model of the state is a 'push' model, the latter is a 'pull'. In this, the consumer or, more likely, the citizen (an altogether more rounded being) becomes a key agent. In truth, a more sustainable political economy cannot be conceived of as imposed in a top-down way. Far from implying a more centralised, dirigiste state or social order, a sustainable political economy re-asserts an older model of the relationship between economy and society, one where social relations assert primacy over economic rules of engagement, rather than the other way round. This is the framework for the present chapter.

What would a more sustainable food system entail? For the food system to move in a more sustainable direction, there would have to be change in at least four key respects:

- how food is produced and distributed (the nature of production);
- what people eat and consumers demand (consumer culture);
- a broadening of the definition of the environment to include medical notions of health (environmental health);
- modernisation and transformation of institutions and policies (institutional reform).

All of these raise problems of considerable complexity.

THE HALTING MARCH TO SUSTAINABILITY WITHIN FOOD POLICY

Thinking about how to turn the notion of sustainability into practical policies is better developed in some policy areas than others. The issues of transport and town planning, for instance, have received considerable attention, in part because there is a structural split between public and private provision, and in part because the Conservative governments (1979–1997) injected such clear ideological support for the private sector that any perceived failures merely high-light the role of government and forward planning. In food policy, by contrast, no such public–private split in production or service provision exists. The food economy is overwhelmingly in private hands. Some welfare catering is perhaps the only relic of public provision, and that was either born or vastly expanded in dire wartime circumstances. Yet in the 1970s and again, more stridently in the 1980s, food policy became a relatively high-profile policy area, with demands for more public policy involvement and controls. The case for putting food production – particularly agriculture – on a more ecological footing moved from the preserve of the hippie and utopian fringes to the policy mainstream in two decades.

UK entry to Europe introduced politicians into the warm waters of the Common Agricultural Policy (CAP) from 1974, but food policy attention really sharpened with the publicity around an apparent attempt by sections of the UK food industry to withhold a health education report by the National Advisory Committee on Nutrition Education (NACNE) in 1983 (Walker and Cannon 1984). This brought to a head a simmering conflict over whether an unfettered food industry could deliver a health-enhancing diet and whether consumers can be given enough information on the health impact of their diet for this to affect demand. This conflict deepened in the 1980s with the extraordinary wave of scandals about adulteration and contamination in 1988–90; but it culminated with the theoretically de-regulatory Thatcher government introducing an interventionist Food Safety Act 1990 (Lang 1998b).

Gradually, over a twenty year period, students of food policy had to re-learn lessons that their predecessors had taken for granted: that planning is important, that the state has, on occasion, to be made to act as an honest broker in commerce, and that unregulated markets have severe limits on what they can deliver with respect to non-economic goals. These lessons are central to any thinking about the role of government and sustainability. Part of the difficulty of turning food policy in a more sustainable direction stems from the fact that food is an intersection point for diverse interests: health, environment, industry, trade, consumers, international relations and culture. It is also big business, with £57 billion annual sales. But this complexity is a challenge, not a barrier.

Despite this difficulty, useful work has begun on how to turn general sustainability policy objectives into operational targets. Much of this work has been conducted by NGOs, which have grown from their origins as campaigning critics into being producers of solutions as well. In Britain this development is now particularly noticeable and is, in part, due to the Thatcher government's ideological commitment to the free market (a euphemism for supporting some economic sectors, but not others).

One area of food policy where there has been most discussion about the case for trying to integrate sustainability goals has been the CAP (Baldock and Conder 1985; Institute for European Environmental Policy 1995). Environmental goals were kept resolutely out of CAP's terms of reference until the MacSharry reforms of 1992–3 (Baldock and Beaufoy 1992). These reforms were not the dramatic change its proponents claimed, but they did introduce a system of environmental payments: a small, but symbolic victory. Another area where there has been both campaigning and analysis is the use of agro-chemicals, a key indicator of intensification of production on the farm, with marked environmental and human health effects. Years of campaigning on pesticides has engendered some degree of consensus on the need to reduce pesticide use, and how to do so (Snell 1986; House of Commons Agriculture Committee 1987; Hurst, Hay and Dudley 1991; Lang and Clutterbuck 1991; Dinham 1993). Options range from wholesale abandonment of pesticides and the adoption of organic or biological pest-control systems, to 'half-way houses' such as Integrated Pest Management.

In food processing, however, there is no consensus between industry, government and NGOs. Government and industry see environmental issues as applying only in fairly restricted terms, such as energy use or packaging, whereas NGOs tend to criticise the nature of production more fundamentally. Arguments over food additives or technologies such as cook-chill or irradiation (Millstone 1985; Miller 1987; Millstone and Abraham 1989) have highlighted this fissure which was institutionalised in the Major government's Technology Foresight document on food and drink (Office of Science and Technology 1995). This was informed by the MAFF's industrial sponsorship function. It excluded consumer welfare issues, and environmental considerations were premised upon an overall industrial strategy of 'backing winners'. In the case of bio-technology, environmental considerations have been more systematically included, but there, too, the assumption is that commerce can best be left to determine the national interest.

In the food retailing sector, attention has focused upon the role of supermarkets and their control over shopping and impact on town centres and green belt development. There is some consensus on the case for reducing reliance upon cars for shopping and on the need to revitalise more local shopping (House of Commons Select Committee on the Environment 1994), but less agreement on whether supermarkets will, on their own, be competent to do this (Raven and Lang 1995; Whitelegg 1995).

In the domestic sphere, there has probably been most interest recently in the issue of cooking. There is consensus that there needs to be a national base of cooking skills – the catering industry is one of the few growth points in employment, albeit on a low-waged basis – but governments have been divided about whether skills should be mandatory or voluntary. There is more clarity about the impact of declining cooking skills on public health. If people cannot cook, they are dependent upon more pre-processed, and therefore more energy-wasteful, foods. They have less control over intake of nutrients. Use of seasonal foods in cooking not only supports general goals such as biodiversity (Jenkins 1992), but also, some evidence suggests, tends to use more local rather than long-distance foods, thereby side-stepping the problem of internalising the full cost of 'food miles' within the cost of goods (Paxton 1994). Currently, cooking is not on the national curriculum, but the Department of Health and MAFF united tacitly against the Department of Education by supporting the *Get Cooking!* campaign (National Food Alliance 1993) which called for cooking skills to be taught to all young people. Cooking remains off the curriculum. This might change now that the Labour government has lent its support to the Royal Society of Arts 'Focus on Food' initiative in which cooks go into primary schools.

Refinement of thinking about the public policy and cultural implications of mundane issues such as cooking skills can be both useful and inspirational, but unless these skills are part of a coherent strategy, they can be dismissed as single issue work within an *ad hoc* food policy, when what is needed is an integrated framework which incorporates rather than 'bolts on' sustainability. The point here is that experience of single issues reinforces the case for re-assessing how governmental institutions and policies help undermine the goal of sustainability which the government espouses elsewhere. The British government may be enthusiastic about reducing global warming, but fails to see the connection with what is taught in its own classrooms. With the exceptions of the reform of MAFF following the 1988–90 food scandals, and the creation of the Food Standards Agency, government committees and institutions mostly date from the post-war era, when the case for the integration of environmental objectives barely registered. Environmental protection is formally part of MAFF's brief, but it is operationally turned into the responsibility of divisions which protect wildlife or monitor pesticides or endocrine disruptors, rather than applied across the whole Ministry. Getting cross-sectoral policy goals adopted and implemented across departments is a perennial headache for government, but in the case of sustainable development goals, it has to be done. Difficulty is no excuse for inaction. How, then, can food policy be moved in a more sustainable direction?

The rest of this chapter explores this question, and suggests that British food policy has suffered from a reliance upon a commercialised view of the food economy and from an official policy assumption that the best role for government is a minimal one. Government rhetoric of non-interventionism is belied by its actions, for instance on regulation, wage rates, research and development policy and other ground rules which affect the food economy. Membership of the EU also gives the lie to non-intervention.

In fact, British food policy can only be understood as the outcome of a complex interplay of forces. As I argued earlier, food policy is a contested domain. Over the last two hundred years, generally, but not always, it has been dominated by trade interests. As a result, from the perspective of sustainability, food policy has been too fragmented. Except in time of war, it has suffered from the separation of economic and other policy domains such as health, culture, employment and the environment itself. The challenge for modern food policy, and sustainability generally, is to develop mechanisms, targets and objectives which integrate all policy demands. In modern times, attempts to integrate policy have been regrettably scarce.[2] We have to turn to earlier periods of interest to draw inspiration for these tasks (Astor and Rowntree 1938).

THE FOOD POLICY CHALLENGE

Part of the attraction, yet also the difficulty, with sustainability as a notion, is that it has been in vogue long enough for governments less wedded to non-interventionism than Britain's to have begun to exert some influence on their food economies. Norway, for example, in the 1970s decided to maintain a viable (but assisted) small farm sector, and to keep people in the countryside. A system of grants to enable small farmers to hire extra labour for a few weeks, to enable them to take holidays, for instance, was instituted. With regard to food processing, tight standards for food quality were set; for instance, a ban on artificial food colours was deemed a way of both ensuring 'real' food and more locally derived food. The more recent German targets for the recycling of packaging provide another example. General policy objectives always need to be turned into specific targets, and equally, before specific targets are set, general policy objectives need to be agreed. For food, globally as well as nationally, these include:

- feeding everyone, not just those with adequate funds;
- security of supply for an increasingly urban population;
- promotion of environmentally-sound food production;
- a good quality, health-enhancing diet;
- stable employment from food production and distribution;
- ensuring that the gap between rich and poor is reduced, within and between countries.

FOOD TRADE AND BRITISH FOOD POLICY

Trade has been the backbone of the British economy for centuries and the food trade provides an interesting case study for the debate about sustainability. Throughout human history, land and food supplies have often been the cause and locus of both military and trade wars, and British history is no exception to this rule. British food history becomes particularly pertinent to the modern sustainability debate in the early to mid-nineteenth century with the repeal of the Corn Laws and the momentous decision to abandon indigenous production for supplies from the colonies. Agriculture entered uncharted waters (Tracy 1982). Although elements of the diet have always been traded – think of sugar, spices and teas (Mintz 1985; Rowling 1987) – this decision meant that for the first time in human history a country was allowing staple food to be a commodity for long-distance, rather than local, trade. British agriculture and the countryside went into decline almost immediately.

Although resistance to the decision continued throughout the nineteenth century, it was not until the next century that the British state seriously began to reconsider its policy, a process brought on by a battery of concerns, ranging from national efficiency to wartime security and social unrest. The 1905 Royal Commission on food in time of war re-assessed, in a typically magisterial fashion, whether the policy since the repeal of the Corn Laws had been right (HM Government 1905). The report might have been better titled 'Food in a time of submarines', because it was their threat to sea traffic which brought into question the reliance upon the colonies (Walworth 1940).

The Royal Commission set the tone for British food policy for this century, and although it focused upon war, it developed two strands of thinking, both still discernible today, and both pertinent to sustainability. The first was a concern about food poverty and the role of food in a fragile social context (Rowntree 1902, 1941; Ministry of Health 1937; Titmuss 1976; Burnett and Oddy 1994). At what point, the Commission asked, after the breakdown of food supplies would the working people begin to express unrest? The second was a more technocratic concern about how to reverse conventional 'free market' systems of food production and distribution in order to maintain security of supply. The Second World War brought both strands of thinking together for the first time (Clarke and Titmuss 1939). The rise of the industrial canteen (Curtis-Bennett 1949) and the explosion of provision of school meals in the Second World War (Burnett 1994) illustrate this merger. Mass catering was both technically efficient at feeding people and in targeting socially 'at risk' populations.

Second World War food policy gave far more prominence to the social dimensions of food policy than the British state had hitherto allowed. Undoubtedly, this was due to decades of campaigning on the dietary aspects of poverty, conducted by an alliance of interests which ranged from women campaigners (Rathbone 1924, 1940; Spring-Rice 1981) to medical interests (M'Gonigle and Kirkby 1936; British Medical Association 1939; Orr 1943) and unemployed workers (Brockway 1932; Hannington 1937, 1977). They had made food poverty a persistent theme of social policy in the first half of the twentieth century.[3] Here, too, scarcity was a theme, but in marked contrast to the efficiency deliberations over food in time of war, which carefully weighed up national, military and morale factors (Rowntree 1921; Curtis-Bennett 1949), thinking about food and poverty was inevitably draped in a more social context. The concern was for morals rather than morale.

Such moral concern, expressed over the mundane issue of daily food, crosses conventional political boundaries. (The English language is replete with food imagery and aphorisms, such as the 'family that eats together stays together', which can in fact be just as well reversed!) It is remarkable to witness the extraordinary capacity of politicians to argue that welfare systems undermine the family and threaten the nation, a theme that crops up throughout the twentieth century to this day. A patronising moral code, for example, featured in the debate on the Education (Provision of Meals) Act of 1906 about the implications of allowing local authorities to levy a rate to pay for school meals: would this meal sap the family unit or would it provide a welcome opportunity to teach the importunate how to wield a knife and fork, and with luck civilise their parents at home (Lancashire School Meals Campaign and Lang 1981; Lang 1983). By the early 1970s, when Margaret Thatcher was Secretary of State for Education, the 'modern' imperative had shifted to how to teach the young to self-serve (DES 1975). Out went so-called family-style meals at school; in came the supermarket revolution.

What is the relevance of this for the contemporary debate about food and sustainability? Even this brief foray into British food policy history suggests, first, that the British state's actions have been narrow and focused upon commerce, although social and cultural consideration have also featured. Second, we can note the definition of food security as strategic rather than environmental. And third, we can see that the spotlight in food policy has been on the state rather than on other social or economic actors. Throughout the twentieth century, it has been the state to which the campaigners have looked to provide welfare, just as in the nineteenth century they did on the issue of food safety. But, as William Beveridge noted in his magnificent official history of the first Ministry of Food (in which he had been a civil servant) and of state intervention in the First World War, the reflex of the British state throughout had been to keep itself at arm's length from commerce (Beveridge 1928). It had to be dragged into acting when, in the words of Lord Milner, it really wanted to restore 'business as usual', a perennial battle cry from the Right throughout the twentieth century.

Advocates of sustainability, by contrast, tend to be ambivalent about whether to look to the state to deliver progress. Some are decidedly anti-statist, viewing the state as almost inevitably interfering, muddled and damaging. Trust the people, they say; the goal should be to decentralise and localise. Others regard the state with more favour. In a world where capital and corporations are considerably more mobile and less regulated, the citizen and the environment can only be properly protected and represented by some kind of intervening power. The political battle is over what form that intervention takes, and how representative state mechanisms are.

THE STATE AND THE FOOD GAP

If, at the start of this century, British food policy had the option to rely upon colonies, rather than domestic agriculture, the Second World War saw the beginning of the end of Empire and a painful period of readjustment (Hammond 1951; Calder 1971; Hennessy 1993). Entry to the Common Market, as it then was, meant the abandonment of the Commonwealth and of the colonial era of deficiency payments for farmers and marketing boards, left over from the 1930s. It meant entry to a new world of higher cost food and an internationally co-ordinated food and agriculture policy (Neville-Rolfe 1984; National Consumer Council 1988). Europeanisation has provided the background for British food policy ever since, and policy has certainly not been static. The CAP has undergone more changes than almost any EU sector. From the moment Sicco Mansholt, on his first day in office, sent a secretary out to buy six filing cabinets and a desk, determined never again to allow hunger to stalk European soil,[4] policy has been one of adjustment to new demands: oversupply, labour policy, prices, fiscal burden, expansion of the European Community (now Union) and latterly, globalisation via the Uruguay Round of GATT.

A main plank in the British approach to European food and agriculture policy was a decision to 'Europeanise' its traditional trade policy. Fresh from wartime reminders about the stupidity of relying on unnecessary external suppliers, Labour's Agriculture Minister in the Attlee government, Tom Williams, MP, took the 1947 Agriculture Act through Parliament with the goal of ensuring a decent supply of food. Entry to Europe both accelerated and altered this policy. Home production of key supported commodities, such as cereals and some dairy products, rose. Instead of encouraging national production, policy encouraged Europeanisation. Farmers and food were supported, and protection at borders was implemented on a Europe-wide basis. The 1974 White Paper *Food from our own Resources* was a misnomer; it should have stated 'Food from European resources'. For Britain, this meant that whereas in the pre-war period there had been external food trade, mostly imports, there was to be internal trade within Europe. The pro- and anti-Europe factions were born.

In 1983, as part of its vision for a re-invigorated, efficient Britain, the Minister of Agriculture, Fisheries and Food, Peter Walker, set up Food From Britain (FFB), a 'quango', whose brief was to promote British food exports. In recent years, the food and drink trade gap has been considerable. Superficially, FFB's promotions and marketing support schemes, such as the encouragement of producers to attend foreign food fairs, have done little to stem the haemorrhage. At inflation-adjusted prices, the trade gap was in deficit throughout the 1980s, a consistent £6 billion. These figures disguise other trends. First, although each year food imports have risen, exports have also increased by fractionally more. For instance, in 1992, exports rose by 13 per cent and imports were up by 8 per cent, a big jump on the previous year. But from a national trading perspective, such as the FFB's, the picture is not as gloomy as the figures suggest. Whereas in 1971 exports were 25 per cent of imports by value, by 1994 they were 60 per cent. Even though both imports and exports were growing, and the trade gap was high, proportionately it was narrowing, if slowly.[5] In 1996, however, the trade gap jumped considerably, partly but not wholly due to the beef ban after the BSE link with Creutzfeldt-Jakob Disease emerged. A huge proportion of the overall gap is accounted for by imports of fresh fruit and vegetables.

Many of the imports are of goods which could perfectly easily be grown or processed locally: products such as beer, sausages, yoghurts. Half of poultry meat imports, for instance, in 1992 came from France (FFB 1992a: 19). According to Department of Transport figures, over the period 1979–94, food, drink and tobacco, which collectively account for less than 10 per cent of GNP, were responsible for nearly 40 per cent of the increase in freight transport. The same amount of food by weight is being transported as in the late 1970s, but it is going 50 per cent further. Internationally, food imports by air more than doubled in the 1980s and, after falling during the recession in the early 1990s, they rose by 15 per cent during 1994 (Paxton 1994). The increase in 'food miles' travelled is an indicator less of comparative advantage than of cheap diesel and motorways.

When the Commons Agriculture Committee investigated the food trade gap, this provided one of the first formal occasions when sustainability issues entered the heart of contemporary food policy and an overview of food policy was attempted (House of Commons Agriculture Committee 1992). Why, the Committee, wanted to know, was the British food industry allowing unnecessary imports? The problem was defined in nationalist terms, but it could be defined in environmental terms (Raven and Lang 1995: 7–24). For its submission, FFB calculated that of the £13.4 billion of imports, £7.5 billion were unavoidable, but £5.9 billion could be produced in the UK. To paraphrase Herman Daly, former environmental economist at the World Bank, no-one conceives of growing man-goes in inappropriate Northern climes (Daly and Goodland 1992), so why import lettuces or spinach or apples in autumn or summer when they can be grown equally well more locally? The traditional – and appropriate – answer from environmentalists is that the full costs are not internalised in the price of the food, but there are other factors. FFB argues that there are four reasons why the UK cannot produce all the food and drink its consumers require:

- climate prevents production of certain foods;
- the UK season for many fruits and vegetables is limited;
- quotas in production of some products necessitate imports;
- consumer demand for 'authentic' imported products (FFB 1995: 6).

A former FFB chief executive, Derek Garner, has tacitly blamed the grower, arguing that the problem is that British farmers do not grow for the market.[6] For example, the UK imports vast amounts of vegetables, accounting for £1 billion of the annual national food trade gap, one-fifth of the total (FFB 1992b: 3). Some of this is importation of vegetables the UK cannot grow, but many could be grown in the UK, as the 371,000 UK hectares planted to vegetables each year testify. The reason for this failure, argued FFB, was poor marketing, an inability to handle surpluses and increased supermarket shopping for vegetables. Dutch produce was imported because the Netherlands had a better system of auctioning vegetables.

This sober analysis of marketing failure should have suggested a connection with rising supermarket power over what was grown and sold, but the Committee did not consider other aspects of changing consumer culture.

THE GLOBALISATION OF A FOOD CULTURE OF ILL HEALTH

Defining what is meant by food culture can be a tiresome task, but we can point to what people do, as well as what they think (Mennell, Murcott and van Otterloo 1992; Tansey and Worsley 1995). Most, but not all, cultural commentators under-standably celebrate the explosion of choice in the modern British diet. At one level, globalisation enables a working-class family in London or Manchester to eat food from far-off places. The diversity of the British diet has been enormously improved by inflows of Asian, particularly Indian and Pakistani, people and their cuisines. One moment people can eat Italian, Japanese or Indian; the next moment they are listening to Latin American music, rock and roll, folk music, while dressed in clothes which take their inspiration from the rest of the world. It is easy to see how easily this cultural analysis of globalisation can be presented as liberating; it is, it can be. The spread of environmental consciousness owes much to television, for instance. Television brings the fragility of ecosystems in far-off lands into people's homes. There is also nothing new about the transfer of foods and cuisines. But questions are justly asked about the environmental impact, about who controls the process and whether people are losing control (if they had any), and about whether globalisation is a misnomer for Westernisation and a change in the nature of production (Sklair 1991).

Globalised food brands on offer in the international supermarket are generally pre-cooked or pre-processed. Cooking is transferred from home to factory. At one level, this can be appealing, especially to those – women – with prime responsibility for domestic food. But now in Western societies, generations are being produced which possess few or even no cooking skills. Far from trade creating freedom, people are actually being rendered more dependent. They are gaining skills in some spheres of their lives and not in others. In Britain, for instance, a survey of 7- to 15-year-old young people found that 93 per cent knew how to play computer games; 77 per cent could use a compact disc or music centre; 61 per cent could programme a video to record something on television; 54 per cent could bake a cake; and 38 per cent could cook a jacket potato in the oven (MORI 1993). As a vignette of modern life, this suggests a food culture in transition, gaining and losing at the same time.

In his study of consumer patterns, Alan Durning, of the Worldwatch Institute, concluded that new, global consuming classes were emerging (Durning 1992). He suggests a categorisation of the world's 5.4 billion people into three consuming classes, for which food is a key characteristic (see Table 9.1). Consumer culture, not just in food, is driven by the ecologically overconsuming class, he argues. Although icons such as McDonald's tend to hog the headlines, it is important to recognise that a deep and powerful transformation of society is under way. Ritzer has called it McDonaldisation (Ritzer 1993). Others have called it coca-colonialism (Levinson 1979). Aspirations for a lifestyle are translated into dietary form; they may be driven by the affluent but copied by the less well-off. This pattern includes, for example, an emphasis on meat eating as an indicator of progress, and a disregard for more local foods. 'Peasant' becomes a term of abuse, synonymous with the past. (The numbers of farmers in Europe has in fact halved in the last two decades.)

Similarities of lifestyle bond the rich of North and South, as well as the poor

Table 9.1 World consumption classes, 1992

Category of consumption (Population)	Consumers 1.1 billion	Middle 3.3 billion	Poor 1.1 billion
Diet	meat, packaged food, soft drinks	grain, clean water	insufficient grain, unsafe water
Transport	private cars	bicycles, bus	walking
Materials	throwaways	durables	local biomass

Sources: Modified from Durning (1992: 27).

(Gabriel and Lang 1995; Watkins 1995). The rich, Durning's consumers, eat in an unprecedently copious way. They – we – can chose from 20,000 items on the hypermarket shelves, drawn from around the world in a brilliantly efficient system of production and distribution. This delivers fresh green beans in mid-winter, flown in from Kenya or the Gambia. Biodiversity on the shelves is not necessarily reflected in the contract fields whence this abundance comes.[7] And the poor continue to starve. According to the United Nations Children's Fund (UNICEF):

> one in five persons in the developing world suffers from chronic hunger – 800 million people in Africa, Asia and Latin America. Over 2 billion people subsist on diets deficient in the vitamins and minerals essential for normal growth and development, and for preventing premature death and such disabilities as blindness and mental retardation.
>
> (UNICEF 1993: 1)

While such facts are sobering, inadequacies of income affect dietary intake in affluent countries too (Dowler and Rushton 1993). The emergence of global consuming and underconsuming classes is accompanied by a globalisation of inequalities.

Thirty years ago, the combined incomes of the richest fifth of the world's people were thirty times greater than the poorest fifth. Today their incomes are over sixty times greater. The rise in numbers of dollar billionaires has been estimated by the Institute of Policy Studies, Washington, DC, as 358 by 1994 (Cavanagh and Broad 1994). This relatively tiny number of people was calculated to be collectively worth some US$762 billion, which is approximately equivalent to the combined income of the world's poorest two billion citizens, or well over one-third of the world's population. This sharp division within the globalisation of consumer food culture is the result of the rapid concentration of national and international economies everywhere.

The assets of the largest three hundred firms in the world are now worth approximately a quarter of the productive assets in the world (*The Economist*, 27 March 1993: 5–6). Transnational corporations now account for 70 per cent of total world trade (in all goods, not just food). Of those corporations, the top 350 now account for around 40 per cent of trade (Daly and Goodland 1992). In food, such power is common, according to research by the United Nations Centre on Transnational Corporations (1981), and high levels of concentration are common in the food system (Tansey and Worsley 1995). Cargill, a family-owned commodity trader, has 60 per cent of world cereal trade (Lang and Hines 1993: 35). The largest five corporations control 77 per cent of the cereals trade, the largest three have 80 per cent of the banana market, the biggest three have 83 per cent of cocoa and 85 per cent of the tea trade (Madden 1992: 46). In Europe, small, craft and local food producers and traders are under pressure. As a result, between 1980 and 1990, 11 per cent of UK farmers and 34 per cent of farm workers stopped farming, continuing a process, it should be stressed, begun long before the EU's CAP.[8] Nevertheless, the fiscal impact of CAP is considerable. For instance,

80 per cent of farm support that actually gets to farmers (as opposed to traders or storers) goes to the largest 20 per cent of farms (House of Lords Select Committee Report 1992).

To health specialists, a key contemporary cultural indicator is not the number of farmers and growers, but fruit and vegetable consumption. Generally, there has been a shift from fresh items (unprocessed, uncooked materials) to frozen or precooked foods. Illustrative of this trend is the declining consumption of fresh potatoes and a rapidly expanding market for value-added potato products such as frozen chips (MAFF 1993: 8). This shift in consumption patterns has ecological implications. The food travels further (see below), but also its energy use rises. The British eat fewer vegetables than any other European country, at least half the amount of France, Spain and Italy. This is a significant factor in the UK's lamentable record of food-related ill-health (HM Government 1992). Vegetables (and fruits) contain many of the protective factors for coronary heart disease and some cancers (World Health Organisation 1990) which are Britain's main sources of premature death. A government study of the health of the Scottish diet, for instance, found that Scottish children's diets were 'the worst in the western world' (Scottish Office Home and Health Department 1993). A high proportion of children eat neither green vegetables nor fruit. If this is the picture today, in 1960 it was even more marked, with Scotland eating over 60 per cent less vegetables, for instance, than the national average (MAFF 1991: Figure 4.11).

After rising proportionally from the 1950s to the 1970s, expenditure on fruit and vegetables declined from 1980 to 1990 (MAFF 1991: 35). In fresh green vegetables, there has been a decline from 14–15 oz per person per week in 1960 to 12 oz in 1980 to 10 oz in 1990. Consumption of other fresh vegetables has risen from 14–15 oz per person per week in 1960 to 16–17 oz thereafter. While fruit consumption appears to have increased significantly since the mid-1970s this is largely accounted for by the very sharp rise in purchases of fruit juice which does not provide equivalent nutrition to its fresh counterpart. This fruit juice consumption, however, is often of juices from long-distant fruit, notably oranges from Brazil. A study by the Wuppertal Institute in Germany calculated that 80 per cent of Brazilian orange production is consumed in Europe. Annual German consumption occupied 370,000 acres of Brazilian productive land, three times the land down to fruit production in Germany. If this level of German orange juice consumption was replicated world-wide, 32 million acres would be needed just for orange production (Kranendonk and Bringezau 1994). The increasing range of fruit available throughout the year also contributes to this rise in consumption.

Reviewing half a century of the national diet, MAFF's National Food Survey concluded that 'better communications, more uniform prices and changing tastes have all contributed to a degree of convergence in consumption levels' between the regions. Although diets have changed in unimaginable ways, in nutritional terms they have changed far more patchily. Fat intake, for example, has remained almost static, but the source of the fats has not. People might be drinking less full fat milk, but the fat is consumed in different forms.

The epidemiological evidence on the contemporary diet is clear. Having conquered hunger in the West, food is now the primary cause of premature death. Food is implicated in the West's great killers, heart disease and some cancers (breast, colon: World Health Organisation 1990). Eating a more 'Western' diet is seen as a cultural yardstick for development, when probably it ought to be seen as cultural failure. The huge medical study of the Chinese diet undertaken by researchers in China, England and the USA has shown conclusively that Western diseases are associated with changes from the peasant diet which is low in saturated fats (Junshi *et al.* 1990). Compared to, say, Americans or British, the Chinese eat a diet low in animal fats. But even within the Chinese population, those who ate a higher saturated fat diet had more medical problems than those who did not.

There is near unanimity in the scientific literature about the ideal diet for humans (Cannon 1992). Sometimes this is referred to as the Mediterranean Diet, in honour of the work by Ancel Keys and colleagues comparing the diet and disease rates of seven countries, which first provided evidence for the failure of the 'advanced' diet (Keys 1970, 1980). The population of Crete and Greece provide the model, a diet high in fruit, vegetables and carbohydrates, low in meats and with some fish.

Today, as food styles are exported and – let us not pretend otherwise – taken up by people, the desirable diet seems a luxury. People are being encouraged to think of food and drink as coming not from farmers or the earth but from giant corporations. A study by opinion pollsters Gallup found recently that 65 per cent of people in China recognise the brand name of Coca-Cola; 42 per cent recognise Pepsi and 40 per cent recognise Nestlé. This change is not just one of brand items, but of how work and social exchange is organised. McDonaldisation, Benettonisation, whatever the names researchers give, they all point to a similarity of process, the triumph of distribution (Murray 1985). In the post-Fordist economy (marked by flexible specialisation systems of production), the distributor not the consumer is sovereign (Gabriel and Lang 1995).

In the UK five food retailers control around 60 per cent of the consumer market,[9] while in Finland, the top five have 95 per cent (Hughes 1994). Every decade the number of grocers goes down by half (McGrath 1995). In almost every processed food sector, one or two manufacturers now dominate. The main concern of these giants is not saturated fats, but saturated markets.

A review of the impact of this emerging food economy conducted in the UK showed how the hypermarket economy has led to the same amount of food travelling further, up and down the motorways (Raven and Lang 1995). A German study of strawberry yoghurt found ecological absurdities in the system of processing, packaging and distribution, such that a theoretical truckload of 150 gram yoghurts would travel 1,005 kilometres (Boege 1993; Paxton 1994). Independent small retailers tend to source their food more locally, whereas giant stores want the regularity of supply that can only be given by large factories, large contracts and large growers.

This changing nature of global contracting and distribution has enormous implications, not just for consumption and shopping patterns but also for the position of the producer on contract, who might be more or less distant. There are signs that developing countries are being set against each other to compete for the favour of feeding affluent areas of the globe, for instance Kenya against the Gambia on vegetable production (Barrett and Browne 1994). This also has the effect of institutionalising the 'ghost acres' phenomenon, where the supposed efficiency of Northern farming is in fact subsidised by cheap inputs from abroad, notably in the form of animal feeds.

The average European weekend shopping trolley contains goods that have already travelled 4,000 kilometres before we take them home (Griffiths 1993). In the USA, one study calculated that each food item in their trolleys now travels an average 2,000 kilometres (1,300 miles) between grower and consumer (Clunies-Ross and Hildyard 1992). The European Commission's Task Force on the Environment calculated that there would be a 30–50 per cent increase in trans-frontier lorry traffic from 1993 following the opening of national borders within the Single European Market (European Commission n.d.). Total lorry traffic was expected to double between 1989 and 2010 (Griffiths 1993).

The reality of hypermarkets is that people have to use their cars to get food. According to the UK government's National Travel Survey, the number of shopping trips in Britain rose by 28 per cent between 1975/6 and 1989/91 and the total distance travelled increased by 60 per cent over the same period (Raven and Lang 1995: 8). Instead of shopping locally, often on foot, an environmentally damaging type of transport is used. The number of car-dependent trips and the distance travelled have gone up rapidly. In 1985, 62 per cent of people used their car for their main shopping trip. By 1993 this was up to 73 per cent (Henley Centre 1994).

This change in distribution not only gives retailers power over the entire food system, but also affects what the farmer grows and how she or he grows it, by the use of contracts and specifications. It also affects poor consumers as they have to pay for transport that they can ill afford. Needless to say, the specifications stipulate that food is unblemished, of a certain size, uniformity, and so on, which only a narrow form of farming can produce.

STANDARDISATION VERSUS DIVERSITY: THE EFFECT OF CHOICE

No-one has contributed more to the process of food standardisation than the supermarkets. Even though there have now been some attempts to introduce local sourcing of speciality products such as cheeses, broadly the rule is that what you see in one outlet of a chain, you can also purchase in another. The style and feel of the chain is deliberately homogeneous. Variations do happen, of course. The customer profile of one store might make it a trial store for new products. And rather like clothes retailing, some stores might be bigger and have a more 'flagship' status within the company than others.

A food culture is not just inherited; it is made, in a complex interplay, by family, friends, commerce, and other factors (Gabriel and Lang 1995; Mennell, Murcott and van Otterloo 1992). Consumers are deluged with food information from companies. By 1990 over £500 million a year was being spent on advertising food in Britain. Food is one of the most heavily advertised of all products. Bodies tell people, after all, that they need food. There is almost no advertising about fresh fruit and vegetables. One-third of food advertising is spent on television (Longfield 1992: 49), and in general food advertising is dominated by the desire to sell processed, usually fatty and sugary foods. A fifth of 'adspend' is on confectionery.

The top twelve retailers spent £46 million in 1986, rising to £72 million in 1990.[10] The figures have risen since. Even something as mundane as the packet design can have drastic effects on product sales. In the USA, the average person is bombarded by all media with 3,000 messages a day and gets 326 direct marketing packages per year, compared to the UK average of 43 (Maves 1991). To the advertiser or direct marketer, this suggests that the UK has room for expansion. In 1994 H. J. Heinz announced that its marketing strategy was changing to direct marketing, in order to build up profiles on consumers. Tesco, the largest UK food retailer, launched its loyalty card in 1995, with the same intent; the other big retailers quickly followed suit. The supermarkets now operate as banks.

Consumers are furiously fought over by food companies. Every year, an estimated 10,000 new food products are launched on to the European food market. One in ten will survive the year, and only one in twenty survive two years (Longfield 1992: 52). The key mediators between what is grown on the farm (wherever that may be) and the consumer is the supermarket. The supermarket has become an icon of the present age. The daily miracle of bringing food from all over the world, whether wrapped or loose, lurid or wholesome, to urban centres is an awesome feat of modern management. No wonder retail captains have been asked to conduct major state work. In the early 1980s Rayner (Marks & Spencer) reviewed Civil Service Catering. In the mid-1980s Griffiths (J. Sainsbury) reviewed Community Care. And in 1994 Lord Sainsbury, deregulation adviser to the President of the Board of Trade, himself introduced the government-wide assault on red-tape (DTI 1994). One of the few big food industry chairmen to support Labour, Chris Haskins of Northern Foods, is chair of the Better Regulation Task Force for the new Labour government.

Demand for a uniform product translates into pressures for uniform plants and growing conditions. Standardisation has resulted in a huge loss of genetic variation in our main food crops (Jenkins 1992), which has reached its apogee in the case of apples: there are 2,000 varieties of apple in the National Collection of the UK[11] but today just nine dominate in our commercial orchards (Common Ground 1991). Within the limited range of varieties in demand by the large food retailers, typically single ones will be grown on a very large scale. The 'use of a restricted range of varieties over large areas approaches genetic monoculture. This has profound effects on the interaction of crop plants and their pathogens, and can lead to epidemics of disease and to calls for new disease-resistant varieties' (Holden and Peacock 1993). The tendency of genetic uniformity to optimise conditions for both pest and disease attack further increases pressure for pesticide usage.

At the same time, supermarkets are demanding products out of season: 'shopping anywhere in the world at world surplus prices' (*The Grower*, 23 January 1992). Stocking policies and promotions are no longer 'planned according to crop development to coincide with periods of peak production. Now they seem to be at the whim of the sales director, imposed on a pre-programmed calendar basis for marketing purposes' (*The Grower*, 11 March 1993).

THE FOOD SYSTEM

The picture being painted of the sustainability of the present food system is one which is both dynamic and multi-dimensional. Figure 9.1 constructs a typology of the key dimensions. According to this schema, the thesis advanced in this chapter is that the current food system is being pushed inexorably to the left-hand side of each dimension, when in theory, if we desire sustainability, policies are needed to encourage the food system to veer more towards the right-hand side.

SUSTAINABILITY: NEW FORMS OF GOVERNANCE FOR OLD?

The above arguments underline the enormity of the challenge posed by the simple, but elastic, notion of sustainability. Food policy is one area where some thought has been expended over the last twenty years on what a more sustainable food system would look like. It may be summarised as a challenge of immense difficulty and complexity. The adherents of old-style central state dirigisme could well argue at this point that this complexity merely proves the value of having a

globalisation	vs.	localisation
long trade routes	vs.	short trade routes
intensification	vs.	extensification
monoculture	vs.	biodiversity
processed (stored)	vs.	fresh (perishable)
open systems	vs.	closed systems
cost externalisation	vs.	cost internalisation
de-skilling	vs.	skilling
standardisation	vs.	'difference'
people to food	vs.	food to people
food from factories	vs.	food from the land
fragmented (diverse) culture	vs.	common food culture
global decision-making	vs.	local decision-making
harmonised standards	vs.	diversity of standards
consumer dependency	vs.	consumer self-reliance
consumer	vs.	citizen

Figure 9.1 Dimensions in the food system

strong state which can cut through the difficulties and impose its will on the recalcitrant parties. At times of slow progress one can sympathise with such a view, but it is ultimately wrong. This chapter has argued that sustainability in food requires a tremendous shift in both production and distribution, culture and politics, economics as well as environmental thinking. This amounts to a truly revolutionary change. To have recourse to tried and failed draconian government would be inappropriate, which is why the green movement has consistently argued for a 'softer' state. The vision of the state propounded by green theorists from Michael Jacobs to Paul Ekins is not the currently fashionable 'hands off' variety but does in fact argue for tough regulations, particularly on the issue of cost internalisation. Much of the critique I have made of contemporary food systems could be addressed by the rigorous application of higher energy costs. The politics of this approach suggest that this will not happen. Wherever there have been attempts to introduce tough carbon taxes, for instance, there has been furious resistance from big business (Lang and Hines 1993). It is more realistic, barring some unforeseen new oil crisis, to argue that sustainability can be approached on multiple fronts rather than through a Big Bang approach such as an energy tax.

What would this entail?

First, there would have to be reform of the institutions of government. The Blair Government has set up the new Food Standards Agency and is planning reform of the MAFF rump left behind. Such reform is to be welcomed, but it will not succeed in promoting a more sustainable food system if it, as at present, excludes the environmental dimension of food policy. The huge super-ministry of the Department of the Environment, Transport and the Regions has functions which crucially affect food sustainability. The committees which monitor and regulate food quality also have narrow terms of reference. These should all be reviewed.

Second, sustainability is not acheivable if the current CAP is left intact. Since the MacSharry Reforms of 1992 some acknowledgement of environmental goals is now made, but environmental protection is really an excuse for other ways of paying marginal farmers to leave the land to be intensively farmed in larger holdings: the 'efficiency' argument by another name. For sustainability to be realistic within CAP, the subsidy system would have to be radically overhauled. The Agenda 2000 reform document of 1997 shows little sign of entertaining this. Pressure is unlikely to subside, however. There is considerable public support for integration of environment and food and farming policies, judging by public opinion polls.[12] The UK has been particularly slow to help farmers in the transition from chemical to organic systems, compared, say, to Germany. Ideally, organic farming should be subsidised rather than high-input farming or set-aside, if there are subsidies at all.

Third, environmental goals would have to be included within the agriculture regime GATT. Despite considerable lobbying during the 1987–94 Uruguay Round, the final text's approach to agriculture was narrowly economic; there was no conception that nearly three-fifths of humanity inhabit rural areas. And despite evidence that Africa, the poorest region of the world, would lose (Goldin, Knudsen and van der Mensbrugghe 1993), the agreement was pushed through. *Realpolitik* determined that this was a treaty which favoured and was brokered by the USA and Europe. In addition, the disputes procedures and food standards-setting systems were far from desirable. The agreement accorded key decision-making power to a UN body, the Codex Alimentarius Commission, in need of serious reform.

Codex is a meeting of governments; but a study of a two-year cycle of meetings, 1989–91, found that a quarter (26 per cent) of participants were from industry and only one in a thousand from consumer groups, and none from environmental groups; that there were more multinationals present than countries; that 20 per cent of the pesticides committee, for instance, was from giant agro-chemical and food companies and none from environment organisations; that Nestlé sent more representatives than the majority of countries; and that representatives from the USA and Europe outnumbered the rest of the world (Avery, Drake and Lang 1994). This situation should be rectified. The WTO does, however, have a trade and environment section, inherited from GATT. The GATT environment committee did not, however, meet for twenty years after it was set up; but now it does.

My fourth proposal is on territory closer to home for traditional conceptions of planning. The analysis of the food system given in this chapter suggests that much could be gained from the implementation of a tougher retail planning and competition policy. It has been argued elsewhere that food retailing concentration should be judged more in local terms and that environmental objectives should be written into the terms of reference of a reformed Office of Fair Trading and Monopolies and Mergers Commission (Raven and Lang 1995). Food sold in corner shops is often more expensive than that retailed in large supermarkets, but the latter are now often located on out-of-town sites and are difficult for those without transport to get to. The full cost of transport is also externalised. The trend towards locating food retail outlets out of town should be discouraged by changes to planning and competition policy. There needs to be a review of national policy on food retailing. Ironically, as the most traditional form of home delivery such as the 'door-step pinta' (milk) declines, many retailers are now actively considering home delivery, utilising the Internet to place orders. Farm diversification – through, for example, farm shops and community supported agriculture (CSA) and direct deliveries – is of increasing importance.

Fifth, the present analysis argues that the current food system is being driven in an unsustainable direction not by any hidden hand on levers that could be thrown into reverse, but by a complex interplay of desires and tastes. These are both economic and cultural in kind. The consumer 'demanding' (that is, buying) fresh green beans in mid-winter is a key factor in unsustainability, yet she or he would probably be horrified to think of her/himself in those terms. We are all 'green' now, after all. The missing link in this respect is a dearth of consumer information. Consumer education in the UK is weak, and with the decline of home economics, will weaken further. Reliance upon market mechanisms, such as labelling, to deliver sustainability goals is inadequate to the task (Lang 1995). It might be more realistic to plan on the basis of a thirty-year strategy to re-direct food culture. Imaginative schemes experimenting with new forms of education and training for life skills are proliferating world-wide; these range from re-invigorating ways of communicating practical cooking skills, to classwork where children learn to 'read' advertisements, to realise that they are marketing targets, objects not subjects (Dibb 1993).

Finally, what about traditional planning, as conducted by planning departments in Town Halls up and down the land? The Local Agenda 21 (LA21) movement, inspired by the 1992 UN Conference on Environment and Development, has led to a mushrooming of interest in Chief Executives' departments in new ways of popular consultation and involvement. LA21 programmes attempt to involve local communities in helping 'envision' the locality in a more sustainable way. Many have chosen to focus on food, auditing, for example, the availability of foods grown as regionally as possible. Their experience warrants more attention than this chapter can give, but suffice it to say that the LA21 movement appears now to be well ensconced in many Town Halls. But it is still marginal where it matters most, namely in relation to the budget process within local authorities. Unless local authorities have more autonomy over budgets, community involvement might peter out.

When faced with a public health crisis at the end of the nineteenth century, local authorities were empowered to act in a variety of ways, ranging from setting up covered markets (that is, direct food provision) to health monitoring. With the modern food supply so concentrated and in private sector hands, what can the local state do? It is financially stretched already in meeting its legal requirements to monitor and enforce hygiene standards under the Food Safety Act 1990. Environmental Health Officers have led the local authority debate about what a more sustainable civic role could be, but unless central government liberates local government to undertake this role, the vision will remain fantasy (Commission on Environmental Health 1997).

Our conclusion must therefore be that in food policy, at least, the promise of sustainability is greater than the reality. A new vision for food is emerging, in which the consumer is beginning to flex his and her muscles. The catastrophe of BSE could not be hushed up because consumer attention was focused on this issue (Lang 1998a). New forms of planning are bound to emerge. They are certainly required. Although concerned citizens can be important in this process, we should be cautious about leaving all the effort and responsibility to individual consumer action at the point of sale. Information and education are currently too patchy and restricted to be effective in meeting environmental goals as speedily as is desirable. Ultimately, I have argued, to shift the food system in a more sustainable direction requires a new involvement for the state.

Only the state, as a voice for the public interest, can be a sufficiently powerful lever against unfettered commercial interest to set new economic rules. Already powerful interests within the food industry are beginning to recognise that if everyone were given the same targets and if these were gradualist enough, sustainability and the market need not be incompatible. Although market mechanisms can deliver more sustainable food production, this is unlikely to happen unless the state encourages a new framework. This requires international as well as local action. Herein lies the opportunity for planning. The two key-words for this new planning will almost definitely be co-ordination – to cover the inter-sectoral nature of the food system – and appropriateness.

While I have stressed in this chapter the strong case for re-localisation of the food system, it should be recognised that a blanket localism would be just as inappropriate as the current worship of the globalisation god. The truth is that while food supply might be better if pushed in a re-localisation direction, some issues in food governance can only be addressed at the local level and others at the regional or international. The distinction between the food system and its govern-ance is critical to any new notion of planning. The key issue is to allocate appropriate powers to the appropriate level of governance and to do this in a way that carries food culture with it. This, as I have argued, requires state action. It may be unfashionable to talk of state action, but that is the uncomfortable reality.

Notes

1 One attempt to face the planning problem is Conway (1997).
2 An exception is the Scottish Office Home and Health Department (1993).
3 Interestingly, they learned a key lesson from the anti-adulteration campaigns of the mid-nineteenth century, namely that broad alliances work best. See Paulus (1974).
4 Interview with Dr Mansholt, Brussels, 1991.
5 Jay Fletcher, Food From Britain, personal communication, September 1995.
6 Interview with David Garner, Food From Britain, November 1992.
7 The earliest study of this process of contracting and year-round production and distri-bution for affluent consumers was Feder (1977).
8 MAFF and DAFS (Department of Agriculture and Food, Scotland) census figures, quoted in Briefing Paper by SAFE Alliance for Rural Lobby, London, 3 February 1993: 1.
9 March 1992 figures, quoted in Crosthwaite (1992: 1).
10 Figures from Economist Intelligence Unit, 1990, quoted in Henson (1991: Table 20).
11 Figure from Brogdale Horticultural Trust, Faversham, Kent.
12 MORI poll for Sustainable Agriculture, Food and Environment (SAFE) Alliance, 1992; see also BBC Country File (1995: 17).

References

Astor, Viscount and Rowntree, S. (1938) *British Agriculture: The Principles of Future Policy*, London: Longmans, Green & Co.
Avery, N., Drake, M. and Lang, T. (1994) *Cracking the Codex*, London: National Food Alliance.
Baldock, D. and Conder, D. (eds) (1985) 'Can the CAP fit the environment?', London: Council for the Preservation of Rural England / Institute for European Environmental Policy.
Baldock, D. and Beaufoy, G. (1992) *Plough On! An Environmental Appraisal of the Reformed CAP*, Godalming: WWF.

Barrett, H. and Browne, A. (1994) 'The internationalisation of vegetable production: the incorporation of sub-saharan Africa with particular reference to the Gambia', unpublished, Coventry University, School of Natural and Environmental Sciences, Geography Division.

BBC Country File (1995) *The Great Debate: Viewers Respond to the Challenge of the Rural White Paper*, Birmingham: BBC.

Beveridge, W. (1928) *British Food Control*, Oxford: Oxford University Press.

Boege, S. (1993) *Road Transport of Goods and the Effects on the Spatial Environment*, Wuppertal: Wuppertal Institute.

British Medical Association (1939) *Nutrition and the Public Health: Medicine, Agriculture, Industry, Education; Proceedings of a National Conference on the Wider Aspects of Nutrition, April 27–29, 1939*, London: BMA.

Brockway, A. (1932) *Hungry England*, London: Victor Gollancz.

Burnett, J. (1994) 'The rise and decline of school meals in Britain, 1860–1990', in Burnett and Oddy (1994).

Burnett, J. and Oddy, D. (eds) (1994) *The Origins and Development of Food Policies in Europe*, London: Leicester University Press.

Calder, A. (1971) *The People's War: Britain 1939–1945*, London: Panther.

Cannon, G. (1992) *Food and Health: The Experts Agree*, London: Consumers Association.

Cavanagh, J. and Broad, R. (1994) 'Understanding North-South Political Economy in the 1990s', Washington DC: Institute for Policy Studies, mimeo.

Clarke, F. and Titmuss, R. (1939) *Our Food Problem*, Harmondsworth: Penguin.

Clunies-Ross, T. and Hildyard, N. (1992) *The Politics of Industrial Agriculture*, London: Earthscan.

Commission on Environmental Health (1997) *Report of the Commission*, London: Chartered Institute of Environmental Health.

Common Ground (1991) 'Apple Day' and 'Community Orchard' leaflets, London: Common Ground.

Conway, G. (1997) *The Doubly Green Revolution*, Harmondsworth: Penguin.

Crosthwaite, H. (1992) *Food Retail* 10 (30 June).

Curtis-Bennett, N. (1949) *The Food of the People*, London: Faber & Faber.

Daly, H. and Goodland, R. (1992) 'An ecological-economic assessment of deregulation of international commerce under GATT', Washington, DC: World Bank Environment Department.

DES (Department of Education and Science) (1975) *Catering Arrangements in Schools: Report by a Department of Education and Science Working Party*, London: HMSO.

Dibb, S. (1993) *Children: Advertisers' Dream, Nutrition Nightmare?*, London: National Food Alliance.

Dinham, B. (1993) *The Pesticide Hazard*, London: Zed.

Dowler. E. and Rushton, C. (1993) *Diet and Poverty in the UK*, London: Centre for Human Nutrition, University College London.

DTI (Department of Trade and Industry) (1994) *Deregulation Task Forces Proposals for Reform: the detailed proposals of the seven Business Deregulation Task Forces* (with an introduction by Lord Sainsbury of Preston Candover), London: Department of Trade and Industry.

Durning, A. (1992) *How Much Is Enough?: The Consumer Society and the Future of the Earth*, London: Earthscan.

European Commission (n.d.) *1992: The Environmental Dimension*, Taskforce Report on the Environment and the Internal Market, Brussels: European Commission.

European Parliament (1997) 'Report on alleged contraventions or maladministration in the implementation of Community law in relation to BSE' (rapporteur: Mr Manuel Medina Ortega), DOC EN\RR\319\319544, Strasbourg: European Parliament.

Feder, E. (1977) *Strawberry Imperialism*, The Hague: Institute of Social Studies.

FFB (1992a) *Poultrymeat Sector Group Report*, London: FFB.

FFB (1992b) *Vegetable Sector Group Report*, London: FFB.

FFB (1995) 'A quick guide to the UK food and drink deficit', briefing on food and drink trade gap, unpublished.

Gabriel, Y. and Lang, T. (1995) *The Unmanageable Consumer*, London: Sage Publications.

Girardet, H. (1976) *Land for the People*, London: Crescent Books.

Goldin, O., Knudsen, O. and van der Mensbrugghe, D. (1993) *Trade Liberalisation: Global Economic Implications*, Paris: OECD, and New York: World Bank.

Griffiths, J. (1993) 'A freer flow of goods', *Financial Times*, 12 March.

Hammond, R. (1951) *Food*, London: HMSO, vol. 1.

Hannington, W. (1937) *The Problem of the Distressed Areas*, London: Victor Gollancz.

Hannington, W (1977) *Unemployed Struggles 1919–1936*, London: Lawrence & Wishart.

Henley Centre (1994) *Planning for Social Change*, London: Henley Centre for Forecasting.

Hennessy, P. (1993) *Never Again: Britain 1945–1951*, London: Vintage.

Henson, S. (1991) 'Increases in the Concentration of Food Retailing in the UK and the Implications for Consumer Choice', a report for the National Consumer Council, mimeo, University of Reading.

HM Government (1905) *Royal Commission on supply of food and raw materials in time of war*, Cmnd 1643, London: HMSO.

HM Government (1992) *Health of the Nation*, London: HMSO.

Holden, J. and Peacock, J. (1993) *Genes, Crops and the Environment*, London: Cambridge University Press.

House of Commons Agriculture Committee (1987) *The Effects of Pesticides on Human Health*, vol. 1, Report and Proceedings of the Committee, HoC Paper 379–1, London: HMSO.

House of Commons Agriculture Committee (1992) *The Trade Gap in Food and Drink*, London: HMSO.

House of Commons Select Committee on the Environment (1994) *Shopping Centres and their Future*, Fourth Report, Session 1993–94, London: HMSO.

House of Lords Select Committee Report (1992) *Development and the Future of the Common Agricultural Policy*, HL Paper 791, London: HMSO.

Hughes, D. (1994) *Building Partnerships and Alliances in the European Food Industry*, Wye: Wye College.

Hurst, P., Hay, A. and Dudley, N. (1991) *The Pesticide Handbook*, London: Journeyman.

Institute for European Environmental Policy (1995) *The 1996 Intergovernmental Conference: Integrating the Environment into other EU Policies*, London: Institute for European Environmental Policy.

Jenkins, R. (1992) *Bringing Rio Home: Biodiversity in our Food and Farming*, London: SAFE Alliance.

Junshi, C., Campbell, T., Junyao, L. and Peto, R. (1990) *Diet, Lifestyle and Mortality in China*, Oxford: Oxford University Press.

Keys, A. (ed.) (1970) 'Coronary heart disease in seven countries', *Circulation* 41 (suppl.1): 1–211.

Keys, A. (1980) *Seven Countries: A Multivariate Analysis of Death and Coronary Heart Disease.*, London: Harvard University Press.

Kranendonk, S. and Bringezau, B. (1994) *Major Material Flows Associated with Orange Juice Consumption in Germany*. Wuppertal: Wuppertal Institute.

Lancashire School Meals Campaign and Lang, T. (1981) *Now You See Them, . . . Now You Don't: A Report on the Fate of School Meals and the Loss of 300,000 Jobs*, Accrington.

Lang, T. (1983) 'The school meals business', *Critical Social Policy* 8: 117–28.

Lang, T. (1995) 'The contradictions of food labelling', *Information Design Journal* 10: 15–25.

Lang, T. (1996) 'Food security: does it conflict with globalization?', *Development* 4: 45–50.

Lang, T. (1997) *Food Policy for the 21st Century*, Discussion Paper 4, Centre for Food Policy, London: Thames Valley University.

Lang, T. (1998a) 'BSE and CJD: recent developments', in S. Ratzan, *The Mad Cow Crisis: Health and the Public Good*, London: University College London Press.

Lang, T. (1998b) 'Going public: food campaigns during the 1980s and early 1990s,' in D. Smith (ed.) *Nutrition Scientists and Nutrition Policy in 20th Century Britain*, London: Routledge, forthcoming.

Lang, T. (1998c) 'Towards a food democracy', in S. Griffiths and J. Wallace (eds), *Consuming Passions: Food in the Age of Anxiety*, Manchester: Manchester University Press.

Lang, T. and Clutterbuck, C. (1991) *P is for Pesticides*, London: Ebury.

Lang, T. and Hines, C. (1993) *The New Protectionism*, London: Earthscan.

Lang, T., Millstone, E., Rayner, M. and Raven, H. (1996) *Modernising MAFF*, Discussion Paper 2, Centre for Food Policy, London: Thames Valley University.

Leather, S. (1996) *The Making of Modern Malnutrition*, London: Caroline Walker Trust.

Levinson, C.(1979) *Vodka-Cola*, London: Gordon & Cremonesi.

Longfield, J. (1992) 'Advertising and labelling: how much influence?', in National Consumer Council, *Your Food, Whose Choice?*, London: HMSO.

Madden, P. (1992) *Raw Deal*, London: Christian Aid.

MAFF (1991) *Household Food Consumption and Expenditure 1990 with a Study of Trends over the Period 1940–90*, Annual Report of the Food Survey Committee, London: HMSO.

MAFF (1993) *National Food Survey 1992*, London: HMSO.

Maves, G. (1991) 'Creative pressure', *Marketing* 7.

McGrath, M. (1995) *Grocery Retailing 1994: The Market Review*, Letchmore Heath: Institute of Grocery Distribution.

Mennell, S., Murcott, S. and van Otterloo, L. (1992) *The Sociology of Food*, London: Sage.

M'Gonigle, G. and Kirkby, J. (1936) *Poverty and Public Health*, London: Victor Gollancz.

Miller, M. (1987) *Danger: Additives at Work*, London: London Food Commission.

Millstone, E. (1985) 'Food additive regulation in the UK', *Food Policy* 10: 237–52.

Millstone, E. and Abraham, J. (1989) 'Food additive controls: some international comparisons', *Food Policy* 14: 43–57.

Ministry of Health (1937) *Advisory Committee on Nutrition, First Report*, London: HMSO.

Mintz, S. (1985) *Sweetness and Power: The Place of Sugar in Modern History*, New York: Viking.

MORI (1993) *Survey for Get Cooking!*, London: National Food Alliance.

Murray, R. (1985) 'Benneton Britain: the new economic order', *Marxism Today*, November: 28–32.

National Consumer Council (1988) *Consumers and the Common Agricultural Policy*, London: HMSO.

National Food Alliance (1993) *Get Cooking!*, London: National Food Alliance.

Neville-Rolfe, E. (1984) *The Politics of Agriculture in the European Community*, London: Policy Studies Institute.

Office of Science and Technology (1995) *Technology Foresight: Food and Drink*, London: HMSO.

Orr, J. (1943) *Food and the People: Target for Tomorrow* (no. 3), London: Pilot Press.

Paulus, I. (1974) *The Search for Pure Food*, Oxford: Martin Robertson.

Paxton, A. (1994) *The Food Miles Report*, London: SAFE Alliance.

Rathbone, E. (1924) *The Disinherited Family*, London: Edward Arnold.

Rathbone, E. (1940) *The Case for Family Allowances*, Harmondsworth: Penguin.

Raven, H. and Lang, T. (1995) *Off our Trolleys?*, London: Institute for Public Policy Research.

Ritzer, G. (1993) *The McDonaldization of Society*, Thousand Oaks: Pine Forge Press.

Rowling, N. (1987) *Commodities: How the World was Taken to Market*, London: FAB Books/Channel 4.

Rowntree, B. (1902) *Poverty: A Study of Town Life*, London: Macmillan.

Rowntree, B. (1921) *The Human Factor in Business*, London: Longmans.

Rowntree, B. (1941). *Poverty and Progress*, London: Longmans, Green & Co.

Santer, J. (1997) 'Speech by Jacques Santer, President of the European Commission at the Debate in the European Parliament on the report into BSE by the Committee of Enquiry of the European Parliament', 18 February 1997.

Scottish Office Home and Health Department (1993) *The Scottish Diet*, Report of the James Committee, Edinburgh: Scottish Office.

Sklair, L. (1991) *Sociology of the Global System: Social Change in Global Perspective*, Hemel Hempstead: Harvester Wheatsheaf.

Snell, P. (1986) *Pesticide Residues – the Case for Real Control*, London: London Food Commision.

Spring-Rice, M. (1981) *Working Class Wives*, London: Virago.

Tansey, G. and Worsley, T. (1995) *The Food System*, London: Earthscan.

Thrupp, L. (1995) *Bittersweet Harvests for Global Supermarkets*, Washington, DC: WRI.

Titmuss, R. (1976) *Essays on the Welfare State*, London: George Allen & Unwin.

Tracy, M. (1982) *Agriculture in Western Europe: Challenge and Response 1880–1980*, London: Granada.

Trienekens, J. and Zuurbier, P. (eds) (1996) 'Proceedings of the Second international conference on Chain Management in Agri- and Food Business', Wageningen: University of Wageningen.

United Nations Centre on Transnational Corporations (1981) *Transnational Corporations in Food and Beverage Processing*, New York: United Nations.

UNICEF (1993) *Food, Health and Care: The UNICEF Vision and Strategy for a World Free from Hunger and Malnutrition*, New York: United Nations Children's Fund.

Walker, C. and Cannon, G. (1984) *The Food Scandal*, London: Century.

Walworth, J. (1940) *Feeding the Nation in Peace and War*, London: George Allen & Unwin.

Watkins, K. (1995) *The Oxfam Poverty Report*, Oxford: Oxfam.

Whitelegg, J. (1995) *Driven to Shop: Transport Intensity and the Environment*, London: SAFE Alliance.

World Health Organisation (1990) *Diet, Nutrition and the Prevention of Chronic Disease*, Technical Series, no. 797, Geneva: WHO.

Index